Applause for Pete Hamill's
Downtown

"With his reporter's eye for detail and a tough-but-tender lyricism, the Brooklyn-bred Hamill brings modern-day New York to life by illuminating its colorful past.... Hamill's winning take on the city he loves is a tale for the ages."
—Scott Stephens, *Cleveland Plain Dealer*

"Rich and thoroughly engaging."
—Larry Lebowitz, *Miami Herald*

"This book is an homage to the immigrant spirit.... Hamill reminds us of the satisfactions of walking the city with our eyes wide open."
—Vincent Cannato, *New York Post*

"Hamill's years as a journalist 'walking the pavement' yield a richness of detail.... In a plainspoken but always compelling style, *Downtown* is part history book, architecture book, and travelogue—all jam-packed with facts, figures, and addresses."
—Erin Hanafy, *Associated Press*

"The task of *Downtown* is to slow things down a bit, peel back the facade of old buildings and new fashions, and reveal the mercantile heart of the city. No other writer could be so well equipped to do this than Hamill."
—John Freeman, *Boston Globe*

"A vicarious walking tour of the city Hamill knows so well and loves so deeply. It's the kind of book you tell your friends they ought to read. When you put it down, you'll pick up the newspaper and see what airfare is to New York these days."
—Dan Danbom, *Rocky Mountain News*

"A delightfully personal, robustly informative portrait of New York.... Hamill knows how to keep his eyes and ears open for the good story, the telling detail, and the quirky but exemplary character.... A marvelous read for anyone who has a hometown."
—Brad Hooper, *Booklist*

Also by Pete Hamill

NOVELS
A Killing for Christ
The Gift
Dirty Laundry
Flesh and Blood
The Deadly Piece
The Guns of Heaven
Loving Women
Snow in August
Forever

SHORT STORY COLLECTIONS
The Invisible City
Tokyo Sketches

JOURNALISM
Irrational Ravings
Piecework
News Is a Verb
Tools as Art

MEMOIR
A Drinking Life

BIOGRAPHY
Diego Rivera
Why Sinatra Matters

Downtown

MY MANHATTAN

Pete Hamill

BACK BAY BOOKS

Little, Brown and Company

NEW YORK   BOSTON

*This book is for
Bill Phillips,
who carries his own nostalgias*

Back Bay Books / Little, Brown and Company
Time Warner Book Group
1271 Avenue of the Americas, New York, NY 10020
Visit our Web site at www.twbookmark.com

Originally published in hardcover by
Little, Brown and Company, December 2004
First Back Bay paperback edition, November 2005

The complete text of "It All Started with *Bomba the Jungle Boy*,"
an interview with Pete Hamill that appears in the reading group guide at
the back of this book, was originally published on December 26, 2004,
in the *Birmingham News*. Copyright © 2004 The Birmingham News.
Reprinted with permission.

Library of Congress Cataloging-in-Publication Data

Hamill, Pete.
    Downtown : my Manhattan / Pete Hamill. — 1st ed.
      p. cm.
    Includes bibliographical references.
    ISBN 0-316-73451-9 (hc) / 0-316-01068-5 (pb)
    1. Hamill, Pete. 2. Authors, American — Homes and haunts — New
York (State) — New York. 3. Manhattan (New York, N.Y.) — History.
4. New York (N.Y.) — History. I. Title.
F128.3.H25 2004
974.7'1'092 — dc22

2004011737

10 9 8 7 6 5 4 3 2 1

Q-FF
Book design by Bernard Klein
Map by G. W. Ward

Printed in the United States of America

CONTENTS

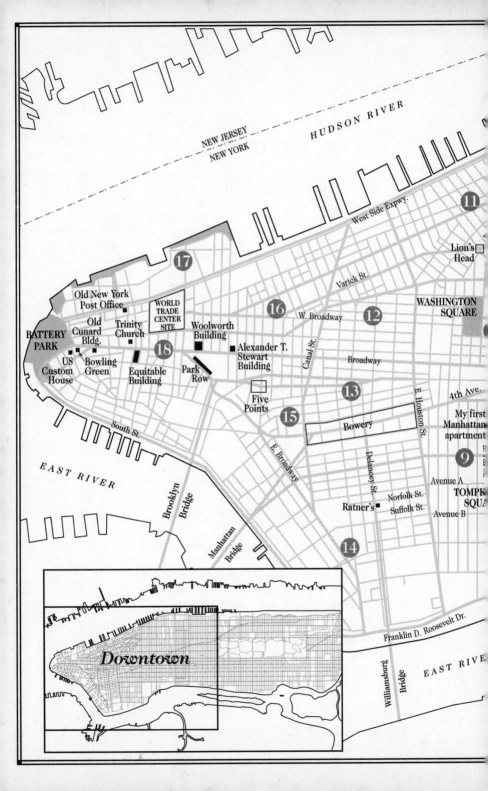

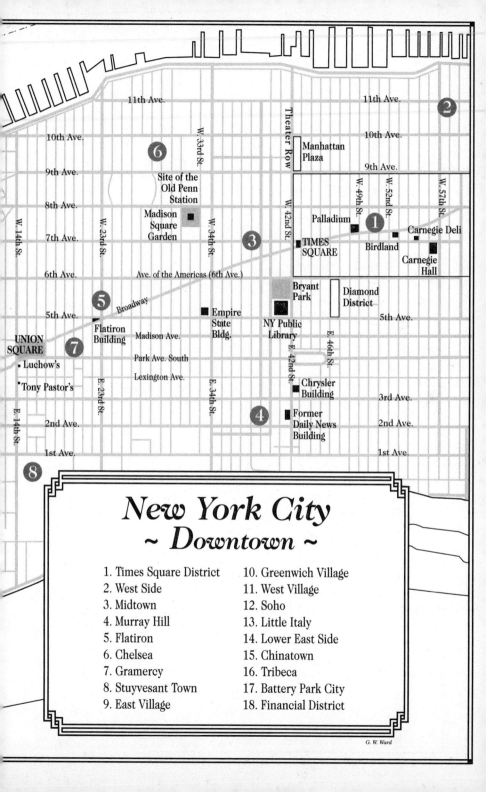

New York City
~ Downtown ~

1. Times Square District
2. West Side
3. Midtown
4. Murray Hill
5. Flatiron
6. Chelsea
7. Gramercy
8. Stuyvesant Town
9. East Village
10. Greenwich Village
11. West Village
12. Soho
13. Little Italy
14. Lower East Side
15. Chinatown
16. Tribeca
17. Battery Park City
18. Financial District

G. W. Ward

I too lived, Brooklyn of ample hills was mine,

I too walk'd the streets of Manhattan island, and bathed in the waters around it,

I too felt the abrupt questionings stir within me . . .

Walt Whitman, "Crossing Brooklyn Ferry"

There are certain sections of New York, Major, that I wouldn't advise you to invade.

Rick to Major Strasser, *Casablanca*

Downtown

Chapter One

THE CAPITAL OF NOSTALGIA

THIS IS A book about my home city. I was born in the immense and beautiful segment of it called Brooklyn, but I've lived and worked for much of my life in its center, the long skinny island called Manhattan. I live here still. With any luck at all, I will die here. I have the native son's irrational love of the place and often think of William Faulkner's remark about his native Mississippi, and how he loved it "in spite of, not because." New York is a city of daily irritations, occasional horrors, hourly tests of will and even courage, and huge dollops of pure beauty. For any native the home place is infused with a mixture of memory, myth, lore, and history, bound together in an erratic, subjective way. That's as true of the natives of New York as of the natives of Oxford, Mississippi. That mysterious mixture is why so much of this portrait is personal. Past and present are merged in its pages, as they are in my consciousness. But something else is in the mix too. Something magical. And certain moments of magic are always present tense.

In my earliest memory, I am five years old, coming home from the Sanders Theater in Brooklyn. I am with my mother and we have just seen *The Wizard of Oz*. The year is 1940. In the safe darkness of the movie house I've seen emerald castles and a lion that talked and a road made of glistening yellow bricks. But in memory all of that is a blur. In memory, my mother takes my hand and the two of us are skipping all the way home singing "because because because because *because!*"

On this wonderful evening, my mother still has brown hair. She is laughing and exuberant, clearly made happy by going to a movie with her eldest son. I remember nothing else, except the word *because*. Later, I will learn that the woman I call Mom is actually Anne Devlin Hamill, an immigrant from the hard, dark city of Belfast, in Northern Ireland. She arrived in New York, with perfect Irish timing, on the day the stock market crashed in 1929. She was then nineteen. The calamity of the Great Depression did not dismay her. She went immediately to work for a rich Manhattan family as a domestic servant, glad of the work, joyous about being again in the city of New York. In all the years that followed in the life of Anne Devlin, that city would always be a wonderland. Why? Because.

Above all, because her journey in 1929 was Anne Devlin's second migration to the place that would be her home until her death at eighty-seven. On these streets, she had once been five too. I would learn that in New York, many stories begin somewhere else, for people who be-

come center fielders and for those who start as domestics.
Her father was named Peter Devlin, who went to sea as a
youth, became an engineer, traveled as far away as
Yokohama and Rangoon, worked for years as an expert in
refrigeration for the Great White Fleet in the banana trade
with Central America. He was a Belfast Catholic, and at
sea he was free of the accumulated bigotries that went
with the endless religious quarrels that began in the Irish
seventeenth century. When he married in his thirties and
soon fathered two children, Peter Devlin decided that it
was time to live again on land. He had seen many places in
the world, but he and his wife chose New York. The young
family of four settled in the Red Hook section of Brooklyn
in the parish of Mary Star of the Sea, hard by the harbor.
There he would work on the ships of the Cunard Line but
live on land with his family. The Devlin children (the other
was my uncle Maurice) would be raised in a city where
nobody cared about their religion. They would grow up in
the greatest metropolis in America, where everything was
possible, if only you worked. Above all, they would grow
up free of the iron certainties of the European past, the
first requirement for creating an American future.

Then, in 1916, while the slaughters of the Great War
raged in distant Europe, disaster struck in Brooklyn. My
grandfather Devlin fell from the deck of a ship and was
crushed between hull and dock. My mother was then five,
and remembered later the tumult and the tears in the flat in
Red Hook but few of the details. She did remember New
York fading into fog and the long voyage home across the
vast Atlantic. Her mother must have known that German
submarines were prowling the approaches to Ireland and

5

England, but she chose to risk any danger to get back among her own people. One of the few consolations in any life is a sense of the familiar, with all of its imperfections.

The widow and her small children made it safely across the Atlantic, but that year Ireland was seething with violence and sectarian hatred. At Easter, there had been a nationalist rising in Dublin against the British rulers of Ireland, with deaths and executions. For many people, Irish nationalism was exclusively Catholic (it wasn't), and in the North, all Catholics were accused by some citizens of stabbing England in the back while the men of Ulster were dying in vast numbers at the Somme. The theory wasn't accurate (many Catholics fought under the British flag), but the fury was real, and so was the fear. But the anger had its own justification. After all, the sons of Ulster were filling the graves of France. It was no surprise that the bitterness, and its local violence, would continue in Northern Ireland long after the Great War finally ended, long after civil war had run its course. Too many Irish corpses would fill the graves of Ireland.

Somehow, in the midst of so much turbulence and fear, young Anne Devlin managed to do what few women, and almost no Catholic women, ever did in those years: she finished high school. That same year, her widowed mother died of a stroke at age forty-seven. And Anne Devlin, now an orphan, decided that it was time to return to the city she had last seen slipping away into fog. Her brother, Maurice, would stay in Belfast for another thirty years. But my mother would sell the family piano, buy a steamship ticket, and go back to the place where she had last seen her father, long ago, when she was five.

My own father, Billy Hamill, was also a child of Belfast. He was twenty when he arrived at Ellis Island, to join two older brothers who had already fled the bitterness of the Irish north. He had only completed the eighth grade when he was apprenticed as a stonemason, but he carried other credentials to America. He was a wonderful singer of songs: Irish rebel songs, the songs of English music halls, jaunty tunes of human foolishness, and songs of sad longing. I grew up hearing those songs and can remember many of the lyrics to this day. He was also a wonderful soccer player. Years later, his friends told me about his magical legs, those legs that carried him across playing fields, that seemed to have an intelligence of their own. The Irish novelist Michael McLaverty, who chose to stay in the Irish north, told me in 1963, "God, he could play that game."

In 1927, his fourth year in America, Billy Hamill was playing for an Irish team in the immigrant soccer leagues that were then common all over New York. There was a Jewish team called House of David, and German teams, English teams, Spanish teams. One wintry Sunday, in the year that Babe Ruth hit those sixty home runs, Billy Hamill played in a game against the Germans. He was viciously kicked in the left leg (almost surely by accident) and fell to the frozen earth with a double compound fracture, splintered bone jutting through flesh. He was taken to Kings County Hospital, the largest in Brooklyn. Because it was a Sunday, there were not enough doctors. There was certainly no penicillin. By the following morning, gangrene had set in. His left leg was amputated above the knee.

The years immediately after that calamity must have been filled with misery, but I never heard him say so. Among the many immigrant codes, spoken and unspoken, there was one that was absolutely clear: The only unforgivable sin was self-pity. He must have felt it. He must have throbbed with rage, too, against his terrible luck. After all, he would never again play the game he loved more than all others. But he would play no other games either. He was deprived, too, of the American opportunities for honest manual labor, those jobs in shipyards and the construction trades that employed so many other immigrants, not all of them Irish. Those jobs made everything possible in America, starting with a family.

And yet he went on with his American life. He would sing his songs for his friends in dozens of Prohibition speakeasies. He designed a bathing suit that covered the stump of his vanished leg and went swimming in the summer sea at Coney Island. And he worked. His penmanship was excellent, and so he worked as a clerk in the home office of a grocery chain. And, with his friends, he even went to dances.

In 1933, after the election of Franklin D. Roosevelt and the end of Prohibition, he went to such a dance in Webster Hall, just below Union Square. There he met Anne Devlin. They started going around, as the Irish said, and eventually they were married. Anne Devlin did not drink. But she must have loved his endless repertoire of songs, his stoicism, his optimism. He surely was attracted by her brown-haired good looks, her sense of humor, and, above all, her intelligence. No child, of course, ever truly knows what brings parents together. Or why a marriage lasts in

8

spite of bouts of poverty, inevitable quarrels, occasional at-
tacks of despair on one side or the other. But they were together until the day my father died at eighty.

I was their first child, eventually the oldest of seven
American children, and as a boy, I gradually understood
that my father was not like other fathers in our blue-collar
neighborhood. Billy Hamill could not take us to play ball
in Prospect Park. He could not take us on long walks
across that park to the sacred precinct of Ebbets Field.
The subway was always a challenge, with its long flights of
stairs leading to the street, and the need to be agile, and so
he almost never went to Manhattan. He could not even
march in the Saint Patrick's Day parade. His America was
limited to a dozen square blocks in our small neighborhood.

My mother's New York world had no such limits. She
was a quick, determined walker of the city, starting with
the streets of our own metropolitan hamlet. In her company, my younger brother Tom and I learned that the only
way to get to know a place was by walking its streets. We
went with her as she shopped. We soon knew where the
church was and the police station and the schools. But
she was always expanding our frontiers. She would show
us the main public library, where books were free, right
there on the other side of the great arch of Grand Army
Plaza. She showed us the Brooklyn Museum and the
Botanic Garden. Sometimes she showed us visions that
stayed with us for all of our lives.

One Saturday in the summer of 1941, while my year-old
sister Kathleen stayed home with my father (she was born
on May 1, his birthday, and he adored her), my mother

took me and Tom on one of our longest walks. We ended up at the entrance to the pedestrian ramp of the Brooklyn Bridge. We had never before seen this great span. From the Brooklyn side, the bridge rises in a graded arc. The central walkway and the roads for automobiles are flanked by its soaring suspension cables. As my mother pointed out the distant ships in harbor and river, from that great height the size of boats in bathtubs, we reached the top of the rising arc. Then, for the first time, I saw them: spires aimed at the sky. Dozens of them. Hundreds of them. All gilded by morning sun.

"What *is* it?" I said in a stupefied way (as my mother told me years later).

"Sure, *you* remember, Peter," she said. "You've seen it before." And then she smiled. "It's Oz."

And so it was.

This book is about what I learned in Oz. It is about the places where I lived and about myself, among others. To my astonishment, I've known the Manhattan streets and many of its people for almost seven decades. The day before yesterday I was five, crossing that amazing bridge. We moved in 1943 to a new flat with a breathtaking view from our kitchen windows of the harbor and the skyline, and I could gaze in all seasons at the towers. I seem to have been eleven for a very long time, in days and weeks of an endless languid summer. Then time started to rush, through adolescence and high school and a job as a sheet metal worker at the Brooklyn Navy Yard and finally into the US Navy itself. Then, after discharge and a sojourn in Mexico on the GI Bill, I was at last a kind of grown-up, living in the buildings of Oz itself. Living, that is, in Manhattan.

As it turned out, my life in Manhattan had its own geographical limits, and they are central to this book. That is why these notes are limited to those parts of Manhattan in which I have truly lived. My own city, the one that feels like home, is the one I've always called Downtown. To me it extends—in defiance of the conventions of guidebooks—from the Battery to Times Square. There is a dense, rich New York beyond the limits of my Downtown, and I've spent some time in its many parishes. But it was never mine in the same way that Downtown became one of my personal possessions. So these notes are personal too. Over the years, I have paid rent at fourteen separate addresses in Downtown, and I live now in a loft in Tribeca that was built in 1872. It stands just below Canal Street, that most exhilarating of New York bazaars. I know Mr. Singh, who sells me newspapers. I know the man who runs the corner variety store. I know the people with whom I share my building. Each day, I exchange hellos with a dozen people who work on my street. When the drivers of cars with New Jersey plates honk too insanely on their horns, I shout at them: "Knock it off! We live here!"

There are other levels of the familiar in the dailiness of my life here. My Downtown is also the place where the city was created. It is where, across the long, turbulent nineteenth century, today's New York character was formed. I look at other people and the places where they live, and the things they do or say, and I learn something about myself too. As a geographer, I'm as idiosyncratic as the early explorers of the New World. My interior maps are jagged and personal, often resembling in spirit the famous *New Yorker* cover by Saul Steinberg showing Ninth Avenue larger than the state of California. My Downtown includes the Carnegie Deli and Carnegie Hall, which on most maps are firmly nailed into Midtown. For me, Rockefeller Center between Forty-eighth and Fifty-first streets, Fifth and Sixth avenues, is triumphantly Midtown, but P.J. Clarke's saloon, at Fifty-fifth Street and Third Avenue, is a treasured fragment of Downtown. The differences have to do with the patina of time, of course, the colors that time gives to brick, slate, copper, stone, and wood. I am always delighted to find something new, or strange, or unusual within the familiar. But I'm happiest in those places where generations have passed before me.

The bunched towers that I first saw as Oz are better viewed from Brooklyn or New Jersey. Up close, they climb out of view. Some Downtown skyscrapers have their own kind of beauty, of course, but I feel more a part of the older city, the one that was lower, that could be seen in one glimpse, that is more horizontal than vertical, that allows us to absorb the light of the city sky, the city of walkers and the city of horses. That is, I cherish the Downtown city. I have been looking at that New York for decades now. The place seems as fresh as it did when I was twenty-one. On its streets, I am always a young man.

It is a standing joke, of course, that New Yorkers are the most parochial of Americans, and that commonplace contains a small amount of truth. For parts of my life, I've wandered far from my home parishes, to live in Mexico

City and Rome, Barcelona and Dublin and San Juan, and
have also paid rent in New Orleans, Key West, Los
Angeles, and Santa Fe. But I've come to realize that I lived
in all those places as a New Yorker. I gazed at their glories
and tried to learn their histories, to define those elements
that made them unique, but always I measured them
against my own city. In unexpected ways, they each taught
me something about New York, its strengths and terrible
flaws, its irritations and its triumphs, the way learning another language teaches you about your own. But in spite
of their many seductions, I always knew I would go home.

In some ways, my experience of the city has been
unique, even for a native. After the summer of 1960 I was
a newspaperman, paid to move through many neighborhoods with pen and notebook in hand. No other experience can be so humbling. You think you know the city
where you were born; each fresh day as a reporter teaches
you that you know almost nothing. I could go to the scene
of a murder and record the number of gunshot wounds,
the caliber of the bullets, and the name of the person
whose corpse was sprawled before me. I'd talk to the police, the relatives, and the neighbors, including the nearest
bartender. I could listen while the victim's relatives wailed
their laments. Trying to rescue the human reality from the
murder statistics, I was often instructed by the street-
smart photographers, who were paid, above all, to *see*.

"Look at this guy's socks," a photographer named Louis
Liotta said to me one morning at a murder scene. "One
brown sock and one blue sock. What's *that* tell you?" I
didn't know what it told me. Liotta explained: "This guy
got dressed *in the dark*." He paused. "Or someone dressed

his body in the dark—and at *home*, or there wouldn't be two different socks."

When I talked to a detective about the socks, he said: "Look, the socks tell you he probably got dressed at home. Or his body was dressed at home."

But as I got better at seeing and describing what was directly in front of me on a Manhattan street, a troubling dissatisfaction began to grow within me. I acquired enough craft to get the facts and then write a story for the next edition that would give the readers a sense of what I had seen and heard in a place where the readers had not been present. But I was nagged by doubt, knowing that I'd only skimmed the surface of the story and some larger truth was always eluding me. Who were all these other people in the neighborhood where one of them had now been killed? How did they live? Where did they go to school and what were their jobs and how did they find their way to these buildings? What was this neighborhood itself? How did it get here? And what about certain abiding New York mysteries: Why was the Bronx called the Bronx? How did Harlem get its name? Who was Major Deegan? From the specifics of a newspaper story, I was learning how little I knew about my own city.

Sometimes I would explore these mysteries in the library of the newspaper, using slow time to take out envelopes of crumbling clippings. Or I'd ask older reporters and editors. Sometimes I'd be told, "Major Deegan was a Tammany hack who served in World War One and lived until the 1930s." Then I'd confirm this with the clippings. The Bronx was named for a guy named Jonas Bronck, a rich Swede who owned most of it as a private farm.

Harlem was named Harlem for the same reason Brooklyn was called Brooklyn: The Dutch got there first and named one place Haarlem and the other Breuckelen after places in the country they'd left behind.

In short, I was educating myself as a reporter, but also as a New Yorker. Much of my reading never found its way directly into newspaper stories, of course. For one thing, I was young and having too good a time in the company of people I loved. For another, the original stories had faded from the newspapers and my discoveries were irrelevant. On newspapers, we believed we were all writing history in a hurry, and after the first few days, even the most appalling stories gave way to the shock of the new. Still, it was clear to me that the only way to try to know this city (or any other) was on foot. I didn't learn to drive until I was thirty-six. Who needed cars when you had two good legs and the subways moved under the traffic?

Even today, I wander through the city as if I were a young man. Something always surprises me. Something else fills me with wonder. I pass a building I've passed a thousand times before and see it suddenly in a new way. In good weather, I like to stand and watch the passing show, a flaneur lounging in a doorway. I see a burly black man help a blind woman across a street. I talk to him later and discover he is from Togo, "all the way in Africa," and he works for one of the fabric wholesalers on Walker Street. He tells me why he came to New York. "For my kids," he says. "I want them to be free and, you know, healthy. In Togo, lots of things are green and beautiful, but the neares' doctor, he was seventeen kilometers away, man." I see a cop flirting with a pretty girl, a tourist from Italy. "Hey, you want me to walk you?" he says. She smiles a dazzling smile and moves on. He sees me watching, smiles in a conspiratorial way, and says, "Makes you wanna live forever."

The New Yorker learns to settle for glimpses. There are simply too many people to ever know them all, to unravel all of their secrets. Nobody in such a vast and various place can absorb everything. You know the people you love and the people with whom you work. The rest is glimpses. And on certain days, yes, you want to live forever.

And yet, in many separate ways, the people of the city express certain common emotions. The forms and details are different for every generation and every group, but certain emotions have continued to repeat themselves for centuries. One is surely greed, the unruly desire to get more money by any means possible, an emotion shared by citizens from stockbrokers to muggers. Another is sudden anger, the result of so many people living in so relatively small a place. Another is an anarchic resistance to authority. But far and away the most powerful of all New York emotions is the one called nostalgia.

The city is, in a strange way, the capital of nostalgia. The emotion has two major roots. One is the abiding sense of loss that comes from the simple fact of continuous change. Of the city's five boroughs, Manhattan in particular absolutely refuses to remain as it was. It is dynamic, not static. What seems permanent when you are twenty is too often a ghost when you are thirty. As in all places, parents die, friends move on, businesses wear out, and restaurants close forever. But here, change is more common than in most American cities. The engine of greatest change is the cramped land itself. Scarcity can create a holy belief in the possibility of great riches. That's why the religion of real estate periodically enforces its commandments, and neighborhoods are cleared and buildings hauled down and new ones erected, and all that remains is memory.

This book is littered with casualties of time and greed and that vague reality called progress. Just one example here: I was in high school in Manhattan when I came to know the Third Avenue El. Sometimes I took it as a ride, not just a means of getting from one place to another. I loved its rattling noise, the imagery associated with the 1933 movie *King Kong*, the stark shadows cast by its beams and girders, and the rows of tenements and Irish saloons that I could see swishing by from its windows. I had no memory of the Second Avenue El, or the Sixth Avenue El, or the Ninth Avenue El. They were all gone. But in some ways, the Third Avenue El seemed as permanent as the Statue of Liberty, and for me it provided a ride through more than simple space. It hurtled me through time as well. They started tearing it down in 1955. By the time I returned from Mexico in 1957, the Third Avenue El was gone too.

There would be many other disappearances, including too many newspapers. Buildings went up, and if you lived long enough, you might see them come down, to be replaced by newer, more audacious, more arrogant structures. I came to accept this after the el had vanished and some of the worst office buildings in the city's history began rising on Third Avenue. There was no point, I thought, in permanently bemoaning change. This was New York. Loss was part of the deal. In the same year that the Third Avenue El disappeared, so did the Brooklyn Dodgers and the New York Giants. The demise of the Third Avenue El was a kind of marker, the end of something that had outlived its time. But for many people, the flight of the baseball teams was an example of unacceptable losses. Some never got over it. After a long while, I finally consoled myself about the Dodgers by saying, Well, at least I had them once and I will always have them in memory. That nostalgia lives in me today. It erupts whenever I see a fragment of black-and-white newsreel showing Jackie Robinson heading for home. But to talk about the Dodgers' departure without cease would be to live as a bore. New York teaches you to get over almost everything.

Our losses would culminate, of course, with the violent destruction of the World Trade Center. For many New Yorkers, now including the young (who grew up with the twin towers), even such a ferocious human toll can provoke nostalgia. Months after the murderous morning of September 11, 2001, I kept hearing New Yorkers speaking in tones of regret about the loss of the buildings themselves, even people who didn't care for them as architecture. For me, the twin towers were *in* Downtown but never *of* Downtown. That is, they were detached from my sense of the home place. And yet most New Yorkers missed their position in the skyline, the sense of dominance they suggested, and longed for the comparative innocence of the brief years in which they existed.

"I hate to admit this," one close friend said, "but when I look at the old photographs of the Trade Center, I'm sometimes choked with nostalgia."

Nostalgia. The word itself, as critic and educator Nathan

Silver has pointed out in his fine book *Lost New York*, is an imperfect one to describe the emotion itself.

"The word in English is hopelessly wishy-washy," he wrote in the revised 2000 edition of his 1967 book. "It seems to denote something between a handwring and a tearjerk, referring as it does to a wistful, regretful feeling. Nowadays most urban dwellers accept that a city's past vitalizes a coherent sense of the present, but calling that 'nostalgia' evokes the approximate reaction that one would get from mentioning heirlooms or embroidery."

The New York version of nostalgia is not simply about lost buildings or their presence in the youth of the individuals who lived with them. It involves an almost fatalistic acceptance of the permanent presence of loss. Nothing will ever stay the same. Tuesday turns into Wednesday and something valuable is behind you forever. An "is" has become a "was." Whatever you have lost, you will not get it back: not that much-loved brother, not that ball club, not that splendid bar, not that place where you once went dancing with the person you later married. Irreversible change happens so often in New York that the experience affects character itself. New York toughens its people against sentimentality by allowing the truer emotion of nostalgia. Sentimentality is always about a lie. Nostalgia is about real things gone. Nobody truly mourns a lie.

That is why, in a million small ways, New Yorkers behaved so well on September 12, 2001. Millions of us wept over the horrors of the day before. Many mourned their own dead and the dead of the larger parish. More millions grieved for the world that existed on September 10, knowing it was forever behind us. For a while, at least, all felt various degrees of fury. But nobody ran. We knew that at least we had lived once in that world before the fanatics changed it forever. With all its flaws, horrors, disappointments, cruelties, we would remember that lost world all our days and most of our nights. And now we would get up in the morning and go to work. Our only consolation would be nostalgia.

That tough nostalgia helps explain New York. It is built into our codes, like DNA, and beyond the explanation of constant change, there is another common thread in our deepest emotion. I believe that New York nostalgia also comes from that extraordinary process that created the modern city: immigration.

Every New York history stresses the role of immigration, because the tale simply can't be told without it. Starting in the early nineteenth century, the city absorbed millions of European immigrants, many arriving in waves: the Irish in flight from the desperate famine of the 1840s; Germans and other Europeans after the political furies of 1848; the immense flood between 1880 and 1920 of Italians, Eastern European Jews, and others in flight from debasing poverty or murderous persecution. We know much about them, and yet we know so little. Many were illiterate and wrote no memoirs or letters; memoir was a genre practiced by their children. We do know that most were young and poor, for the old and the rich don't often emigrate to strange countries. We know that a common mixture of overlapping hopes served as their personal engines: the desire to raise their children in a place where they'd be healthy and educated, a longing for honest work in a place where they would not be tested about religion or origins, the hope for personal freedom in a country where nobody need ever bend a knee to a monarch.

But many paid an emotional price for their decisions, and that shared sense of disruption would lead to the second stream of New York nostalgia. For the rest of their lives, those first-generation nineteenth-century immigrants would carry with them what their American children could not fully comprehend: the things they left behind. Those things were at once objects, people, and emotions, and they were part of what almost all immigrants came to call the Old Country. The place where they were children. The place where they ran with friends on summer mornings. The place where all spoke a common language. The place of tradition and certainties, including those cruel certainties that eventually became intolerable. For a long time in the age of sail, most knew they were leaving the Old Country forever. In Ireland, when still another son or daughter prepared to depart for America, families often held what became known as "the American wake." Their wailing was a lament, as if for the dead.

Similar rituals marked the departures of many Germans, Jews, Italians, and Poles as they traveled across land to the ports of Europe and then on to the scary Atlantic and the distant harbor of New York. Parents were certain they would never see their children again, and children surely felt that way about their parents. That rupture with the immediate past would mark all of them and did not go away as the young immigrants grew old. If anything, the nostalgias were often heightened by the coming of age. Bitterness often faded, but not the sense of loss. Some would wake up in the hot summer nights of New York and for a few moments think they were in Sicily or Mayo or Minsk. Some would think their mothers were at the fireplace in the next room, preparing food. The old food. The food of the Old Country.

Many of their nostalgias would be expressed in music. There were hundreds of nineteenth-century songs, in all languages, about vanished landscapes full of well-loved streams, or golden meadows, or the slopes of remembered hills, peopled usually by girls or boys who were left behind. The songs were often calculated treacle written in a cynical way for the immigrant market, but they triggered genuine emotions. With their labor, the immigrants who were singing these songs had purchased their tiny shares of New York. Most saw their children grow tall and healthy and educated. To be sure, some immigrants did little singing or remembering; they collapsed into alcohol, drugs, or criminality. Some were broken by New York and its hardness and returned in shame to the Old Country. Or, if the shame of failure was too much to admit, they moved west, to the empty land Out There, vanishing into America.

And yet . . . and yet, for those who prospered and those who did not, the music was always there. Those immigrant songs were sung in tenement kitchens and in dance halls, and at weddings and funerals. They ensured that from the beginning of the immigrant tides, loss and remembrance were braided into the New York character. Every immigrant knew what Africans had learned in the age of slavery: that there was a world that was once there in the most intimate way and was now gone. Part of the past. Beyond retrieval. On the deepest level, it didn't matter whether you had that past taken from you, as had happened to the Africans, or whether you had decided personally to leave it behind. At a certain hour of the night, the vanished past could be vividly alive.

That double consciousness—the existence of the irretrievable past buried in shallow graves within the present—was passed on to the children of the immigrants and, with diminishing power, to many of the grandchildren. All were conscious of time and its accompanying nostalgias. Events in the larger world often imposed that sense of time. I know a few old New Yorkers who still divide time into three epochs: Before the War, During the War, and After the War. They mean the Second World War. Each of the three periods shaped by the war has its own nostalgias, its own music, its own special sense of hope, anguish, or loss. New Yorkers on the home front experienced that war in a way that was different in the details from the way it was experienced in California or Mississippi or Florida. Other New Yorkers still mark a great shift in the personal consciousness of time by the departure in 1957 of the Brooklyn Dodgers and the New York Giants. Many conversations still can begin, "Before the Dodgers left..." Others mark time by the murder of John F. Kennedy in 1963, the event that was the true beginning of what became known as the sixties.

But the old immigrants themselves lived through that one great defining rupture: between the Old Country and the new. That wrenching break did not happen only to others; it was not forced upon them by history; the immigrants lived it themselves and thus made their own history. And their passage would cut a permanent psychological template into the amazing city they helped to build. In the age of the jetliner, there are no more American wakes. The departed emigrant children can now visit the Old Country, carrying their own American children with them, to celebrate holidays and weddings or to mourn for their dead parents. If they can afford the airline tickets, they can show their children the places where they were young. They can show off their photographs of New York streets, New York schools, New York apartments, New York graduations, New York ball games, and New York picnics. This, they can say in the Old Country, is their America. But the sense of the drastic break, of things left behind, remains with them, and therefore with us. Their nostalgias are familiar. They are the nostalgias that every one of their predecessors felt in the darkest hours of their Downtown tenement lives.

Here among us now in New York are the Dominicans and the Russians, Indians and Pakistanis, Mexicans and Chinese and Koreans, and others from what a visitor to New York in colonial days once called "all the nations under Heaven." Even from Togo. Some have moved into Downtown neighborhoods that once provided imperfect nurture to the Jews, Irish, Italians, and Germans before them. Some are settled in Brooklyn or living in newer places in Queens and the rehabilitated Bronx, and travel by subway to jobs in Downtown. Their presence always cheers me; they are proof that in the city of constant change we also have our continuities.

If they are lucky, the new immigrants will get to know

New York the way so many others did, long ago. They will discover that the easiest way to know this place is to start at the beginning. That is, to go on foot to Downtown. They will walk its streets. They will recognize its ruins and monuments. They will inhale the dust of the past. They will celebrate living in a place that is filled with people who are not, on the surface, like them. They will stroll with their children across the Brooklyn Bridge and see the spires of Oz gilded by morning sun.

Such experiences need not be limited to the newcomers in the city. Sadly, too many third- and fourth-generation children of the old European migration don't know much about the city that helped make their lives possible. This is as true of Denver as it is of New York. The tale is not taught in any powerful way in most public schools. The culture of television has deepened passivity, discouraging the active search for understanding. But true students, driven by simple curiosity, can still find the places where their grandparents or great-grandparents once struggled for them without even knowing their names. In New York, the student (of whatever age) can enter the surviving streets, gaze at the tenements, visit the Lower East Side Tenement Museum, and embrace the story. In New York, most of that old narrative took place Downtown.

So does the newer narrative. All around Downtown, the new immigrants can be seen today, literally from morning to night. They are working on the reconstruction of old buildings. They are delivering Chinese or Thai or Italian food through snowstorms. They are preparing sandwiches in Korean delicatessens. They are cooking in restaurants. They are taking their young American children to their

American schools. And late on Saturday nights in summer, when so many windows are open to the cooling air, the stroller can hear familiar music in unfamiliar languages, those aching ballads of loss and regret.

Chapter Two

THE FIRST DOWNTOWN

BEFORE THERE WAS a Downtown, there was the harbor. It is the reason for the city's existence and remains the liquid heart of the city.

The word *harbor* itself implies safety and welcome, what Bob Dylan once called shelter from the storm, and that is the way I always feel in its immense watery presence. On days of gray drizzle or dazzling October sun, I often wander to the Battery, to the place where all of this started not that long ago. On those visits, I'm part of a kind of international fiesta. Americans of all generations mingle with tourists from France and Germany and Japan and other nations of the world, people who believe New York is one of their treasures too.

"Look, Jimmy," says a woman from Minnesota to a teenage boy. "Right out there? You see that island just past the Statue of Liberty? That's Ellis Island, Jimmy. That's where your great-grandfather landed when he came from Germany."

A dozen feet away, a French couple peers across the water at the Statue of Liberty, the man with field glasses, the woman with a camera. I hear the name Bartholdi, the French sculptor who designed it. I hear the words Alsace-Lorraine, where Frédéric-Auguste Bartholdi was born in 1834. The full conversation is blown away in the breeze.

The overheard talk along the promenade always contains the same proper nouns: Ellis Island, the Statue of Liberty, and New York. I wander through those twenty-three acres of our grassy little Babel, and no matter what the language, the tone is one of awe and embrace. Peddlers are everywhere, with Statue of Liberty ashtrays, cheap little versions of the statue made of tin and plastic, and photographs of the statue with the twin towers in the background, along with Statue of Liberty T-shirts and jackets and pamphlets. But the Statue of Liberty Enlightening the World (its full title) seems forever safe from kitsch.

"What do you think?" I ask a bearded well-dressed man in his thirties, who turns out to be an architect from Bologna.

He smiles. "In every modern way," he says in excellent English, "we should laugh at it. But we don't, because it's beautiful. In spite of everything, it's beautiful. Because the *emotion* is beautiful."

Before all of us lies the Upper Bay, five miles long, three miles wide, in many places fifty feet deep. It is one of the great natural harbors of the world, protected from the open sea and yet part of that sea too. The water gives off the pervasive odor of salt, for while one powerful river flushes the Upper Bay each day from the north, and smaller ones feed it from the Jersey shores, the sea also rolls in on ceaseless tides. It moves up through the Hudson for miles.

I don't go to the Battery with hopes for adventure. I go in search of the familiar. Like many New Yorkers, I'm a creature of habit. I usually walk directly to the railing of the Admiral George Dewey Promenade, a name that no New Yorker ever uses, and I face the harbor. Almost always, I'm alone among strangers. There are many New York places where I prefer solitude: any museum, the pedestrian ramp of the Brooklyn Bridge, and here, where my city began. Sometimes I lose myself in counting waves on days when the wind is blowing in from the west and I can hear those waves breaking with a growling whoosh upon the granite seawalls. I look up at the flocks of seabirds, urban and sly, locked in a perpetual reconnaissance, rising, swooping, forever searching. Occasionally, I even see a falcon, fresh from a nest in one of the skyscrapers, alive again in the New York sky after years of death from chemicals. Flags, on their orderly flagpoles, are slapped and flopped by the breeze. On the wide lawns, kids eat ice-cream cones. Lovers hold hands. Solitary old men sit on benches, reading newspapers or watching the young with melancholy eyes. About once a year, I try a hot dog, in hope of recovering a lost pleasure of my childhood. They are always terrible, but I'm sure it's me, not the hot dogs. So I retreat into passive observation. The Staten Island ferry, all orange and squat, slides with surprising grace into its mooring, like a caravel on steroids. On some days I pass the hawkers of souvenirs, many of them now from Nigeria or Senegal, and think of those first Africans who arrived here in chains on the second Dutch ship in 1626.

In some unplanned way, part of the Battery is now a necropolis. Here we can pause and remember the dead of various wars and other calamities, or we can move past them in an indifferent hurry. The largest monument to the dead is the East Coast Memorial, dedicated to the 4,601 servicemen who died in the Atlantic coastal waters during World War II, defending, among many other places, the Port of New York. Visitors stand before each of eight huge granite slabs, examining the carved lists of the names divided by branch of service. "I had an uncle in the marines, died in the Pacific," a middle-aged woman said one afternoon. "I never knew him, but I've seen his pictures for years. He's not here, I guess. The Pacific, that's where he died. Not the Atlantic." Then she shook her head. "It's so damn sad." She glanced at the names of all the dead young Americans and walked away. A marker explains that the memorial was dedicated by President John F. Kennedy on May 23, 1963. Six months later, he was dead too.

The park holds other memorials. There's one for the wireless operators who died doing their work, including a man who went down on the *Titanic*. One is a gift to the American people from the sailors and merchant mariners of Norway, who used New York as a home port while the Nazis occupied their homeland. The Hope Garden is filled with rosebushes to memorialize those who live with HIV or have died from AIDS. Down near the ferry terminal is the US Coast Guard Memorial, erected in 1947, showing two young men helping a third, who is badly wounded.

The Korean War has its black obelisk with the stainless steel outline of a soldier cut into the polished granite, disembodied, faceless, epitomizing the Forgotten War. There's even one honoring the Salvation Army.

The most original lies thirty feet out in the water south of Pier A. This is the American Merchant Mariners Memorial by Marisol Escobar (1991), and I've seen nothing like it anywhere else. It's made of bronze and stainless steel, and shows merchant seamen on the tilted deck of a sinking raft. One seaman is kneeling. A second is shouting for aid. A third is on his belly, reaching into the water for the extended hand of a drowning man. The rescuer's hand falls short by less than an inch. At high tide in the harbor, the drowning man vanishes below the water. The simplicity of the conception includes the repetition of the tides, coming and going day after day, traveling from the hope for life to the certainty of death. Sometimes, Escobar says, there are no happy endings.

The most powerful memorial, in some ways, is also the most unplanned. It is the large sphere by German sculptor Fritz Koenig that stood for almost thirty years in the plaza of the World Trade Center. It was battered, twisted, and torn on September 11, 2001, but not destroyed. The ruptured parts have been reassembled here with all of their wounds showing, while an eternal flame burns before it on a patch of earth. Hundreds of visitors pause each day before this fiercely eloquent symbol of the city's worst calamity, the monument itself an alloy of various metals, and of past and present.

On most days, the park is noisy with people who are indifferent to the memorials. They are too busy being young.

They erupt into heart-stopping stunts on skateboards. They walk on their hands to impress girls. They smoke cigarettes. They hug each other, pet each other, and tell lies that are thousands of years old. Sometimes they even lean together on the railings and gaze out at the water.

Walking around the Battery, I know I'm almost always on landfill. All twenty-three acres of Battery Park were placed there by human beings, starting with the seventeenth-century Dutch. Beneath the trimmed grass surface lie the granite bones of today's park: boulders, clusters of rock, small reefs. Over the years the landfill even closed the gap with the old red sandstone fortress now called Castle Clinton. This was built in 1811 on a small man-made island a hundred yards off shore, with the sea serving as a kind of moat. At the time, tensions with the British were building toward war, and Castle Clinton was part of a system intended to defend the harbor. But the War of 1812 never came to New York. Before, during, and after that war, the Battery remained a zone of tranquillity.

In some ways, toward the end of day, the zone also feels washed with sadness. One monument is missing down here, one that should memorialize all those nameless women who came here to deal with loss. Down here, in the age of sail, wives and lovers often came to the shore to pray for the return of their seagoing men, many of whom never came back. They waited here for men who had gone off to war. Sometimes I can feel their melancholy presence and the sadder ghosts of those women who became reluctant prostitutes. With husbands gone or dead, they were forced in a hard world to do what they felt was necessary if they were to feed and shelter their children. Charity was elusive; there was no such thing as state welfare; jobs for women were almost nonexistent. So they accepted the stigma and the shame, trusting that God would be more forgiving than self-righteous human beings, and in all weathers they moved around the trees of the Battery. Across the 117 years of the British colony, they were here, servicing British officers and soldiers and various be-wigged worthies. They were here long after the triumph of the American Revolution. They should be remembered too.

In all seasons now, tourists cluster to the simple old cir-cular fort, picking up maps and leaflets or buying excur-sion tickets. The most curious visitors learn about the way this old fortress served as a clearinghouse for immigrants from 1855 to 1890, before the opening of Ellis Island, or how P. T. Barnum created a sensation in 1850 when he im-ported Jenny Lind, the Swedish Nightingale, to give a concert within the fort, whose name was then Castle Garden. I first saw the building in 1941, the last year of its existence as the New York Aquarium, a place filled with imprisoned squid and sharks and other ferocious creatures of the deep. That day, too, my mother held my hand.

From certain spots along the promenade, you can see the Verrazano Narrows Bridge, the last of the city's great sus-pension bridges (opened in November 1964). It serves now as a kind of man-made visual border announcing to arriv-ing vessels that they have entered the harbor of New York and to those departing that they have left the home precincts of Oz. I've sailed on transatlantic liners in both directions, and from the top decks, as you pass under the bridge, you feel as if you can reach out and touch it. The span passes over the mile-wide channel called the Narrows, connecting the Brooklyn end of Long Island to Staten Island, and I remember being told as a boy during the war that a steel mesh had been strung across this passage, hidden below the surface, to block any Nazi U-boats with dastardly notions of creating havoc in our harbor. Ships could pass over it, but no submarine could pass under it. That news thrilled me, as did the knowledge that we had anti-aircraft guns too, in Fort Hamilton in Brooklyn and Fort Wadsworth in Staten Island, aimed out at the Atlantic, and others on rolling tracks carved into the hills above the meadows of Prospect Park. Of one thing we were certain: Hitler and Göring would never get away with attacking our harbor and the great city that it served. Nobody would. This was a harbor. All harbors were safe. Or so we believed.

Out past the Narrows and its bridge lies the Lower Bay, another roughly one hundred square miles of water that leads from the open sea into the harbor. Both the Upper and Lower bays are part of the same system, and the Lower Bay is bounded by Sandy Hook, a curving five-mile-long sand spit seventeen miles south of the Narrows. For centuries, mariners have approached New York and seen Sandy Hook and followed its curving shape into the harbor. Even today, in the age of jetliners, the familiar channels of entry and departure are better known to some seagoing people than our streets and avenues. And the harbor itself is busy in a new way. We are an island now served by almost thirty ferry lines, like sleeker, more powerful versions of vanished craft from the nineteenth century. Pleasure craft follow the channels, seen and unseen. From the Battery I can't see that distant Lower Bay, but I can sense its existence sometimes in the liquid shimmer of the distant Atlantic sky.

On any given day at the Battery, I can see arriving freighters scabbed with old paint or powdery with rust. They move across the surface of the Upper Bay and turn to their left into the piers of New Jersey or continue past the tip of Manhattan into the North River, heading for Albany or Troy.

I am part of the last New York generation that calls the lower Hudson by its older name, the North River. A man across the street from us in Brooklyn once worked at Pier 1, North River, which was already gone when I met him, and other neighbors commuted each dawn to the elite piers of the passenger liners. In those days, there were seventy-five piers jutting from the island all the way to Fifty-ninth Street; today only thirteen are left. When as a boy I first heard the North River named in the accents of Brooklyn, I thought they were talking about the Nought River and wondered why it would bear such a title. Today, with all those vanished piers, that version of the river's true name seems fitting at last. As the plain North River, it passes all of Manhattan and doesn't become the Hudson to old New Yorkers until it passes north of the Tappan Zee Bridge.

I would learn later that the name connects us to the earliest years of the city. It was given to the river by the Dutch, not because it moved north to the fabled (and nonexistent) Northwest Passage to Asia, but because the early Dutch colonizers worked on two principal rivers. One was the Delaware, which they called the South River, and the other was the lordly Hudson, which was crucial to their northern settlement of New Netherland. The northern river is short by the standards of great rivers: a mere 350 miles long from its source in the Adirondacks. Still, it is a superb river. Geologists tell us that the Hudson and the North River were surely cut by a glacier through the frozen world that existed many centuries before history. The grinding power of that glacier was, of course, enormous. When the river passes Manhattan, where the glacier cut the sheer cliffs of the Palisades on the Jersey side, the depth is almost sixty feet. The ancient river channel itself moves out past the Narrows another sixty-odd miles into the Atlantic, suggesting to some geologists that it was once a longer, deeper river in a world where all oceans were much lower.

And there was much other history, all of it younger than the tale of the river. Some of it inadvertently revealed something of the city's later spirit. When Giovanni da Verrazzano° arrived at the Narrows in the middle of April 1524, after a voyage of more than fifty days, he sensed the power and surge of the underwater river and assumed that the harbor was a vast lake. He was a Florentine who sailed out of the French port of Dieppe and that year he was thirty-eight years old. As captain of the three-masted *La Dauphine,* he was in the employ of the French king, Francis I, who had enormous respect for Florentines, having given employment and shelter to Leonardo da Vinci in the artist-

°In most histories, Verrazzano is spelled with two *z*'s. Only the bridge named in his honor uses the single *z*. Go figure.

engineer's final years (Leonardo died in 1519). The purpose of the voyage of *La Dauphine* was to find that elusive Northwest Passage to the silks and spices of Asia, and to claim any unclaimed lands for France. Verrazzano failed in both tasks, but he did become the first European to find the great harbor. On July 8, he wrote a report to Francis I and described what he saw:

> As we were riding at anchor in a good berth, we would not venture up in our vessel without a knowledge of the mouth. Therefore we took the boat, and entering the river, we found the country on its banks well peopled, the inhabitants . . . being dressed out with feathers from birds of different colors. They came toward us with evident delight, raising loud shouts of admiration.

The Indians were almost certainly Lenape. In the following year, another visitor came through the Narrows from the world beyond the horizon. His name was Esteban Gomez, a black Portuguese sea captain who was searching for gold and silver or that elusive Northwest Passage. He returned the hospitality of the Indians by taking fifty-seven of them as slaves and hurrying off to peddle them in the slave markets of Lisbon. Then for a long time there were no recorded visits from strangers. A few shipwrecked sailors might have reached Lenape country, or the odd fur trader, or confused travelers headed north or south. But essentially, for more than eighty years after the Gomez visit there was no news of any kind. Then, on September 12, 1609, an English seaman named Henry Hudson sailed a Dutch ship called the *Halve Maen* (Half

Moon) into the harbor. Again, the local Indians were reasonably friendly. But Hudson kidnapped two of them for display back in Amsterdam, and when he reached Albany and the river narrowed and he knew there was no Northwest Passage, he turned back. One of the Indian prisoners died, the other escaped, and word spread on the island known as *Manna-hata* that these white people could not be trusted. Hudson departed swiftly under a shower of angry arrows.

By then, the Indians must have regretted their innocence in those early years of the seventeenth century. Those first Manhattanites had offered welcome and paid for their naïveté. Centuries would pass before their initial impulse was revived, by people who came across oceans.

Today, at the railing of Battery Park, I can see the ridge in Brooklyn where we lived. Up there in 1944, over on the left, I saw from our rooftop the skyline erupting into brilliant light after the Allied landing at Omaha Beach. The blackouts were over! The war would be next! My father said so. "Those Nazi bastards are finished!" And part of the deal, if you lived where we lived, was that the skyline would be ours, night after night, forever.

Here at the railing, my consciousness always shares this piece of the Battery with that place in Brooklyn. Two places separated by water. Two eras, separated by ten thousand small things. For a moment, and sometimes longer, I fill with certain shards and fragments from the summer of 1945, after the war was won in Europe. That summer was the beginning of the era we called After the

War, even though the era was not official until mid-August, when Japan surrendered. Most vivid of all to me was (and is) the sound of foghorns and ships' whistles and endlessly pealing church bells on the day that the old *Queen Mary* came steaming into the harbor. She was bringing home 14,526 of the men and women who had beaten the Nazi bastards. While crossing the Atlantic, they had slept on the floors of old cabins. They had slept on open decks. They had slept in engine rooms. But what the hell: If you had come out alive from the Battle of the Bulge or Anzio or Bastogne, nothing mattered except going home.

In *Manhattan '45*, the British writer Jan Morris brilliantly re-creates that day, reminding me of the navy dirigible I saw from our roof. It floated above the great ocean liner, moved over the Narrows and the hidden underwater mesh that had stopped the Nazi U-boats, and then was in the Upper Bay. The *Queen Mary* was followed, flanked, and preceded by a flotilla of smaller vessels: tugboats and fishing boats and small cargo ships. They passed the Statue of Liberty, and the roar of New York must have been heard in heaven. Thousands of those returning soldiers were surely the children or grandchildren of other brave people who had come across an ocean long ago, determined to become Americans. I like to think that some of the soldiers cheered those old immigrants too. As the harbor exploded with joy and celebration and triumph, I was four days short of my tenth birthday. I believed, as did those men and women on the *Queen Mary*, that all the wars were over. Few of us could have imagined the new monuments that would someday face that same harbor or the many places that young Americans would visit with guns and flags.

As the Dutch trading post became a Dutch settlement, the hamlet soon had quaint yellow-brick houses with steep gabled rooftops built out of the memory of Amsterdam. Some housed craftsmen and their apprentices and a few contained well-off burghers attended by African slaves. There were many rowdy taverns, much smoking of tobacco in clay pipes, plenty of naughtiness. The streets were mud. Pigs roamed freely. There were even a few windmills.

Most of us know that the Dutch built a wall across the top of their tiny settlement to keep out unfriendly natives, and when the threat was over and the wall was torn down, the place became Wall Street. We know that the Dutch, who loved canals, dug one along Broad Street that led to the sea, a canal later filled in by the conquering British. We know that on cold winter days they went ice skating on the Collect Pond, just above today's Chambers Street, then in the open countryside. That vanished hamlet deserved a painter like Franz Hals, even more than Vermeer or Rembrandt. The Dutch in New Amsterdam never got the painter that would bring their outpost to life, full of laughter and defiant optimism.

Those Dutch settlers, and the people they persuaded to join them, must have possessed an extraordinary loneliness too, of the kind Ray Bradbury expresses in his chronicles of Mars. After all, the journey from Holland to New Amsterdam averaged four and a half months. Nothing was familiar except what they built. They were perched on a tiny sliver of an island on the edge of a totally unknown, uncharted continent. It was no wonder that they huddled for warmth through those first winters in the few churches and the many taverns.

But the physical evidence of their presence is gone, except for those streets laid out long ago. Fire was the great agent of erasure. The great fire at the beginning of the American Revolution destroyed 493 houses down here (along with the early version of Trinity Church). Most were British; many were Dutch. The Great Fire of 1835, which leveled 700 more houses, erased what was left. The remnants lie under the skyscrapers. Even Fort Amsterdam, much of it built by slave labor, the place where Peter Stuyvesant expressed his rage and his authority, was long ago reduced to rubble, and the spot is now partially occupied by the muscular marble solidity of the Custom House.

The one exception to the erasure of the Dutch town is the small triangular park called the Bowling Green. Nobody bowls there anymore, although the Dutch and English once did, but it stands as a green marker to the creation of the city, right down at the beginning of Broadway. The grass is protected by an iron fence, which itself has gone through as many mutations as the little park. This triangular spot was once much larger, serving as a produce market for the early settlers, as a cattle fair, and as a marching ground for inept amateur soldiers.

Occasionally, it was the scene of trading with visiting Indians. The street that became Broadway was adapted to an existing, much-traveled Indian trail. Right up to the arrival of the Europeans, and for twenty years afterward, the

native Americans retained the old habit of visiting Manna-
hata in summer from their home precincts high on the island or out on Long Island. They left no written records,
of course, but all were under the general anthropological
umbrella of the Lenape. Some were Canarsees from Long
Island. Some were Weckquaesgecks whose home base
was in present-day Westchester. Some were Mahicans
from the west side of the river. For centuries they had
feasted here on the bounty of the harbor: oysters and
clams, lobster and terrapin, and every manner of fish. One
study estimates that oyster beds covered 350 square miles
of the bay and the North River. There were occasional dolphins in the harbor and a rare visiting whale who had
taken a wrong turn at Sandy Hook. Before the eastern
shore of the island's tip was expanded by landfill, there
were great mounds of oyster shells along the river edge,
some washed ashore by the currents of the estuary, some
left behind by the summering Lenape. They were
smoothed out by early settlers to make a street, which
some forgotten Dutchman with a sense of irony dubbed
Pearl Street. The street lives on with that name. It is the
street where Captain Kidd once lived and where Herman
Melville was born.

There were few pearls to be discovered in early Dutch
New York. The basic trade involved beaver pelts gathered
in the forests up the North River, and there were never
enough of them to create profit. The Dutch did not, as
they had hoped, establish a major rivalry with the Russian
fur traders who helped clothe wintry Europe. But in their
North American settlement, certain practices became a
founding component of all future New York generations.

New Amsterdam's basic mission was to make money for the West India Company, its directors, and its shareholders. The company (not any king) assigned the directors, calling them governors, and some of those early New Amsterdam governors had private missions. They were not there to proclaim the truth of any Christian sect. They were not there to create a modern civilization among people they saw as savages. They were there to get rich. Almost from the start, corruption was woven into the enterprise.

Standing at the iron fence of today's Bowling Green, I sometimes imagine Willem Verhulst nodding at friends or acquaintances gathered at this spot, his mind feverish with deals. He was the first director of the trading post, or governor, ruling in the name of the West India Company. His residence stood within the confines of the fort that he had ordered built. There is no surviving portrait of the man, but with Hals and Rembrandt in mind, I imagine him as thick necked and blustery, wearing his authority as a weapon. He was, by all surviving accounts, a bully and a drunk. But more important to the New York tale, he was also a man with a passion for crookedness. He created the future city's first known set of double books, one for the company, one for himself. He cut himself into various other deals (primarily in real estate) around his small but growing domain. The company directors finally got wise and recalled him, replacing him with Peter Minuit, a forty-year-old French-speaking Walloon born in Germany, who was to formalize the title to the island with the company's "purchase" of Manna-hata for twenty-four dollars' worth of beads and trinkets. This was almost certainly a double

swindle, with visiting Canarsee Indians unloading an island to which they had no genuine claim. Minuit served
for only thirteen months, but his name endures thanks to
that land transaction, a fitting claim to fame, after all, in a
city that would be driven so ruthlessly by the future brig-
ands of real estate.

Those who soon followed Minuit were either crooked or
stupid. None matched in flamboyance the British governor Lord Cornbury (1661–1723), who after 1702 loved
strolling the ramparts of the fort dressed in drag and had
himself painted as Queen Anne. Then, in 1647 arrived that
extraordinary human bundle of flaws and virtues named
Peter Stuyvesant: a brave soldier, a tough commander, his
peg leg banded with silver, his mind filled with certainties
and iron will and his share of nasty little bigotries. His
frown seemed permanent. His rages about human weakness were legendary. Stuyvesant arrived in Nieuw
Amsterdam in 1647, aged thirty-seven, expecting to stay
for three years; he stayed for fifteen. Even when the
British took the town in 1664, even after his own son had
joined those citizens—a majority—who urged him not to
resist the British forces, Stuyvesant stayed on. He retreated to his immense farm, or bouwerie, up the east side
of the island, and is buried at St. Mark's-in-the-Bowery,
parts of which served as the farm's chapel. The church is
at Second Avenue and East Tenth Street, and for years
kids from the wrong side of town made failed raids on the
cemetery hoping to steal Stuyvesant's silver-banded leg.
(One of them was Rocky Graziano, the middleweight box-
ing champion in the 1940s.) Stuyvesant surely would have
seen such expeditions as additional proof of human iniq-

uity. But after his death in 1672, he became one of those permanent New Yorkers, his bones staying on forever in the island that in some cranky, fierce way he loved more than the land where he was born.

Today, more than three centuries after his death, Stuyvesant's name and image are welded to the alloy of Manhattan. His name adorns the finest public high school on the island. It is the name of an eighteen-square-block housing project on the East Side, built in 1943. Apartment houses carry the name, and at least one public square, one florist, and one oil burner company.

There are no public traces of his corrupt predecessors, and no memorials. In a way, there should be, for their legacies are part of the New York alloy too.

The Bowling Green is now a tranquil secret garden. It is difficult to imagine the Dutch here, grunting, smoking, and bowling. Outside its fence, at the northern tip of a traffic island that includes the tiny park, stands a bronze statue of an angry bull twisting its horned head north toward unseen Wall Street. The three-and-a-half-ton bull is the work of a sculptor named Arturo DiModica, cast by a man named Domenico Ranieri. The statue was not commissioned by anyone. It simply turned up, sixteen feet long, under a Christmas tree in front of the Stock Exchange in 1989. The parks department later arranged to move it to the present location, where it seems certain to remain, deep in the heart of the capital of capitalism. The reason is simple: New Yorkers and their guests love it. Every day of the week, platoons of visitors clamber around its head while posing in rain or sunshine for the cameras of their friends. At the rear of the statue, teenage girls pose beside the bull's immense testicles, now polished by thousands of enthusiastic hands. At first, the posing girls always giggle. Then they laugh in a roguish way. And sometimes they erupt in gales of laughter. On one afternoon, I saw four French nuns behaving just like the teenage girls while a fifth nun immortalized them with a digital camera. Surely no statue in Manhattan has brought more joy to strangers.

DiModica's bull has its back to the secret garden of the Bowling Green. Inside the fence, there are smooth-topped tables with slatted chairs, and benches where solitary visitors read books or watch the platoons of tourists following leaders carrying yellow bats or furled American flags. At one summery table not long ago, three homeless men argued loudly over a chessboard, their words a slurred yawp. A man in a business suit licked a Dairy Freeze ice-cream cone in isolated pleasure. Another stood silently beside a gurgling fountain, staring into the water.

"I come here," said an older man named Richard Hewitt, "because nothing ever happens when I'm here. That's exactly why I come here."

A sign on the fence now explains that the green was leased under British rule in 1733 as the official bowling green (for a rent of one peppercorn a year), with the fence itself erected in 1771. Originally each picket of the fence wore a replica of a British crown. But on July 9, 1776, when the Sons of Liberty and other young Americans heard a reading in what is now City Hall Park of the Declaration of Independence (signed five days earlier in Philadelphia), a mob descended upon the park. They did

a bit of damage. The prime object of their patriotic exu-
berance was a huge, gilded, seven-year-old equestrian
statue of George III, the mad king of England. The design
was based on the famous statue of Marcus Aurelius in
Rome. The mob ignored all noble antecedents. They toppled the metal George III from his marble pedestal, as-
saulted him with clubs and axes, beheaded him. Witnesses
remarked that there were no shouts of triumph or singing
of revolutionary songs. The dismantling was manual labor.
According to historian Rodman Gilbert, some patriots
then took the various pieces by cart off to distant hideouts
(almost certainly in Connecticut) and melted down the
statue's four thousand pounds of lead into 42,088 bullets
(in his 1936 account, *The Battery*, Gilbert did not explain
who did the counting). We do know that the battered head
came to a tavern in Kingsbridge, where it was soon captured by British soldiers, then briefly buried for safekeep-
ing, dug up, and sent off to England, where it was shown
to some citizens as proof of the savagery of the Americans.
The tail of the horse and three other fragments were found
on a Connecticut farm in 1871 and are now at the New-
York Historical Society.

The mob also wrenched the crowns off each picket in
the Bowling Green fence. The fence itself has survived,
but after more than two centuries, nobody has ever found
those missing crowns.

From the entrance to the little park, a visitor can look
south toward the harbor and see, a few hundred feet away,
the splendid pile whose official name is the Alexander
Hamilton US Custom House. Since the 1990s, it has

housed the George Gustave Heye Center of the National Museum of the American Indian, which contains many fine things, and a good bookstore. Most New Yorkers simply call it the Custom House.

The designer was Cass Gilbert, a midwesterner who became one of the finest of all New York architects (his masterpiece is the 1913 Woolworth Building). The building is only seven stories high, in a neighborhood of giant structures, but the Gilbert design, in the French beaux arts style, has an enduring, muscular power. Gilbert has been called a "modern traditionalist," adhering to the surface styles of traditional European architecture but drawing on advances in technology, including the use of steel frames and, later, the elevator. Unlike the modern Bauhaus-inspired blankness that was to dominate mid-twentieth-century New York, this was a building to be looked upon, studied, even read. Gilbert wanted to please his client, and himself, and the New Yorker who strolled by on a summer afternoon. He pleased all three.

The exterior stone is a dark gray Maine granite, with forty-four Corinthian columns spaced around the entire building. Out front, too, stand four white limestone sculptures by Daniel Chester French, in striking contrast to the darker building itself, the groups of figures representing Asia, America, Europe, and Africa. High above the main entrance are smaller statues dedicated to the world's greatest mercantile nations, as perceived in those confident early years of the twentieth century: Greece, Rome, Phoenicia, Genoa, Venice, Spain, Holland, Portugal, Denmark, Germany, England, and France. Clearly this is a building designed to be used (one of Gilbert's tasks was to find storage space for the growing bulk of bureaucratic documents). But it also was imagined as a monument to trade. That is, as a monument that expressed the triumphant spirit of the booming port of New York.

Today, a visitor can climb the same wide stairway that existed when the building opened in 1907 and inhale the salt air of the harbor or gaze north along Broadway. Inside is the elliptical rotunda, 135 feet long, with a dome that rises almost 85 feet above the floor. The marble columns and marble mosaic floors add a sumptuous, even sensual flavor to the room and an echo that is almost ghostly. The fresco murals here were painted by Reginald Marsh in 1937. In the early 1920s, Marsh was a sketch artist for the tabloid *New York Daily News,* but he had moved on from journalism to become the visual poet of the city's subways, dance halls, and burlesque palaces. Faced with those high unadorned walls — eight horizontal spaces, eight vertical — he must have understood what most New Yorkers come to understand: the harbor is everything. The art historian Lloyd Goodrich described his solution:

> For the central theme of the large space he chose to represent eight successive stages in the arrival of an ocean liner at New York: the ship passing Ambrose lightship; taking on a pilot; being met by a coast guard cutter; being boarded by officials; passing the Statue of Liberty; on deck, the press receiving a female celebrity (probably Greta Garbo); tugs warping the ship into dock; and finally, discharge of cargo at the pier. This was a modern saga, both real and epic; clear and logical in its unfolding, and completely appropriate for the building.

Marsh froze the present in these 1937 paintings, which is why today they give off such a powerful aura of nostalgia. In New York, the present becomes the past more rapidly than in any other world city. Look up at the paintings in a certain mood and you can hear Rudy Vallee singing. You can see Fred Astaire delivering the gift of grace to those maimed by the Depression. You can see Mayor La Guardia kicking slot machines into a river. You can see people walking down gangplanks and reaching for that day's *New York Times* or *Daily News*. Or you can hear romantic young F. Scott Fitzgerald, in his autobiographical essay "My Lost City," remembering the first time he came through the Narrows on such a ship, after three years in Europe: "As the ship glided up the river, the city burst thunderously upon us in the early dark—the white glacier of lower New York swooping down like a strand of a bridge to rise into uptown New York, a miracle of foamy light suspended by the stars." And then arriving again after the Crash, almost a decade later, like the passengers in the Marsh paintings: "We passed through curiously polite customs agents, and then with bowed head and hat in hand I walked reverently through the echoing tomb. Among the ruins a few childish wraiths still played to keep up the pretense that they were alive, betraying by their feverish voices and hectic cheeks the thinness of the masquerade."

The well-heeled passengers in the Marsh paintings of 1937 might have been chastened, as Fitzgerald was, by reality. But Marsh grants them the right to a mask. They could pretend to care more for the ball scores and the stock market than the news of Hitler or the civil war in

Spain or the permanent scars of the Depression. For most of the passengers, adjustments appear to have been made. They had come through the bad time after the crash in 1929, when stockbrokers were shooting themselves in the bathrooms of speakeasies. Some had trained themselves to resist pity. But in the paintings, even they have a kind of pleased innocence, as they return to a New York that had three major league baseball teams and nine newspapers.

The world symbolized by the great liners seemed certain to last forever, with all its arrogant adherence to the privileges of class. When Marsh was painting them, he could have walked out the door of the Custom House and seen the flagship buildings of the major shipping lines, solid and impregnable. They were bunched together on those few blocks of lower Broadway that had been called since the middle of the nineteenth century "Steamboat Row." The buildings are still there, although the ships have all gone.

Marsh must have walked where a vendor now sells lemonade and coffee and snacks, and looked at number 1 Broadway. On this spot in the perilous early days of the American Revolution, George Washington briefly pitched his headquarters in the home of one Archibald Kennedy. The historian Thomas Jefferson Wertenbaker described it this way: "Its classical front entrance, Palladian window, ornate cornice, spacious rooms, grand staircase, elaborately decorated walls and ceilings, its great banqueting hall bespoke both good taste and opulence."

Washington didn't stay long in the comfort of that house. Within months, he retreated from New York with most of his amateur army in the face of overwhelming

British seaborne power, to fight again another day in other places. After the war, the site evolved from private home to tavern to small hotel and then in 1848 into the larger Washington Hotel. For more than thirty years it remained a hotel, serving the growing international clientele that passed through the booming harbor, or Americans from other states coming to New York to embark for Europe or other parts of the world.

Then, in 1881, Cyrus W. Field, famous for being in charge of the successful laying of the Atlantic cable, decided to convert the site into an office building. The planned building started at ten stories, then was increased to twelve stories, with a tower and a mansard roof. Rising 258 forbidding feet above Broadway, the building offered views from the offices that were said to be spectacular. But in photographs, the imposing building, with its dark red-brick facade, looks gloomy at best, spooky at worst. The real estate men eventually agreed. In 1921, it was given a face-lift, with much of the ornament removed and the facade covered with a white limestone veneer. Until 1969, it would serve as the proud headquarters of the United States Lines. That year, the American flag vanished from the passenger line business.

Today the building still carries marks from the vanished world in which it existed. Carved into the Broadway facade are escutcheons of the outposts of a swaggering capitalist empire: Capetown, New York, Melbourne, Queenstown, London, Plymouth. They remind us that globalization is nothing new. Around the corner on the long Battery Place side there are carved seashells and dolphins, along with doors still marked Cabin Class and First

Class. Those doors no longer offer passage to distant places. Now they enter upon a row of ATMs operated by Citibank. On hot summer days, when the city is wilting, everybody looks like cabin class.

At 25 Broadway stands another building from the lost world. A sign informs us that it is now the Bowling Green Station of the United States Post Office, which it has been since 1977, but for decades 25 Broadway served as the New York headquarters of the mighty Cunard Line. This was once the largest, grandest, most important passenger ship line in the world, which had been sailing to New York since 1840. One hundred and five years later, when the *Queen Mary* arrived with all those returning troops, there must have been people here who wept. And before his death in 1916, my grandfather, a valued employee of Cunard, must have visited here too. To step inside the building, as Reginald Marsh surely must have done while working at the Custom House, is to be astonished.

The bronze doors open into a high vaulted vestibule that in combination with the great hall beyond has been described by the New York writer Gerard R. Wolfe as "certainly one of the most beautiful interior spaces anywhere." I agree. The vestibule, with ornament designed by Ezra Winter, is a kind of overture for the great hall. The visitor pauses and then enters the main room, the place where travelers once booked passage. This chamber is shaped like an octagon and is 185 feet long and 74 feet wide, with a dome that rises 65 feet above the floor. It forces you to look up. And there on the groined, vaulted ceiling is a riot of figures and designs, all swirling with energy into ocean-like arabesques. There are mermaids and dolphins, starfish and sea horses, waves and wind, ships bearing many flags. Frescoes, bas-reliefs, painted maps, unreadable signs, obscure symbols, with visiting Neptunes and sirens and even an albatross: All struggle for space in this man-made vision of the sea. There are the ships of Columbus. And Leif Eriksson. And Sebastian Cabot. All as remote now, even to schoolchildren, as the legend of the Flying Dutchman. In some odd way, this baroque storm of a ceiling has an almost angry feeling to it now, as if the sea gods resent their abandonment by the puny mortals who are lined up below them, buying stamps.

By comparison, the murals of Reginald Marsh, just down the block, are sedate, even happy. In the turbulent art of the Cunard Building, you still feel the presence of drowned sailors and lost ships, betrayed by wind and stars and luck. Waves can be murderous, the images tell us. Tides can be remorseless. All voyages are filled with the peril of the unknown. The Cunard murals are about the adventure and romance of going away. The Marsh murals in the Custom House remind me always of those soldiers in 1945. They too are about coming home. And home, for Marsh, is always New York.

Chapter Three

TRINITY COUNTRY

IT IS A bright Saturday afternoon in late summer, with a cooling breeze blowing up Broadway from the harbor. On the western sidewalk, I gaze down the slope of Wall Street, its entrance barricaded against terrorists with ugly concrete blocks. In the distance I can see the dark band of the East River. Sharing the sidewalk with me is a Middle Eastern man peddling hot dogs and roasted nuts from a cart with an umbrella. Ten feet away, another man sells New York sweatshirts, and they chat away in Arabic as the tourists pass them, fresh from looking at the site of the destroyed World Trade Center. A few yards downtown, toward Rector Street, huddled against the entrance to the subway station, an African man sells handbags and watches.

My mind teems with those who have passed this way, the posturing aristocrats, the illustrious people from John

Adams to Edith Wharton, the vanished merchant princes of the early nineteenth century, Alexander Hamilton and his deadly rival, Aaron Burr, mechanics and their apprentices, slaves and freedmen. I try to imagine the vanished Dutch town. We retain several Dutch words, such as *boss* and *stoop*, along with a few other remnants. As noted, those early Dutch bosses established the long New York tradition of corruption. The most famous boss, Peter Stuyvesant, waged a bigoted war against human weakness and, of course, lost, thus establishing another New York tradition. But there was one enduring legacy from the Dutch, one that even Stuyvesant could not destroy: the spirit of tolerance.

That legacy of tolerance was not created by starry-eyed Dutch idealists. The Netherlands in the seventeenth century was the most religiously tolerant country in Europe because the Dutch were pragmatists. Paradise could wait; what mattered was making money today, this week, or this year. That in turn meant that everybody must have a share in the nation's enterprise. When Stuyvesant wanted to expel Jewish refugees from New Amsterdam, the true bosses back home, the directors of the Dutch West India Company, told him, in effect, Forget it; we have Jews on our board. Tolerance was more than an ideal. It was good business.

Most of the Dutch physical presence was erased by the great fires of 1776 and 1835. Time changed other things too. Across the long years of British rule, the old Dutch families slowly merged with their British conquerors, creating the first human alloy in New York, which was given its name in 1809 by Washington Irving: the

Knickerbockers. On the whole, the Anglo-Dutch were a haughty, pretentious group, with constricted, mannered social lives, given to careful public display of aristocratic values. Irving was making fun of them in his *A History of New York from the Beginning of the World to the End of the Dutch Dynasty.* But the name stuck, and even the subjects of his humor came to embrace it. I'm always cheered when I think that those who are today called Knickerbockers have included such men as Patrick Ewing, Latrell Sprewell, and Stephon Marbury.

The old Knickerbockers had their nostalgias too: for moving in grand carriages driven by slaves, or ballrooms in Georgian houses blazing with candlelight, or flirtations in Sunday morning places of worship. But nothing could last forever. The Bowling Green got smaller and smaller, more a park than a place for actual bowling. The splendid Georgian-Federal houses that faced it became places of trade, almost all of it concerned with the business of the port. Down the slope of Wall Street, in the direction of the East River, fine private homes gave way to countinghouses and brokerages and insurance companies, and later to skyscrapers. Down there, at the end of Wall Street at the river's edge, stood the slave market. It too was part of the business of the port, and most of the prominent Knickerbocker families took part in it without shame. Many convinced themselves that God approved. Most didn't care. This was New York, where money ruled.

On today's stroll north on Broadway, I pause, as always, when I reach Trinity Church. It's a day free of appointments or deadlines. I can surrender for a while to this marvelous piece of human evidence. I'm not a religious man, but I'm always moved by Trinity and the land upon which it stands in such Gothic majesty. It is hard to imagine New York without it. Even its location speaks to our origins as a city, for Trinity faces Wall Street, creating a symbolic crossroads of God and Mammon.

I enter the wide gates in the fence to the grounds and walk around to the left into the churchyard. I go directly to the monument that marks the grave of Alexander Hamilton. For several years in the early 1960s, coming up from the subway after midnight and walking down Rector Street toward West Street to go to work, I passed this monument and thought about the man. Almost certainly I'd have voted against Hamilton and his notions about the absolute need for an American aristocracy. But still I cherished him. In 1801, he had founded, with some political allies, the newspaper called the *New York Post*. In 1960, I started to work there as a reporter, thus beginning my adult life. I was like most other young men, profoundly ignorant of the past, even that part of it that had some marginal relevance to my own life. But I knew enough to thank Hamilton for starting his newspaper. I still offer him my gratitude.

The Hamilton monument rises to a pyramid, the base of the pyramid bearing four stone lamps. Words and dates are carved into the face, but they only suggest the complexity of Hamilton's life, of course, starting with his birth in the West Indies in 1755. At the foot of this monument is the grave of his wife, Elizabeth, who as the daughter of Philip Schuyler was part of the Knickerbocker elite. By comparing the dates on both graves we learn that

Elizabeth lived for almost fifty years after Hamilton was shot dead in his foolish 1804 duel with Aaron Burr across the North River in Weehawken, New Jersey. The former Elizabeth Schuyler surely had heard the tales of her handsome husband's infidelities, real or merely rumored, but she ended up beside him in the graveyard at Trinity.

Off to the right is the grave of Robert Fulton, who died in 1815 and thus did not see the enormous changes that came to New York in the wake of his steamboat, originally called the North River Steamboat, later the *Clermont*. This first successful steam-powered ship sailed from the foot of Cortlandt Street in 1807 and made it to Albany in a record thirty-two hours. At the time, most of the city's seaborne commerce was clustered along South Street on the East River. That river (or estuary) was generally free of ice because of tides and salt from the harbor, and captains preferred to avoid the hard winds that often howled from north or west along the North River. Fulton's passenger steamboat changed all that, gradually at first and then with a great triumphant surge in the later decades of the nineteenth century. That little steamboat opened the North River to commerce and development. Until his invention, Fulton, a child of Irish immigrants from Kilkenny, was better known as a gifted painter, a student in Paris of the American expatriate Benjamin West, one of the most important painters of the turn of the century. On Fulton's monument, the bas-relief is based on a self-portrait. But Fulton's remains are not beneath his monument; they are in the vault of the Livingston family. His wife, Harriet, was a Livingston, and the *Clermont* was named for the family's Hudson Valley estate.

Today the tombstones and monuments, like so much about Trinity, exist as testimony. The earliest graveyard is north of the church itself, granted to the parish in 1697. The second, where the monuments to Hamilton and Fulton stand, was added in 1705. The north yard is dominated today by a brownstone Gothic monument erected in 1852 in memory of those hundreds of Americans who died as British prisoners during the Revolution in the old Sugar House two streets north of Trinity on what is now called Liberty Street (formerly Crown Street). Together, north and south are said to hold 1,907 graves, with others in private family vaults inside the church. They tell us something about mortality and vanity, of course, as all graveyards do, but they also speak to us about history and change in the city of New York.

The names and relevant dates of many of the dead have been ground away by time and weather, and in a few cases charred into blankness by the fires of 1776 that toppled the first Trinity itself. Some of the permanent residents were renowned in their time, and for the few years in which they existed in human memory. The north yard holds the remains of William Bradford, who was a printer in Hanover Square beginning in 1693 and in 1752 founded New York's first newspaper, the *New York Gazette.* He lived to be ninety-two. Also here is Francis Lewis, the only signer of the Declaration of Independence to be buried in Manhattan; he lost almost everything in the Revolution but is better known now through the boulevard in Queens that bears his name. Albert Gallatin is here too, twice secretary of the treasury, the man who stabilized American finances during the presidency of Thomas Jefferson and helped forge the settlement that ended the War of 1812. He was a founder of New York University. In a way, they too are examples of the New York alloy. Bradford emigrated to New York from England. Lewis was born in Wales. Gallatin came to New York from his native Switzerland.

But with the probable exceptions of Hamilton and Fulton, even those whose names remain legible are now as forgotten as those whose names have been erased. Many of them were children, dead of cholera, dead of smallpox, dead of yellow fever in a town that had an inadequate water supply and no sewage system at all, a town where wild dogs contended for garbage with free-running pigs. The aristocrats who rented pews at Trinity did what they could to immunize themselves and their children from the dangers around them. Some of those tombstones tell us that none was ever truly safe.

Trinity has its own rich New York history, in its way as indomitable as the city itself. The first church was granted a charter as part of the Church of England in 1697 by King William III, appropriately an imported Dutchman. The British strongly believed in welding church to state in the interests of preserving power. The first small, squarish church opened the following year, its construction aided by block and tackle loaned by Captain William Kidd from Pearl Street, who in 1701 would be hanged in London for piracy. Kidd would not be the last New Yorker whose friends insisted he was framed.

The future of Trinity was truly secured in 1705, when Queen Anne made a land grant for a "church farm" that extended from Broadway to the North River and from what became Fulton Street all the way to Christopher Street in the west of today's Greenwich Village. Such an immense grant was not unusual for the day. The Dutch had granted enormous tracts to well-connected patrons, arrangements validated by the shrewd British conquerors. The British understood that New Amsterdam was an outpost of a company, not a country, and thus free of nationalist obligations. They brought the Dutch settlers into the life of the colony they had renamed New York.

In London, the British crown also understood that its distant colony needed institutions that would bind it permanently to the mother country. Trinity was selected to become one of those institutions. The grant was surely intended to ensure the dominance of the Church of England, although in far-off London in 1705, this was largely a game of maps and speculation, like handing out land on Mars.

But that land, the essential secular patrimony of Trinity, was to ensure its survival in the postrevolutionary town where churches came and went, too often reduced to rubble to make way for banks or brokerages. Even their graveyards were paved over by the agents of Mammon. As the city expanded from the hamlet below Wall Street, the land grant became even more valuable (today it would be worth billions). This gave Trinity a sense of security, so that it never succumbed to religious fanaticism in the years when conflict between Protestants and newly arrived Irish and German Catholics sometimes left corpses in the streets. The good vestrymen of Trinity had learned the virtues of patience that came from surviving tumult and disaster. When the church was reduced to ashes in 1776, there was no doubt in the minds of the vestrymen that they would rebuild as soon as the Revolution ended. During that great upheaval, Trinity remained loyal to the British crown. As part of the Church of England, it had no choice. But there was no unanimity in the congregation itself. Some good Anglicans vanished from their rented pews and went off to join the forces of independence. Others remained, certain that the rebels would be crushed and life would return to normal. But nothing is normal about a revolution. In 1783, many of the Tories of Trinity, including the rector, joined the exodus to England and Nova Scotia.

The ruined church was rebuilt. During the construction, most of the depleted congregation worshipped at St. Paul's Chapel, a branch of Trinity that had opened in 1766, five blocks to the north on Broadway. When George Washington was inaugurated as president in 1789, he walked from Federal Hall to St. Paul's, where a pew was decorated in his honor; it can still be seen there. The choice of St. Paul's that historic day was dictated by one simple fact: The new Trinity was not finished until the following year. But the spare simplicity of St. Paul's was fitting for a president who represented republican values. It remains the oldest continuously used structure in Manhattan. After September 11, 2001, the chapel served its city with great honor, providing food, drink, and rest to hundreds of rescue workers and hard hats, and its fences were decorated by thousands of spontaneous messages from those who came downtown to find lost relatives, friends, or lovers, or simply to mourn. St. Paul's has been witness to more history than Trinity itself.

The 1790 Trinity can be seen in old prints, with its 200-foot spire rising above every other structure in sight. This second Trinity was, alas, an imperfect structure. In 1839, the roof was badly damaged by a heavy snowstorm. The vestrymen and their advisers looked carefully at the problem and decided that it would be more sensible to tear down the entire church and start over than to try to repair it. This time they hired a young architect named Richard Upjohn, who had emigrated from England as a child and was a former cabinetmaker. He got it right.

If you stand facing Trinity today, the brownstone church of Richard Upjohn soars before you with a kind of muted grandeur. The tower rises 284 feet above the street. This surely must have inserted an unacknowledged model into the New York imagination from the day of its consecration in January 1846. Its presence, decade after decade, surely said that great buildings must challenge the sky.

The cornerstone was laid in 1841. Over the next five years, Upjohn himself supervised the project, and he was present when it was consecrated. The cost was $90,000, the equivalent of about $1.9 million in today's money. The material Upjohn used was a brownstone quarried in New Jersey, but one subtly free of the chocolate look of many surviving brownstone buildings in New York. Trinity's facade is enriched with a subtle rose color that is most luminous in the mornings when the sun courses up Wall Street. If the church is now dwarfed by the skyscrapers that are its neighbors, it still asserts a sense of phoenixlike triumph, rebirth, and enduring faith.

I wait among the crowds of people entering the church and run my fingers over Trinity's bronze doors. The day is warm. The doors are cool. The doors are modeled after Ghiberti's famous, much-imitated doors for the Baptistery in Florence. These doors were added in 1896, designed by Richard Morris Hunt, the favored architect of the uptown nouveau riche who were insisting on chateaux and grand mansions in Newport and on Fifth Avenue. Hunt chose conventional scenes from the Bible and left their execution to the sculptors Karl Bitter, who did the main door, J. Massey Rhind, who did the right, and Charles H. Niehaus, who sculpted the left. Bitter was an immigrant from Austria who also did the sculpture in the Pulitzer Fountain in Grand Army Plaza, facing the Plaza Hotel. On the night of the day he finished the clay model of the Pulitzer bronze, he left the Metropolitan Opera and was run over by a taxi and killed. In New York, artists have learned not to expect applause.

The doors were paid for by William Waldorf Astor (1848–1919) in honor of his father, John Jacob Astor III, who was known among the Astors as Junior to the day he died in 1890. The original John Jacob Astor, an immigrant from Germany, was not a regular at Trinity, not even conventionally religious, although he was christened as a Lutheran. But he was well-known to the people who ran the church and its properties. Very well known.

After emigrating to America at age twenty in 1784, Astor had an extraordinary career: peddler of musical instruments, ruthless fur trader, war profiteer, opium traf-

ficker in the China trade. But a deal involving Trinity led
him to his truest vocation. This too involved a man whose
ghost lingers over the churchyard: Aaron Burr. The story
is not a simple one. In 1767, Abraham Mortier, paymaster
general of British forces in North America, made a deal
with Trinity to lease 465 acres of land along the North
River, including parts of today's Greenwich Village. For
Mortier, the terms were perfect: $269 a year for ninety-
nine years. It's a wonderful thing to deal with a church
from a position of secular power. On the tract, facing the
North River, Mortier built a mansion called Richmond
Hill, on land between today's King, Varick, Charlton, and
MacDougal streets. Came the Revolution, Mortier fled
New York, and in 1790, Burr acquired the lease. He ran
Richmond Hill in a lavish presidential style (although that
prize always eluded him), and his guests were as varied as
James Madison, Thomas Jefferson, and the man he would
eventually send to the earth of the Trinity graveyard, his
rival Alexander Hamilton. There is no record of John
Jacob Astor attending these festivities, but Burr and Astor
knew each other in the small but growing port of New
York. In those days, New York was still a walking town.

In 1802, Burr was serving as vice president under
Thomas Jefferson and was desperately short of money.
He made a deal with Astor, turning over the Mortier lease
for $62,500. The lease ran until May 1, 1866. Astor began
subdividing the land into at least 241 lots and devised
unique terms for those who subleased the lots from him.
They could do what they wanted on their lots for twenty-
one years. After that, they must renew the lease or Astor

would take back the lot. If they went broke, too bad. Astor cleaned up.

By then, Astor knew that the city was growing inexorably to the north and, with the Mortier-Burr lease in mind, he began buying land out beyond the city limits. Welded to his vision was the stolid virtue of patience. He built almost nothing himself, other than the Astor Hotel in 1830, an ugly pile just across the street from City Hall Park. Within all of his other properties, he owned the land and let others pay him rent. Every major change in the city's life helped him: the first use of gaslight on the streets in 1824 (which extended the New York day), the opening of the Erie Canal in 1825 (which doubled the city's trade and population within a few years), the cholera epidemics downtown during the early 1830s, and then the catastrophic Great Fire of 1835. The filth and congestion of the lower city became intolerable. People began moving north to Greenwich Village and beyond. And the creation of horse-drawn omnibuses in the 1830s made it possible for some New Yorkers to live to the north and still reach their downtown offices.

For the first time, New Yorkers began to live and work in different places. Wall Street itself became a predominantly male neighborhood. Private clubs blossomed. A French import called a restaurant began appearing to serve the hungry stockbrokers, accountants, and insurance men. A version of fast food, served at curbside, appeared on the new sidewalks. It came from the bounty of the harbor: oysters, clams, fish, and (from Long Island) corn in many styles of dress, from plain butter and salt to a version of paprika. Most of the fast food was served by African American women.

By 1834, Astor had given up most of his other businesses to focus on Manhattan property, and he swiftly became the richest private citizen in the United States. He was the country's first millionaire. And the first multimillionaire. Late in life, he said, "Could I begin life again, knowing what I now know, and had money to invest, I would buy every foot of land on the island of Manhattan." Thanks to the desperation of Aaron Burr, he had discovered the true religion of New York: real estate.

In that sense, John Jacob Astor was a true New York founding father. And the people who ran Trinity Church must have looked upon him with a very human mixture of anger and envy.

I enter Trinity and slide into an atmosphere of repose, beauty, and refuge. The great high reach of the building, its muted Vermeer-like light, the discreet sound of ancient music: All suggest a suspension of time and space. Here the clock stops, in spite of the New York imperative about time being money. Here the rushing, colliding, driven energy of the Wall Street neighborhood is left behind. The church has an enclosing genius, shaped by the vision of the architect, bringing the visitor in and leaving the world outside.

There is, in fact, a sense of the medieval about the church, evoking the time before the Reformation and the Counter-Reformation, before the Inquisition and the religious slaughters of Europe. In the Middle Ages in Europe, there was one church, and it was the binding and guiding element of society, more powerful than individuals, merchants, or kings. Or so they believed. That is why, I suppose, to me Trinity has a very Catholic aura, at once simple and lavish. For visitors of any religion, or no religion at all, the interior offers a very special kind of whispered welcome.

Just inside the doors, where pamphlets and books are stacked in rows against the back wall, there is a guest book for signature by visitors. I sign. The three signatures before mine are from Seattle; Middlesburg, Ohio; and Reynosa, Mexico. About twenty tourists sit together in a pew close to the altar, all obeying the injunction against cell phones. There are hymn books in each perfectly carpentered pew, and velvet cushions that allow strangers to ease into solitude. Signs on the pillars state that the hymns at the next service will be 423, 567, 493. The pulpit on the left of the altar carries a banner marked 1696, the year of the first Trinity. The date on the banner is a reminder that time itself is long, even if the time of man is far too short.

Stained glass windows add to the Catholic feeling of the immense space and its luminous sense of continuity. The altar, raised high for maximum theatrical command, also features the crucified Jesus and statues of the apostles. We have seen such imagery in hundreds of churches, and that is the implied point: They are the familiar iconography of the Christian faith. They express a world without schism. It doesn't matter that grander, deeper, or more disturbing versions of the same images exist in many of the churches of Europe, including those in the Vatican. Much of the imagery in Trinity feels like the early Renaissance, before the later triumphs of the baroque. Those windows, paintings, and sculptures are not great art, but the designers in the 1840s were aiming for something other than great art: the expression of enduring faith.

Here too are carved reclining sculptures of somber old men with heads crowned by mitres, looking very papal. Here are votive candles whose smoke waxes the air. Here is a Virgin Mary carved from wood. Here is worn travertine on the floor. The nonbeliever can gaze in admiration at all of this, and silently applaud the craftsmanship, while feeling free of any urgent demand for belief itself.

Sometimes I sit alone in the church and imagine myself in other lives. I am sitting with Albert Gallatin, who will leave in a minute or two to visit with his friend John Jacob Astor while sternly resisting his offers of money. The French-speaking Swiss Gallatin is talking with the German immigrant Astor in English, the lingua franca of all New York immigrants. I imagine Burr, in a back pew, counting the house. I try to see the faces of Livingstons and Van Rensselaers and Brevoorts. Over and over, I see George Templeton Strong.

Strong was one of the greatest of all New Yorkers, which is not to say that he was in any way perfect. He was born in 1820, graduated from Columbia University in 1838, and spent his life as a practicing lawyer. He played and loved music. He became a vestryman of Trinity. During the Civil War, he served on the United States Sanitary Commission, which helped save the lives of thousands of soldiers and civilians. He died in 1875 and is buried in the churchyard.

But such a sketch does not suggest his enduring value.

Starting in his teenage years, Strong kept a diary, one that in the end totaled more than two million words. In its pages (along with the shorter diary kept by Philip Hone) we have at least partial access to much of what we know about nineteenth-century Manhattan. The bulk of the diary remains (disgracefully) unpublished, but after its first publication, in a four-volume abridgment by the historian Allan Nevins in 1952, we instantly understood what a remarkable man Strong was. The writing is lucid, intelligent, brilliantly observant of large-picture politics and the smaller, more revealing details of manners. Strong is the truest voice of the old Protestant elite. He is writing for himself and so expresses his alarm at the flood of immigrants that is changing his New York. He is venomous and bigoted about Catholics in general and the Irish in particular. He is a well-mannered racist, too free to use the word *nigger,* bleak and guarded about abolishing slavery, uncertain that the American children of African slaves would ever have the intelligence to be citizens equal to whites. In those casual bigotries, he almost surely expresses the beliefs of his time and class. He even sketches a patronizing vision of his wife, fitting her into the mindless stereotype of fairy-tale female innocence. About women in general (who should not even be allowed to practice at the bar as lawyers) he's a relentless and cranky male chauvinist. He was surely not alone.

And yet there flows through his work a persistent decency too, a kind of personal rectitude that makes him feel like the central figure in a certain kind of Jamesian novel in which ambiguities and contradictions add to the character's fundamental humanity. A handsome, melancholy man in public life, Strong allows his private angers to erupt in the pages of his diary, and they all sound absolutely true to the way he sees his city. He is not a politician writing for future judgment. He is not a journalist offering his thoughts to the public prints. He is not expecting applause or condemnation. He is trying to set down what he believes is the truth about his life and times. And sometimes no truth is more powerful than one expressed in anger by a melancholy man.

Not surprisingly, the work is suffused with that aching nostalgia that so many New Yorkers carry with them. Above all, he laments the fading of Old New York, the city of his youth, and its certainties of style and place. He regrets, with anger, that he had to leave Greenwich Street, where he grew up, and move in 1848 to Gramercy Park, a new development that was the creation of his father-in-law and would become the capital of the Brownstone Republic. Strong's move to the new neighborhood — roughly between Eighteenth and Twenty-third streets, from Third Avenue to today's Park Avenue South — was dictated by the decay of the old neighborhood, its decline into commercial use, its rowdy immigrant culture of working-class saloons and boisterous street life, its evaporating privacy, its growing lack of rules. He had become a stranger in his own land. He is, in the best sense, a genuine conservative, but he is also more than that. Once this place was good, says the New York conservative, and now it is a ruin. Variations on this lament have been voiced by every New York generation since Strong died.

And yet Strong is never doctrinaire, seldom a narrow voice of orthodoxy. Here is Strong on July 17, 1851, re-

flecting on the growing poverty of the New York under-
class:

Yet we have our Five Points, our emigrant quarters. Our
swarms of seamstresses to whom their utmost toil in mo-
notonous daily drudgery gives only bare subsistence, a life
barren of hope and of enjoyment; our hordes of dock
thieves, and of children who live in the streets and by
them. No one can walk the length of Broadway without
meeting some hideous troop of ragged girls, from twelve
years old down, brutalized already almost beyond redemption by premature vice, clad in the filthy refuse of the
rag-picker's collections, obscene of speech, the stamp of
childhood gone from their faces, hurrying along with
harsh laughter and foulness of their lips that some of them
have learned by rote, yet too young to understand it; with
thief written in their cunning eyes and whore on their de-
praved faces, though so unnatural, foul, and repulsive in
every look and gesture, that that last profession seems ut-
terly beyond their aspirations. On a rainy day such crews
may be seen by dozens. They haunt every other crossing
and skulk away together, when the sun comes out and the
mud is dry again. And such a group I think the most re-
volting object that the social diseases of a great city can
produce. A gang of blackguard boys is lovely by the side
of it . . .

In flight from such depressing and pitiful sights, many
Trinity congregants abandoned the downtown neighbor-
hoods for Bond Street and Washington Square and
Colonnade Row, higher up in the town. Some assembled

even farther up the island, in Strong's Gramercy Park. Many church members continued to pay their pew rentals (which Trinity collected until 1919), but the emptying church itself was forced to question its own reason for existence. Many must have felt the way Strong did, as expressed in the same day's entry:

> And what am I doing, I wonder? I'm neither scholar nor philanthropist nor clergyman, nor in any capacity a guide or ruler of the people, to be sure—there is that shadow of an apology for my sitting still. But if Heaven will permit and enable me, I'll do something in the matter before I die—to have helped one dirty vagabond child out of such a pestilential sink would be a thing one would not regret when one came to march out of this world . . .

The shadow of an apology dominated the debates in Trinity over its future mission. The vestrymen chose finally to take their beliefs seriously. They had great wealth from real estate, including some income from the very slums that were producing the children of Broadway. As Christians, they must use the wealth to try to save these forlorn and broken children. As many of them as possible. Or even, as Strong said, just one vagabond child. The good Episcopalians of Trinity Church began working among the poor, a duty the church continues to perform to this day.

At the beginning, this was not easy. The unforgiving Irish of the Five Points rebuffed them, snarled at them, broke many of their well-meaning hearts. Among the refugees from the Irish famine and their children, few forgot the role of the Anglicans in Ireland, where they made up the official church of their conquerors. Few forgot the punishing Penal Laws of the century before, enacted to break the Catholics of Ireland by barring them from owning property, attending schools, and voting. Among the Irish in New York, there was too much memory and too little forgetting. The poor prostitutes of Corlears Hook on the East River — some say they gave us the word *hooker* — had no desire for upper-class pity or jobs that paid thirty cents a day. Around this time, the word *reformer* entered the New York language as a term of derision. And yet, with Trinity as the engine of compassion, hundreds, perhaps thousands of the young were saved for decent lives. They became literate. They learned trades in vocational schools. They found their way into professions such as journalism that demanded only talent, not credentials or lustrous family trees. They served as policemen and firemen. They formed trade unions. They became the infantry for a surging Tammany Hall and made their votes count. Slowly they moved out of the slums and saw their children graduate from real schools. In short, those outsiders, those wretchedly poor Irish emigrants, became a permanent part of the New York alloy.

Neither George Templeton Strong nor those early immigrants would recognize the modern city, of course, even though they helped create it. Sometimes, walking from the Bowling Green up Broadway, passing coffee shops, restaurants, delicatessens, and deliverymen, I try to imagine the place through nineteenth-century eyes. What is sushi? What are tacos? Or bagels? What, for God's sake, is pizza? The most common foods of today's New York did not then exist. Neither did so many other things that are now too common, from automobiles to skyscrapers. And yet this remains that lost city. The food alone is evidence of the persistence of tolerance.

In the time of the Knickerbocker ascendancy, tolerance was severely tested by the explosion of population. Most of the Knickerbockers thought the world above Fourteenth Street would always be farmland or left wild. Along came the immigrants, including John Jacob Astor. The much less successful immigrants themselves paid little heed to the rigid virtues espoused by the Anglican elite. Trinity and other Protestant churches meant nothing to them. They were Catholics, or were in flight from religion itself. They certainly did not come to America to assume the posture of humble deference. After the opening of the Erie Canal in 1825, the streets started filling with people from the American hinterlands, and from impoverished Europe, all in search of a piece of the American vision. Tammany Hall welcomed them. So did the speculators in shabby housing, the first New York slumlords. The aristocrats could not see their need, their ambition, their intelligence, their hope; all they saw was the rising shadow of the mob.

And so the world changed, and the Knickerbockers too succumbed to nostalgia. They yearned for the intimate town that lay comfortably below Wall Street. They remembered meeting friends on the streets or snubbing their enemies. Now they passed hundreds of people each day they might never see again. They remembered the glittering parties. They remembered the names of much-loved dogs and certain horses, and liveried footmen, and slaves. They remembered the first Tammany Hall meetings on Spruce Street, then at Nassau and Frankfort streets, and how most of their friends laughed at these crude men dressed in such coarse cloth. A few remembered seeing George Washington worshipping in St. Paul's Chapel, in that year when New York was the temporary capital of the new United States. They remembered that Hamilton lived for a while on Wall Street. And that the dreadful Burr lived in Maiden Lane and then at 4 Broadway, facing the Bowling Green. They had seen them often. They remembered lolling in the air of the Bowling Green themselves, watching flocks of birds cross the harbor. They remembered a town that created a certain measure of fear but absolutely no doubt about the way men were destined to live. And then they were gone from the stage.

They were not gone from the city. The Knickerbockers did many fine things once they had assumed a more modest place as part of the alloy and not as the city's true rulers by right of bloodlines. They created Central Park and the New York Public Library and Columbia University. They added intelligence and a certain moral rigor to the New York mixture. But they were also capable of melancholy about the city in which they had been young. In his diaries, George Templeton Strong recorded some of his laments. So did the former mayor Philip Hone, who had begun his own diary in 1826. With all their flaws, they were among Manhattan's finest citizens. But they too headed north, out of their version of Downtown, which had begun to vanish as a precinct for the older families. Strong would live the rest of his life at 74 East Twenty-first Street, where he died in 1875. Hone, who earlier lived on Broadway across from City Hall Park, went up Broadway in 1836 and would live out his days on Great Jones Street, now loosely claimed for the East Village. Strong's final address was the graveyard at Trinity Church.

Chapter Four

VELOCITY

MANY DISCOVERIES, AS the world has known for centuries, come from accidents. Scientists make such discoveries all the time. Others go in search of fabled Cathay and find Staten Island. In 1954, after getting out of the navy, I went to work as a messenger in the art department of an advertising agency called Doremus & Co. I wanted a job anywhere, but I found that one in the heart of the old Downtown, thanks to an accident: It was the first listing I found under "Artists" in the *New York Times* classified ads. To my astonishment and joy, they hired me for forty-five dollars a week. The discoveries would come later.

Doremus specialized in the offerings of stocks and bonds in what were called "tombstone ads." The offices were (in memory) on a high floor at 120 Broadway, better known as the Equitable Building. I would learn that this immense structure had a special place in the history of

New York architecture. According to the historian Keith D. Revell, the Equitable was erected in 1914, despite protests from its sun-starved neighbors, and rose thirty-six stories straight up into the sky, its great bulk throwing a shadow that covered seven and a half acres. At the base, it filled a complete city block, facing Broadway, extending to the limits of Cedar, Nassau, and Pine streets. Its rentable space could contain fifteen thousand workers, making it the largest, densest office building in the city. The public anger over its arrogant theft of sky, sun, and room on the lunchtime sidewalks did have a valuable consequence: In 1916, New York passed the first zoning law in the city's history. This insisted upon setbacks in the upper stories of all future skyscrapers, thus allowing at least some sunlight to reach the citizens on the streets. In 1916, it was too late for the streets around 120 Broadway, but the new law led to the building of all those Manhattan towers that rose to spires, the most beautiful, of course, being the Chrysler Building.

I knew nothing of this when I went to work for Doremus & Co. The immediate neighborhood was full of the towers I could see from Brooklyn, but on the street level, it was also layered with the past, which began to tug at me. That past was most graphically embodied by Trinity Church, which I saw every morning and lunch hour. In its Gothic presence, I began to imagine those forgotten years of its creation. Nobody at Doremus & Co. could answer my questions about Trinity or Broadway or the rise of the towers. "We're getting ads ready for tomorrow's *Wall Street Journal*," one grouchy copywriter said. "Don't worry about that stuff." I didn't worry about it, but I was curious about the world around me. It would take me decades to find answers to my questions.

One thing I slowly learned was that around the time in the nineteenth century Trinity assumed its architectural dominance, the city itself had already assumed a newer character. Life was marked, above all, by the presence of velocity. Speed of movement, speed of change, speed of growth. From 1825 to 1850, the population had risen from 133,000 to more than half a million. Life was quicker, the people more driven, the pace more frantic. Horse-drawn omnibuses added to the roaring jam of traffic on lower Broadway, as men hurried to jobs or to homes while young men called "runners" dodged around pedestrians, carrying urgent messages by hand. Gaslight came to the streets in the 1820s, with lamplighters announcing the coming of a New York night that would never again be completely dark (the last of the gas lamps vanished around 1914). Men worked later than ever in the gaslit countinghouses along South Street and the East River. New wharves were jutting into the North River like immense fingers, and warehouses were rising nearby to handle the trade that came with the steam-powered ships. The speed of change was astonishing. In the early 1840s, the telegraph increased swift communications with the rest of the world. The Atlantic cable, imperfect at first and then increasingly refined, brought European markets closer to the booming marketplace of New York. By 1840, there were sixty-three wharves on the East River and fifty on the Hudson. The clipper ships, the last, most graceful and lofty of all sailing ships, were born in 1843, clipping days off the journeys to Europe. But they were already doomed to become objects of New York nostalgia.

Velocity pervaded everything: ideas, visions, the dailiness of street life. As brusque New Yorkers rushed through their Downtown streets, they acquired a reputation for rudeness that has never gone away. The New York accent became general: clipped, blunt, hard, a fist of an accent. More and more New York men gobbled hurried lunches in packed and primitive restaurants, simultaneously devouring afternoon editions of the newspapers crammed with the latest news. Time was money, and so was information. In good weather, many stood in clusters on the streets at noon, feeding on oysters and clams and corn from sidewalk stalls, the way a century later I fed on hot dogs. Fine old Knickerbocker homes were transformed into malodorous, unruly boardinghouses for the young men who were soon being called "bachelors," while their proud owners retreated to other neighborhoods and their own country of nostalgia.

One place the Knickerbockers carried in their baggage was called St. John's Park. All accounts of this exclusive square describe it as a lovely urban oasis, designed in 1803 on the London West End model of small, elegant places of domesticity, trees, and light. There was a small fenced park in the center (for which only residents had a key), the whole lined with handsome Federal and Greek Revival homes, a kind of early version of Gramercy Park. It was located between Laight, Varick, Ericcson, and Hudson streets, a few blocks from where I now live (in what the real estate people call Tribeca). The name came from St. John's Chapel at the east end of the square, designed in the Georgian-Federal style by John McComb Jr., the Scots builder who worked with the French architect Joseph Mangin on the marvelous new City Hall. At night, the square was illuminated by gas lamps that gave it a warm, intimate glow, and a lone watchman made his rounds. By day, in all seasons, children played, governesses watched, servants shopped for large family meals. In spring and summer, the front and rear gardens blazed with the colors of flowers. The most pervasive sound was made by horses' well-shod hooves on cobblestones.

And then came the changes, starting in the 1830s as the North River was transformed by the steamboat, escalating in the 1840s. The ladies and gentlemen of St. John's Park, many of them descendants of those aspiring aristocrats who were politically defeated forever in the 1820s and 1830s by Andrew Jackson, began to leave. Slowly at first, and then with quickening velocity, the fine houses fell into the purgatory of boardinghouses, their rich owners content to collect rents from the safety of their new homes (some of them located across the river in the heights of Brooklyn). Weeds rose in the green. Disorder alternated with seediness. Warehouses blocked access to the river. In 1869, Commodore Cornelius Vanderbilt (a son of Staten Island) bought the entire site for a railroad terminal. The church was torn down, its graveyard emptied. The Georgian houses were destroyed. The rail yards of the New York Central filled the days and nights with the squeals of steel wheels on steel tracks and the incessant clanking of couplers ramming into each other while cargo was loaded and unloaded. Eventually, even the railroads moved uptown. There is no sign of the elegant old square now, because the area itself was erased in the 1920s for the approaches to the Holland Tunnel. Nobody now alive can even remember Vanderbilt's railroad yards.

During the great days of St. John's Park, rapid change was general all over the city. "The process of pulling down and building up is abroad," complained Philip Hone, the businessman-diarist who also served as mayor. "The whole of New York is rebuilt about once in ten years."

Some things took longer to change. One of them was poverty. The Five Points grew more squalid and danger-ous, even as speculators erected new tenements in other sections to handle, and exploit, the growing numbers of immigrants. The new arrivals were coming up the New York streets from the piers with their own forms of veloc-ity. Most were in flight from the Irish famine or the failed European social revolutions of 1848. The Irish and Germans (along with some French) discovered, of course, that the streets were not paved with gold; that reversal of a cliché became itself a New York cliché. Like most clichés, it was repeated because it was true. Women were paid two dollars a week in a time when a furnished room cost four. It was thus not surprising that more and more prostitutes, many of them part-timers, worked the bal-conies of theaters or the gaslit shadows off Broadway. More and more criminals, working alone or in gangs, chose the quick robbery in preference to the long unpaid apprenticeships of tradition. *Quick. Choose. Do it now. Time is money*. In the 1850s, the Irish accounted for 55 percent of arrests, and that percentage would rise even higher. For many young men, gangs provided solidarity, safety, and even small amounts of money; it was better to be a Dead Rabbit or a Plug Ugly than an underpaid working stiff. Other impoverished immigrants chose the instant nirvana of alcohol or opium. A hundred years later, a writer named

Willard Motley voiced in his New York novel *Knock on Any Door* the slogan that could have been applied to thousands of those young nineteenth-century men and women: *Live fast, die young, and have a good-looking corpse.* Where I grew up in Brooklyn, in a time of street gangs similar to those in Five Points, many apprentice hoodlums used the line without irony. They heard it in the movie version of the novel. It could be used today by many of the city's hardened young men.

But, among rich and poor of the middle of the nineteenth century, there was a growing psychological velocity too. On the eve of the Civil War, thousands of New Yorkers were possessed of the dream of the quick fortune. They believed they could be little Astors, if only they could combine ruthlessness, audacity, and luck. The example of Astor was as vivid as Trinity Church. And so they would conceive elaborate schemes in land speculation. They would gamble in the stock market, or buy shares in the voyages of commercial clipper ships, or dream up inventions they hoped would change the world. The war against Mexico (1846–48) was a kind of metaphor for this impulse: a quick invasion based on fraudulent premises, a war that with fewer than two thousand American deaths led to the acquisition of about one-half of the territory of Mexico including California, which gave the United States a west coast. As a war, it was the equivalent of winning the lottery. And land was not the only thing that mattered. In 1848, gold was discovered at Sutter's Creek in California, a discovery kept from Mexican negotiators until after the conclusion of the peace treaty. When the news of gold reached New York, many young men rushed to the West, joining thousands of other Americans as forty-niners. A half-century later, Mark Twain would say that the gold rush drastically changed the American character, ending the tradition of patient apprenticeships, the gradual mastery of self, talent, and money. Gold created the get-rich-quick mentality that has been with us ever since, most recently during the dot-com bubble of the late 1990s.

Far from the Rio Grande, New York shared the bounty of victory. Gold from California flowed into the banks of New York. Shrewd, hard Downtown men began planning the transcontinental railroad and were willing to bribe the United States Congress to make it real. In a city and country blazing with golden visions, moral debates were only debates, a form of empty talk. If God didn't want the United States to spread across the continent, he would have intervened. Or so it was said among some moral men hurrying from Wall Street along Broadway. These discussions were not prolonged. Amid the culture of velocity, New Yorkers talked fast and walked fast. They still do.

Underneath the great quickening of New York life was a plan. In 1811, the interior geography of New Yorkers was about to change forever, although most people at the time seemed to shrug off the extravagantly ambitious new vision of the city's future. That year, a master plan for Manhattan was released to the public and approved by the state legislature, which had commissioned the plan in 1807 at the urging of Mayor and then Governor De Witt Clinton, the obsessed, authoritarian politician who was also planning the Erie Canal. The plan had taken four

years to complete, and the men who created it—
Gouverneur Morris, Simeon DeWitt, John Rutherford,
and a young surveyor named John Randel Jr.—came up
with a vision of Manhattan so wonderfully simple that we
live with it to this day.

The official name was the Commissioners' Plan. Its central vision was a grid. The designers' plan was an imposi-
tion of rigid order on wildness, glorying in what New York
historians Edwin G. Burrows and Mike Wallace have
called "the supremacy of technique over topography." The
grid would eventually have a decisive impact on the city's
economy, on the evolution of the New York human alloy,
on art, thought, architecture, and even on urban psychol-
ogy. By the time I was first exploring Manhattan, I had already been shaped by the grid.

As imagined by the planners, the future city would rise
from a simple grid of avenues and streets. Each of twelve
avenues, running south to north, would be 100 feet wide,
stretching from about today's Houston Street to the distant end of the island, at what the planners labeled 155th
Street. The streets would move east to west, river to river,
roughly 200 feet apart. Each street would be 60 feet wide,
with the exception of fifteen streets that would be 100 feet
wide: 14th, 23rd, 34th, 42nd, 57th, 72nd, 79th, 86th, 96th,
106th, 116th, 125th, 135th, 145th, and 155th. At the time
the plan was drawn, most of that land was made of farms,
stubborn hills, racing streams, isolated mansions, and
stands of trees that had survived the Revolution. Some
streets were altered or subverted over the coming years, or
blocked by the creation of Central Park. But basically they
are the city's major crosstown streets to this day.

Under the plan, all natural topography would be submitted to the discipline of the grid. Hills were leveled. Ponds and swamps would be filled or drained. Streams would be diverted through pipes to the rivers. There would be no European-style stars, ovals, or circles to impede the velocity of traffic. The grid would rule. Each of those streets and avenues would carry only numbers, rather than names, which were dismissed as examples of human vanity. The commissioners in 1811 claimed that the grid would combine "beauty, order, and convenience." That was a Knickerbocker vision of the future, of course, almost Calvinist in its rigidity.

Not everybody was pleased. Some objected to the arrogant power of the state to determine what owners could do with the land they owned. Clement Clarke Moore, who owned great tracts of real estate in today's Chelsea (and who later was credited with writing "A Visit from St. Nicholas," better known as " 'Twas the Night Before Christmas"), complained bitterly: "The great principle which governs these plans is, to reduce the surface of the earth as nearly as possible to dead level. . . . These are men . . . who would have cut down the seven hills of Rome." A few others shared his complaint about the coming destruction of natural beauty. But at the time, most New Yorkers were indifferent or dismissive, for the plan described an imaginary city, or one that would not exist until most current residents were dead. Almost a century later, Henry James (in his way, a descendant of the Knickerbockers) was to call the grid the city's "primal topographic curse, her old inconceivably bourgeois scheme of composition and distribution, the uncorrected labour of minds with no imagination . . ."

Among other flaws, the grid made few provisions for open recreational spaces, for parks, water courses, leafy hills bursting with outcroppings of granite; it would be another forty years before the first plans were made for Central Park. The 1811 planners shrugged and gestured to the rivers, "those large arms of the sea which embrace Manhattan Island . . ." The rivers (and the harbor), they insisted, "render its situation, in regard to health and pleasure, as well as to the convenience of commerce, peculiarly felicitous."

It was true for a long time that the rivers drew New Yorkers to their shores in mysterious, primitive, almost religious ways. In the opening chapter of *Moby-Dick* (1851), New Yorker Herman Melville (born eight years after the unveiling of the grid) evoked that mysterious pulling effect in the years when he was young:

There now is your insular city of the Manhattoes, belted round by wharves as Indian isles by coral reefs—commerce surrounds it with her surf. Right and left, the streets take you waterward. Its extreme downtown is the battery, where that noble mole is washed by waves, and cooled by breezes, which a few hours earlier were out of sight of land. Look at the crowds of water-gazers there.

Circumambulate the city of a dreamy Sabbath afternoon. Go from Corlears Hook to Coenties Slip, and from thence, by Whitehall, northward. What do you see?— Posted like silent sentinels all around the town, stand thousands upon thousands of mortal men fixed in ocean reveries. Some leaning upon the spiles; some seated upon the pier-heads; some looking over the bulwarks of ships from China; some high aloft in the rigging, as if striving to get a still better seaward peep. But these are all landsmen; of week days pent up in lath and plaster—tied to counters, nailed to benches, clinched to desks. How then is this? Are the green fields gone? What do they here?

But look! Here come more crowds, pacing straight for the water, and seemingly bound for a dive. Strange! Nothing will content them but the extremest limit of the land; loitering under the shady lee of yonder warehouses will not suffice. No. They must get just as nigh the water as they possibly can without falling in. And there they stand—miles of them—leagues. Inlanders all, they come from lanes and alleys, streets and avenues—north, east, south, and west. Yet here they all unite.

That apparently timeless vision of an east-west city in the embrace of two rivers did not last. In New York, few certainties ever do survive.

The template of Manhattan had changed forever by the time the children and grandchildren of Melville's river-bound landsmen were singing, "East Side, West Side, all around the town . . ." In 1894, when James W. Blake and Charles B. Lawlor composed "The Sidewalks of New York," the famous chorus was another reflection of New York's abiding nostalgia. Fewer New Yorkers thought in terms of east and west. As a place to live or to play, uptown was leaving downtown behind. The waterfront was blocked from view by commerce. Central Park now existed, and it was way uptown, above Fifty-ninth Street. A vast tract of real estate that was marginal in the time of Melville was now considered central.

The most enormous changes were made by real estate people, their engineers and architects, and the elites who possessed secular power. A small downtown city became a city that would reach, eventually, the full length of the island. For real estate speculators the island was the new promised land. Each block could be broken into lots, usually 25 feet wide and 100 feet deep, which made investment more attractive to individuals and to large-scale developers. The adherents of the secular New York religion founded by John Jacob Astor saw manna falling from the skies. As the planners themselves said in 1811, it was self-evident that "strait-sided and right-angled houses are the most cheap to build, and the most convenient to live in."

That turned out to be true. North of Greenwich Village (which was such a jumble that planners mercifully left it alone), Manhattan today is an island of right angles in a way that Brooklyn, the Bronx, and Queens are not. The hamlets of the other boroughs have streets and avenues too, but the hamlets themselves shift and wander. Manhattan never wanders, at least above Greenwich Village. This has had its effects on the residents, and even upon those who live elsewhere but work eight or more hours a day in what most still call "the city." In 1964, the British writer V. S. Pritchett wrote, "The physical course of a New Yorker's daily life is a preoccupation with right angles; he is a man conditioned to an automatic process of anxiously going along and inevitably going up."

Inevitably, Manhattan went up. First, uptown. Then to the sky.

In Old New York, the word *skyscraper* described the tallest mast of a sailing ship. And so the word would be used until the last decades of the nineteenth century. But the more *occupied* Manhattan became, the more the real estate men looked up at the sky, beyond the tip of Trinity's lovely Gothic tower, up at the emptiness above the crowded city. They looked at the emptiness with longing.

After the Civil War, the real estate people began a new kind of building, exclusively for offices, at first to replace more efficiently the inadequate old countinghouses that were falling into decay along South Street. A surging capitalism was creating many tons of paper: receipts, records, correspondence, notices from bureaucracies. But the new office buildings were limited by a number of factors: the rising cost of downtown real estate, the generally accepted height limits of five or six stories, and extraordinary technological problems. Truly tall buildings—higher than six stories—had to have creative ways to carry workers from the street to their offices, and to provide them with light, air, and plumbing.

One major solution would come in the 1880s with the development of electric power by Thomas Alva Edison and others. The concept of mechanically moving loads to higher floors was there from the time of the Dutch, but all such devices were operated by ropes and pulleys, powered by human muscle, and, of course, few houses were taller than four stories (I remember hand-pulled dumbwaiters, as they were called, surviving in the four-story tenements of my childhood). The Astor House of 1830 used a primitive steam-powered elevator for baggage (and a few brave passengers), but the hotel was only five stories high, and the elevator was always in danger of falling. Two decades later, a man named Elisha Graves Otis, working and dreaming in Yonkers, invented the spring lock that would break the fall of an elevator if the rope broke, and demonstrated it at the great Crystal Palace exhibition in 1854. Development was coming one small step at a time.

The first Otis elevator was installed three years later in the new cast-iron E. V. Haughwout Building on the corner of Broadway and Broome Street. Steam provided the power. Miraculously, the five-story building is still there, with a large Staples store occupying the ground floor. Its design is simple and elegant. I pass it a few times a week and always think about those men who built it, and whether they understood that they were making one of the first moves toward creating the city we inhabit. Our present was their future. In their New York, height was not truly important to most citizens; it remained a horizontal city. But their elevator made great height possible. The success of that first elevator allowed other men to dream.

Otis, who was born in 1811, continued working, directing his staff, while other New York engineers began making variations on elevators, particularly for use in those new warehouses along the North River. Power was the greatest limitation to their visions, and it was not solved at the time of Otis's death in 1861. After his death, his small company continued working on newer, safer, and better elevators. So did a rival named Charles Pratt. All tried screw, steam, and hydraulics for power. None of these was truly satisfactory. The first great generation of American mechanical engineers was also hard at work on other problems with tall buildings. Even if elevators were able to soar to the upper floors, the conventional load-bearing walls of solid masonry would become so thick at the base that office space on the lower floors would be limited, particularly on the small but desirable plots of land in downtown Manhattan. A few engineers understood the concept of load-bearing steel frames and light curtained walls. But for a long time, that understanding was only theoretical.

All awaited electric power, which was being developed slowly, incrementally, throughout the 1880s. That tale is primarily the story of Edison, who started as an assistant to telegraphers and ended up a tycoon. He lived for a long time in New York before moving his company to New Jersey, but his restless, inventive mind was crucial to the story of the city, and all the cities of the world. There were other creative engineers and inventors involved in the process, of course, but the public face of the electric age belonged to Edison.

In 1889, the Otis Company would finally install its first electric-powered elevators in the Demarest Carriage Company Building at Fifth Avenue and Thirty-third Street. In the climb to the skies, one major problem had been solved. In that same year, the first true New York skyscraper opened at 50 Broadway, near Exchange Place. This was the Tower Building, designed by Bradford Lee Gilbert, which rose eleven stories from a lot only twenty-two feet wide, less than the land under the average New York residence. It featured a steel skeleton and thin exterior walls, inspired by the success of Chicago's Home

Insurance Building of 1884 (designed by William LeBaron
Jenney), which proved that such a technique was no
longer mere theory. The steel frame would bear the load of
all the floors.

Still, many New Yorkers feared the Tower Building
would go over in a high wind. Just before its completion, a
hurricane struck the city with winds of eighty miles an hour.
Gilbert rushed to the building and met the developer, a silk
merchant named John L. Stearns. Crowds were gathered at
a safe distance, and some buildings across the street were
evacuated. My late friend the New York historian Edward
Robb Ellis wrote an account of what followed:

> Gilbert grabbed a plumb line and began climbing a ladder
> left in place by workmen when they had quit work the
> evening before. Stearns followed at his heels. From the
> crowd arose screams: "You *fools!* You'll be killed!" The ar-
> chitect and businessman could barely hear them above the
> shriek of the hurricane. Stearns' courage gave out when
> they reached the tenth floor. There he sprawled full length
> on a scaffold and held on for dear life. Gilbert, who felt the
> risk of his reputation was worth the risk of his life, contin-
> ued to climb the ladder, rung by painful rung, his knuck-
> les whitening with strain and gusts of wind battering him
> unmercifully. When he reached the thirteenth and top
> floor, he crawled on hands and knees along a scaffold. At
> a corner of the building he tugged the plumb line from a
> pocket, got a firm grip on one end of the cord, and
> dropped its leaden weight toward the Broadway sidewalk.
> He later reported, "There was not the slightest vibration.
> The building stood as steady as a rock in the sea."

In that moment of triumph Gilbert rashly jumped to his feet on the scaffold. His hat had been tightly crushed on his head. Now he snatched it off and waved it exultantly. The wind knocked him down. It scudded him toward one end of the scaffold. He gulped. He prayed. Wildly he grabbed about him. Just as he was about to be swept off the end of the board and down to certain death, he caught a rope lashing about in the wind from an upright beam of the tower. His grip held. The rope held. He steadied himself, eased down onto his knees, and carefully picked his way back to the ladder. Climbing down the ladder, he was joined by Stearns at the tenth floor, and the two men then made their way slowly back to street level.

Spectators cheered the heroes of the hour and gave way to let them pass. Locking arms, their chins upthrust, the architect and the businessman marched up Broadway, dumbfounding Trinity Church members just leaving the morning service by singing in unison: "Praise God from whom all blessings flow . . ."

After that, the sky was literally the limit. Up ahead, in the early twentieth century, lay Oz.

While the fabled towers were beginning to rise from the tough granite bedrock of the downtown city, another version of New York was being created. From roughly 1880, and for another fifty years, there was a vivid architecture of New York grandeur. Some have called it the New York Renaissance. Others define it as part of the City Beautiful movement. The name doesn't truly matter. But most of the physical New York I love comes from that era. I cherish certain solitary skyscrapers: the Woolworth Building, the Flatiron, the Daily News Building, the Seagram Building, the Chrysler Building. But I could not live without the various enduring splendors of that older era, buildings created on a more human scale, closer to the ground, buildings I can see without looking up to the sky. I mean these buildings, among others: the Metropolitan Museum of Art, the Frick Collection, the New York Public Library, the old Custom House, the New York Stock Exchange, Carnegie Hall, Judson Memorial Church, the former Police Headquarters on Centre Street, the Little Singer Building, the tower of the Metropolitan Life Insurance Company, the General Post Office on Thirty-third and Eighth, the old B. Altman's store (now part of the City University), the Pierpont Morgan Library, the salvaged Bowery Savings Bank at the corner of Grand Street, the Century Association, the Art Students League, the Metropolitan Club, the Dakota Apartments, the Ansonia Hotel, the Apthorp, Congregation Shearith Israel, the Low Library at Columbia University, and dozens of others scattered through the city. When I think of New York as a visible city, these are the buildings that dominate all others.

Over five decades, I came to know these buildings as an adult New Yorker, not as a student of architecture, and for me they are essential to the idea of New York. They represent continuity with the New York past and the original values that made the modern city such a thing of wonder. They tell us that excellence endures. They offer visions of solidity and power without being even vaguely totalitarian. With their adornments of sculpture or ornament, each displays the work of human hands. All of them can be gazed upon, experienced, *read*, from street level; that is, from the place where all the collisions and surprises of New York life occur. In the city that sometimes prides itself on being vertical, they are triumphs of the horizontal. Over decades, I learned much of the story of the buildings that so captured me when I was young. In my own erratic way, I absorbed the story of how a generation of American architects came to New York after training in the famed nineteenth-century ateliers of the École des Beaux-Arts in Paris. As mature architects, they didn't truly form a "school" in the narrowest understanding of the term. They took different approaches to the work itself, developed their own mannerisms, used different craftsmen to execute their visions. But they had one uniting vision. They wanted to create buildings that expressed the triumphant emergence of one of the great cities of the world. For me, they succeeded beyond all dreams.

They were later called masters of the beaux arts style, but most scholars say that there was no such style. The words mean simply "beautiful arts." As the critic and historian Henry Hope Reed has written: "The key element that identified what we call Beaux-Arts is not the rule of locking façade to plan, the emphasis on symmetry in the plan, or the eclecticism, but the powerful drive for ornamentation." The ornamentation, often executed by very skillful Italian and French immigrant craftsmen, made the buildings unintended expressions of the New York alloy; in the end, New York itself is the supreme example of the strengths of the eclectic.

The architecture also expressed the wider culture of the

late nineteenth century, when Paris was the artistic capital of the world. If Henry James or Marcel Proust had been architects instead of masters of ornamented prose, they'd surely have made buildings that resembled, in their own special ways, those that still exist in New York. Neither, of course, was a student at the École des Beaux-Arts, but each lived in the world of which it was a part. Some École students were painters or sculptors, most were French, not American, and all learned from one another. Most of them lived in the bohemian world made so attractively real in George du Maurier's 1894 novel *Trilby*, a huge bestseller that served as a kind of social training manual for a generation of young artists.

Those who labored in the workshops of the École in Paris were thoroughly educated in the arts of the long European past. Naturally, some rebelled against the disciplines of drawing from casts and copies of masterpieces. But for most, the training was not seen as a hindrance to creativity. Most students acknowledged a continuity between the past and present, and the American past (or so the Americans believed) was also European. For them, all of Europe was the Old Country. They drew on the past for ideas and inspiration in the same way that artists in the Italian Renaissance did when they went sifting through Roman models. If you were an artist, you took what was valuable, made your own variations on the older models, and discarded other models.

By the time I was an art student at Pratt Institute in the late 1950s, almost all of the work of the men from the American Renaissance was being dismissed as "eclectic." It was not "new." It was not "original." It did not adhere to "the law" as set down by the great Chicago architect Louis Sullivan: "Form follows function." It didn't matter that in his only New York building—still there at 65–69 Bleecker Street, just off Broadway—Sullivan didn't follow his own law. The building is a masterpiece of ornamentation.

Sullivan's maxim was used to justify some of the worst architectural junk in the twentieth-century city. These new blank and faceless examples of the International Style, with its roots in the Bauhaus, made the beaux arts buildings even more valuable presences in the city. They were also crucial to the city's sense of itself. That is why the destruction of Penn Station in 1963–66 created such an uproar of protest and rage. I was living in Europe in 1963–64, working as a reporter, and when I returned, the demolition of this great building was already under way. Again and again, I would walk around the periphery or stand across Seventh Avenue wondering how they could destroy that row of columns, the pediments, the simple *grandeur.* Each time I came for a visit to Penn Station, there was less of it. I was not alone, gazing at this immense act of municipal vandalism and whispering, *You bastards. You stupid goddamned bastards.*

The station was designed, as were so many of our treasures, by the firm of McKim, Mead & White. The basic model was the Baths of Caracalla in Rome, but the designers never lost sight of its function as a railroad terminal. It was the first to include electrically powered trains in the original planning, connecting by a new tunnel to New Jersey and the vast continent beyond. The Long Island Railroad was also part of the plan, carrying thousands of commuters each day to the growing suburbs. Construction started in 1902, as existing houses were cleared and work-men began to dig eighteen feet into the site, which stretched from Seventh to Eighth avenues, between Thirty-first and Thirty-third streets. Thousands of New Yorkers came to see the process of construction, including the painter George Bellows. Seen today, his paintings of the site have an eerie resemblance to Ground Zero in the weeks after September 11, 2001, with the deep pit, the rubble, the burning fires. The difference is obvious: Bellows was capturing the construction of beauty, not the mass destruction of human life.

But there were many Penn Stations, not simply the one I remember and Bellows painted. Each was seen through separate eyes, by people of all ages, classes, and races. After the destruction, each of those remembered Penn Stations inflamed the anger of millions of New Yorkers be-fore cooling into nostalgia. There was the Penn Station of memory, of arrivals and departures, of hope and disap-pointment, and the trembling prospects of romance. How many had arrived in that waiting room to begin new lives, passing through a magnificent place that made each arrival feel momentous? Such people were filled with desire for careers, for excitement, for the great velocity of the city. Many found what they were looking for. But how many left through the same vast room in bitterness and defeat italicized by that same dominating majesty? I'd look at the site in 1964 and 1965, and remember the great spaces of the waiting room, with its high, graceful wrought-iron arches and many windows, the whole suffused by day with the light of the city and at night—if you only looked up— with rectangles of a dark, luminous glamour. For generations, young men had waited near the clock for young women arriving for a night together on the town. I was one of them. We could look at the ruins of the station and remember girls in polo coats with snow melting in their hair. We could remember what followed an arrival. Certain tiny restaurants in the Village, or wanderings through the Metropolitan Museum, or trips to the Five Spot to hear Thelonious Monk. We could remember a time when we were so young that we thought the things we loved would last forever.

When it was over, and that Penn Station was gone, and a new, infinitely inferior one put in place on the site, along with the fourth Madison Square Garden, the anger did not go away. The vandals had attacked some core image New Yorkers had of their city and themselves. The landmarks movement rose from the rubble. Now we know: Such a thing will never happen again. My own anger has faded, but I still regret one accident of life. Because I was in Europe at the time of the first assault, I never had a chance to walk through that magnificent waiting room and run my hands over the sensual marble and travertine, and say a proper good-bye.

Chapter Five

THE MUSIC OF WHAT HAPPENS

FOR ME, THIS commonplace is true: Broadway exists as a concrete place and as an idea. As a place, physical, touchable, it stretches the length of Manhattan from the Battery to the Harlem River, just short of thirteen miles, and then moves four more miles into the Bronx and as far into Westchester as Sleepy Hollow, a final destination that would have delighted Washington Irving. I've walked most of the avenue in Manhattan block by block across more than a half century, and certain parts of it live vividly within me no matter where I am. Broadway in my mind is an immense tree, with its roots deep in the soil at the foot of Manhattan, which is why I insist so stubbornly to my friends that the uptown places I cherish on Broadway are actually part of Downtown.

There is the Broadway block on the Upper West Side where the Thalia movie house once stood at Ninety-fifth

Street and where I first saw the films of Kurosawa, Fellini, and Bergman. It drew students and faculty from Columbia University, from the Village (where it resides in time with the Art and Eighth Street theaters as part of Downtown), and from as far away as Brooklyn and New Jersey. There was a coffee shop nearby, its name gone from memory, where knots of people sat up after the movies, drinking coffee and smoking cigarettes, and argued about the French new wave and whether *Black Orpheus* was a drama or a musical, while a few auteurists insisted that Howard Hawks was the equal of Eisenstein.

There are certain Broadway buildings where my friends once lived, full of laughter and passion and intelligence, right up to the hour of their deaths. Other Broadway blocks are a mushy blur of shops and food markets and take-out stores. They offer the cuisine of the New York alloy: sushi and pizza and tacos, or delights from India and Thailand and China. That is, they tempt you with the same food that can be found in the parish of Trinity Church and in all other boroughs, the food that can be delivered to home or office in all weathers. On parts of Broadway, in the mornings and at dusk, hundreds of people walk dogs. Across the afternoons, nannies push baby carriages past the latest outposts of Starbucks. Kids rush around on skateboards, leaping over curbs, terrifying the old. Scrawny guys on bicycles demand passage on crowded sidewalks, their helmeted heads wearing masks of self-righteousness. Everywhere there are dense lines of trucks: delivering groceries to Gristede's or Pathmark, packages from UPS and Fed Ex and the US Postal Service, while police officers from the traffic division lay tickets on illegally parked cars and unattended trucks. *I'll only be two minutes, I swear! You already had your two minutes, buddy. . . .*

But there also exists in me an *idea* of Broadway. It swells with every variety of urban swagger. You see the swagger in the old downtown financial district, where men in conservative suits and overcoats walk toward offices, or clubs, or lunch at India House in Hanover Square as if certain of their destinies. Today, in cold weather, they are once more wearing fedoras and sometimes look like players from the movies of the 1930s. The swagger appears around City Hall, where men and women with agendas hurry out of taxis or limousines and pass the policemen on permanent alert against terrorists and skip up the stairs to meet with the mayor. You see it beyond Chambers Street, among the almost eight thousand federal employees who work in the federal buildings, men and women with the confident stride of those who have attained permanent employment.

The swagger isn't seen among the thousands of immigrants lined up each morning of the week for visits with bureaucrats who will decide whether they can stay in New York or must depart unwillingly for their version of the Old Country. I hope that in a short while the time will come when they can swagger too. Nor do you see the swagger among the last of the men who in the nineteenth century made that part of Broadway the center of the fabric industry. Talk to them and they sound like the exhausted survivors of a once-regal line, their businesses reeling from cheap imports from China and Latin America, their rents rising in the great loft buildings that were built by their mercantile ancestors. They walk in a more tentative way, eyes on the sidewalks before them, like men who know that they will soon go away.

And yet here come the young people who are now filling the emptying lofts: artists, lawyers, designers, computer people. Even in the wake of the dot-com collapse, when you saw SUVs every weekend being loaded up with computers, they have attained the Broadway swagger. They have survived a long season of adversity. They've learned that life here will never be easy, that there will be no long runs of success upon success, that impermanence is part of the deal. Sometimes, New York knocks you down. It also teaches you, by example, how to get up.

And so you see them in the mornings with their children, waiting for school buses or walking with them to the schools of Tribeca. The domestic responsibilities are satisfied, and then they walk to work, often south to Wall Street or north to some of the temporary uptown offices that were opened after September 11. The destination doesn't matter. They walk with the swagger. And it was earned. After the calamity, they did not run.

To be sure, the Downtown stretch of Broadway is not the same as the grand avenue that pushes up through Soho and into Union Square and Times Square and Columbus Circle and through the Upper West Side into Harlem and beyond. Nor is it the generic Broadway of theaters and musicals, haunted by images of Damon Runyon, actually seven or eight blocks long and two blocks wide. Obviously, each of these Broadways is shaped by the neighborhoods through which it passes. Some are centers of retail shopping, or transportation, or entertainment. Others are residential. Many are too mixed for narrow labels. On some streets you can see a heroin addict trying to rent her ruined body to a tourist. You can see peddlers of knockoff Rolex watches or Vuitton handbags or the latest CDs. Or you can see the ghost of Broadway Danny Rose coming toward you from the direction of the Carnegie Deli.

All, in mysterious ways, are meshed in my head. The idea called Broadway is one of mixture, of difference, of a familiar unknowability, and of movement too, of rushing, honking *velocity.* On certain days, I walk the avenue and feel in my arrogance that I know everybody. I know what's on the walls of their living rooms. I hear the talk at their dining tables. I know what they drink and how they vote. And then I cross the street and I'm an alien, knowing nothing. I descend into the nearest subway station for the swift ride home.

Broadway never obeyed the commandments of the grid, and the reason was simple: Broadway was Broadway, and even the planners knew they must not tamper with what it already was. They handled it on the map by leaving it out. Today, it's the only major Manhattan avenue that moves diagonally across the island, from the center to the west. It is the only one that carries us through time from the seventeenth century to the present. It will surely be part of the innovations of the unknowable Manhattan future.

By the 1840s, Broadway was one of several man-made asphalt rivers moving north into the open land of Manhattan. Eventually it would absorb the Bloomingdale Road and the road called the Boulevard, making Broadway the longest street on the island. Downtown in midcentury, above and below Trinity Church, was the city's most illustrious commercial avenue, filled with elegant shops, restaurants, places of entertainment, side-street bordellos, and evolving forms of merchandising. Speed ruled. One primary example of this evolution (and the velocity that drove it) still exists. In 1846, while American soldiers were fighting in Mexico, a diminutive (five-foot-tall) Irish immigrant named Alexander T. Stewart opened the city's first department store on Broadway between Chambers and Reade streets. With that one act of innovation and faith, Stewart radically changed the city.

The store was five stories high (a sixth and seventh floor were later added) and gleamed with its facing of white Tuckahoe marble. Immediately, it became known in the newspapers as the Marble Palace, so distinctive a structure in the downtown city that it did not bear Stewart's name or any other; suddenly, it was just there, the Marble Palace. For a brief period during its construction, it was known too as Stewart's Folly, because he chose to build on the east side of Broadway, and right behind his emerging store lay the Five Points. No decent woman, it was said, would risk shopping there, where thieves and pickpockets and other predators could strike swiftly and then vanish into the lawless alleys of the city's worst slum. At night, it was predicted, armed gangs from the Points would come to loot the place. Stewart was clearly a mindless fool.

But the palazzo-style Marble Palace was an instant success, and Stewart revolutionized New York merchandising. He divided his store into departments that made it easier for customers to choose goods. He insisted on fixed prices, which meant that nobody could bargain for better prices, including clerks who might be privately servicing friends or relatives. He invented the low-priced "sale," offering the remainders of damaged lots of goods (the "fire sale") or out-of-fashion clothing for quick turnovers of cash. He understood that most consumer decisions were made by women and so hired almost two hundred handsome male clerks with impeccable manners. Aristocratic women flocked to the Marble Palace from uptown. New York was abruptly, and permanently, changed.

Other downtown merchandisers began to imitate Stewart, opening new stores on Broadway as it pushed north into what is now known as Soho. These included Arnold Constable, Tiffany, Hearn Brothers, Brooks Brothers, and Lord and Taylor. Window-shopping was born. Business boomed. Eventually, Stewart followed his customers uptown and opened in 1862 a grander store on Broadway between Ninth and Tenth streets, across the avenue from the elegant Grace Church (which was now drawing many refugees from the old Trinity parish). The newspapers dubbed it the Iron Palace, for its cast-iron architecture. Stewart then used the original Marble Palace for the production of clothes by battalions of seamstresses, most of them Irish. The new store had a central rotunda and organ music, and was even more successful than the store he'd built on the corner of Chambers Street. Stewart became a man of such wealth that only the Astors could rival him. For a time (in that era before income taxes), he paid more taxes than any other American. His private mansion on Thirty-fourth Street was for a while the grandest in the city, with a block-long sculpture gallery and a collection of paintings that at least in bulk was one of the most impressive in the city. The old Knickerbocker society never accepted him, with his abrupt Belfast accent, his hard work, his acknowledgment of his Irish roots when he sent food and other aid to those afflicted by the Irish famine. But if A. T. Stewart cared about the approval of the old elite, he never showed it.

The first Marble Palace is still there at Broadway and Chambers Street. It has recently been rehabilitated after years of decay, but there is no sign that tells passersby about Alexander T. Stewart or his extraordinary monument. He is, in fact, largely forgotten by all New Yorkers except students of the city's history. One reason: He left no heirs. There would be no family foundations to perpetuate his name, no doors erected in his memory to decorate a city church, no college scholarships. Even today's department store operators seem to know little about him. After his death in 1876 there was a brief period of lurid publicity when his body was stolen in 1878 from the graveyard of St. Mark's-in-the-Bowery and held for $200,000 ransom. His widow and her lawyer refused to pay. Bargaining ensued, that wretched process that Stewart so despised in life and commerce. Eventually, the widow paid $18,000 for a collection of bones that fit into a gladstone bag. It was impossible in those days to know if the bones were actually those of the richest single individual of the period. But they were buried with ceremony in Garden City, Long Island, a town established by Stewart to provide affordable housing to those who worked for him.

Today, etched into the high face of the old Marble Palace are the words "The Sun Building," added after the building was taken over by the old *New York Sun* in 1917, where it stayed until the paper died at age 117 in 1950. A cube-shaped bronze clock is still in place on the Chambers Street corner, green with age, matched by an elegant temperature gauge on the corner of Reade Street. Both bear the motto "The Sun—It Shines for All." In that building worked some of the finest American newspapermen of several generations, including my friend W. C. Heinz, who was a splendid sportswriter and war correspondent. But even as an old newspaperman, I always think of it as the A. T. Stewart Building. His concept of a department store was the commercial engine of the move uptown, long before anyone called Broadway the Main Stem or the Great White Way. Today there's a Duane Reade store on the ground floor and a bank. In sunshine or snowfall, New Yorkers hurry by on Broadway, walking and talking fast.

After Broadway, a second major street had carved its way into the old empty farmlands of the early nineteenth century and into our present history: the Bowery.

In truth, the Bowery was a kind of tributary of Broadway. Compared to Broadway, the Bowery was short, reaching only fifteen blocks from Chatham Square to today's Cooper Square at Fourth Street. Originally, it stretched to Fourteenth Street, but in 1849 the well-off citizens who resided near the upper Bowery had the name changed to Third Avenue in an attempt to evade the raffish stain of the true name. That name itself derived from the Dutch word for farm, and the street existed before the Revolution. On November 25, 1783, George Washington and his triumphant army of brave amateurs waited on the corner of Canal Street and the Bowery until the British army had departed forever. The date was celebrated for almost a century as Evacuation Day. It was erased as a New York holiday by the Anglophiles who had control of such matters (although it is still celebrated in Boston in March). Nothing, alas, stays the same in New York.

When I was a boy, the Bowery was a squalid avenue plunged into moody, sinister shadow by the Third Avenue El. With the exception of those people who sold restaurant supplies (and lived somewhere else), the population was almost completely composed of alcoholics. The more prosperous could find shelter in the fifty-cents-a-night transient hotels called flophouses, where they slept in locked wire cages. Those who lacked the fifty cents often slept, and too often died, in the urine-soaked doorways of the street. At twelve, I went for my first cautious, solitary peek at the dark street, trying to see the legendary face of the "Bowery bum." I was instantly filled with a mixture of pity and fear. I walked from Astor Place south, the el screeching overhead, and slowly began to feel that I might never escape. There were alcoholics in my Brooklyn neighborhood, of course, often solitaries, castaways from the world of home and work, men who howled at the moon in midafternoon. But here I was the solitary in the grim republic of alcohol. Most of the faces I saw were gullied and ravaged. Their eyes were scoured of life. Their clothes and bodies reeked. Shoes were often taped, or tied with rough twine and stuffed with strips of newspaper. They wore long army surplus coats or Ike jackets. They drooled, or babbled, or reposed silently in the angular bars of shadow thrown upon them by the el. Sometimes they would try to fight each other, in futile caricatures of battlers, their punches almost always hitting air. Later, as a young newspaper reporter, after the el was gone, I would sometimes wander among the dwindling number of rummies and winos (as they were dismissed by the proud drinkers of beer and whiskey), and hear the familiar tales of how they got there: A woman was almost always at fault. Or so they said. At Thanksgiving and Christmas I was usually able to get such sentimental tales into the newspaper.

But even then there were remnants of an older Bowery, a place that once had glittered. A few buildings possessed a grimy majesty. Others rose above tattoo parlors and barber colleges with decorative details cut into lintels over the boarded windows. They were like rummies dozing in frayed Edwardian clothes. I was learning that the Bowery had evolved in the mid-nineteenth century into *the* great avenue of New York popular culture. In a few stray books at the library, I'd seen old woodcuts of the avenue's nightly crowds, with men in sharp clothes, and women with bustles and bonnets, and horse-drawn cabs waiting by the sidewalks. Others waited in the shadows of the gaslights, watching, poised. Along the length of the Bowery, other horses pulled omnibuses on rails. Newsboys came up from Park Row in fierce little platoons, selling the latest editions of the city's newspapers. Many had been orphaned by the Mexican or the Civil War. Dime novels, scandalous magazines, tabloidlike organs such as the *Police Gazette*, and even crude forms of pornography were available everywhere, although most of the more salacious items were discreetly sheltered behind counters.

✾ ✾ ✾

But it was music and theater that gave the Bowery its energy and fame. Between 1840 and 1870, in the stretch between Canal Street and Chatham Square, there were more than a dozen large theaters on the Bowery, along with dance halls, cabarets, and uncountable oyster bars and saloons. The first version of the famous Bowery Theater was built in 1826 on the corner of Canal Street (the present 50 Bowery). It offered three thousand seats and was the first American theater to be fully illuminated by gaslight. On the stages themselves, light was often provided by candles attached to barrel hoops. Gaslight was not always stable, of course, and candles were worse. Fires were common. The Bowery Theater suffered several disastrous fires but kept coming back. The customers always said it was better than ever.

All the new theaters, including the Bowery, offered a variety of productions, highbrow and low-, including Shakespeare for mass audiences. Competition was intense and sometimes deadly. On May 11, 1849, rioting erupted on the streets outside the Astor Place Opera House, between Broadway and today's Lafayette Street. The trigger was the claims for acting dominance between the elegant Englishman William Macready, cherished by the Knickerbockers, and the roaring American Edwin Forrest, who was the hero of the Bowery. Macready was scheduled to appear in *Macbeth* at the white-gloves-only new opera house. Forrest was appearing in the same role at the more populist Broadway Theater. The riot was stirred up by the author of dime novels Ned Buntline, who was a vile nativist and a gifted agitator. The drama of the streets was simple: American versus Englishman.

After a riot inside the opera house on May 7, Macready reluctantly scheduled a farewell appearance for May 10, urged on by prominent New York citizens (including Washington Irving and Herman Melville). On the new date, Forrest's fans, who believed that the Englishman had insulted their hero, began a march from the nearby Bowery. Swirling on the streets was a peculiar combination of anti-immigrant nativists, Tammany bravos, Irish immigrants protesting the appearance of the Englishman, various Bowery b'hoys out for a night's diversion, hundreds of policemen, waiting militiamen, and many curious bystanders. The assembly seethed with class resentments. Protestors charged the police lines and broke them in a great surge. Bricks were thrown. The panicky militia opened fire. When the counting was finished, twenty-two people lay dead. Another nine would die in the following days. About one hundred fifty were wounded. One of the dead was only eight years old. Some were mere passersby or plain spectators from the neighborhood. An old man waiting for a horse car on the Bowery was among those killed. At the time, it was the worst riot in the city's history and the worst theatrical riot in the history of the world.

That night, Macready was spirited away from the theater by friends, and he left the city itself in the dead of night. He would end up in Boston and then leave America forever, recording his furies in his diary. Forrest said nothing in public and finished his engagement down at the Broadway Theater two nights later. Ned Buntline was arrested and would eventually serve a year in prison for his part in the melodrama. The opera house itself was closed for several months of repairs, but it never recovered from the horrors of May 10. The kid-glove atmosphere ended, as the theater was used for magic shows, minstrel shows, and, again, opera. It closed in 1854 and became for many years the site of the Mercantile Library.

Today, when I wander to Astor Place, I often gaze at the northern edge of the street, where an office building now stands. Around the corner is the New York Shakespeare Festival, where Joseph Papp in the 1970s built a permanent home for all kinds of theater, including versions of the Bard in the powerful, human style of Edwin Forrest. On certain chilly evenings, particularly in May, I can see the faces of the furious young roaring boys marching up from the Bowery, the frightened aristocrats fleeing for safety, the panicky policemen and militiamen. I can hear the groans of the dying. Some of them died right there, in front of Kinko's. On such evenings, if there is no rain, I always walk home along the Bowery.

Most Bowery theaters offered staged versions of the stuff of dime novels: melodramas about crime, punishment, and redemption. Some were about cowboys, some detectives. We live with them today because those characters and plots became the basic material of movies and television. There were minstrel shows too, with their racist stereotypes, and sketchy vaudevilles full of dancing girls and acrobats. Much of it must have been great mindless fun. Sometimes, on my walks, I try to imagine them, to see the heroes and the villains and the damsels in distress, to hear the music and the awful jokes. I always fail. I see woodcuts. Or scenes from silent movies. But the teeming theater moments never come clear.

Except for one marvelous historical moment that helped create our present. As I go down the Bowery and cross Canal Street, I can put myself into the Five Points in the 1840s because so much of it was described in newspapers, journals, and the pamphlets of reformers. In spite of the general squalor and climate of despair, there was also entertainment. Some Five Points saloons offered cockfighting, rat-fighting, dog-fighting, and prizefighting. But a few offered an entertainment more exuberant and more beautiful: dancing.

After slavery ended in 1827, there still was no large, compacted black ghetto in the city. Harlem would not become today's Harlem until the second decade of the twentieth century. For most of the nineteenth century, class took precedence over race, and poor blacks and whites lived together at the bottom of the social ladder in the Five Points and other slums. Sometimes they lived together as man and wife or as lovers (which contributed to the racial ferocity that erupted during the Draft Riots of 1863). The close Irish-African presence was adding to the New York alloy. It could be seen in the way they walked, absorbing each other's mannerisms into a unique street style, and heard in the slang they coined together. But the Irish and the Africans were taking other things from each other: music and its brother, dance.

In 1842, a visiting Charles Dickens, then thirty years old and already famous for *The Pickwick Papers,* went down a flight of steps into Afleck's dance hall on Orange Street and saw for the first time the young man he called "the greatest dancer known." The dancer was then sixteen, an African American named William Henry Lane, better known as Master Juba. He was born a free man in Providence, Rhode Island, and in search of greater freedom he found his way to New York. In his book *American Notes*, Dickens described what he saw:

> Single shuffle, double shuffle, cut and cross-out, snapping his fingers, rolling his eyes, turning in his knees, presenting the backs of his legs in front, spinning about on his toes and heels like nothing but the man's fingers on the tambourine; dancing with two left legs, two right legs, two wooden legs, two wire legs, two spring legs—all sorts of legs and no legs—what is this to him? And in what walk of life, or dance of life, does man ever get such stimulating applause as thunders about him, when, having danced his partner off his feet, and himself too, he finishes by leaping gloriously on the bar counter and calling for something to drink . . . ?

In 1844, Master Juba was matched with a young Irish American dancer named John Diamond, who was himself a rising master of the percussive Irish dancing of jigs and reels (as seen a few years ago in the show *Riverdance*). They drew huge racially mixed crowds to the Chatham and Bowery theaters, and as they merged Irish and African rhythms, blending them, topping them, adding steps, "cutting" each other the way jazz musicians would do at jam sessions a century later, they invented what came to be called tap dancing.

Other dancers, theatrical impresarios, and the audiences took notice. This was something new. It wasn't Irish. It wasn't African. This new form of dance could only have been forged in America, and specifically in New York. From those friendly contests and extraordinary perform- ances came, years later, Bojangles Robinson and Fred Astaire, Gene Kelly and Gregory Hines, John Bubbles and the Nicholas Brothers, Bob Fosse, Michael Bennett, Jerome Robbins, and thousands of other dancers and cho- reographers who might never have heard of Master Juba and John Diamond.

There was, alas, no happy ending. After touring the United States (where he was forced to wear blackface in at least one minstrel show), Master Juba became one of the first black artists to seek exile in Europe. He danced in London and in the British provinces, and performed for Queen Victoria. But in 1852, he died suddenly in London (where Dickens had made him famous). He was only twenty-seven. At the time, Juba was performing with an English company, far from the Five Points and the cheers of Bowery crowds. He lives on in theaters all over the world. Nobody now knows what happened to John Diamond.

In certain indirect ways, Master Juba and John Diamond surely added luster to the gaslit New York nights, particularly along the Bowery. But they must have caused some uncomfortable moments among the promot- ers, since African Americans were forced to sit in segre- gated sections of the "white" theaters, if they were admitted at all. This was another dreadful American tradi- tion that would endure for almost a century (in the 1920s and 1930s black patrons were barred, for example, from the Cotton Club in Harlem, until Duke Ellington, through sheer force of character, compelled the hoodlum owners to integrate). But this we do know: After Master Juba and John Diamond, the shows in the Bowery theaters, and later on Broadway, were never the same.

The patrons of those shows—and of the Bowery itself—came from the immediate neighborhood, which included the mainly Irish Five Points to the west of the Bowery and the mainly working-class-German Fourth Ward that stretched east to the South Street waterfront. Thousands of Germans were settling there, in what came to be known as Kleindeutschland, opening beer gardens filled with singing and bawdy laughter. The Germans were, in fact, the second largest nineteenth-century immigrant group after the Irish, and they would soon have their own churches, hospitals, social clubs, and literary societies. They went to the big American theaters too, because they were handy to the Fourth Ward and in some cases dazzling. In certain ways, the large German presence helped shape the italicized styles of the Bowery performers and the physical style of the comedy. The first-generation Germans spoke imperfect English, but as Chaplin, Keaton, and Laurel and Hardy later showed, verbal comedy can't match the glories of slapstick if the intention is to make the whole audience laugh.

But the Bowery theaters were not strictly neighborhood theaters. Increasingly, by foot or in horse-drawn cabs, audiences arrived from the emerging West Side, from what was called the Gap, and later Hell's Kitchen, where the rising commerce of the North River was creating jobs and housing for those who had worked themselves out of the Points. The old aristocratic elites were generally entertained elsewhere, faithful to the old John Street Theater or to the splendid Park Theater until it burned down for the final time at the end of 1848. New theaters were also opening on Broadway, as it moved inexorably north.

But for a long time, the Bowery was the central location of vibrant theatrical life. Saturday night was the biggest night of all, as young men arrived with their pay packets from the labors of the six-day work week. They left behind the rooming houses, with their sour air and bleak furnishings, and did what the New York young have done ever since: They went out. They went out in search of laughter, noise, diversion, illusions, or some form of obliteration. They went out to prove that they could not be conned by confidence men. They went out to drink bad booze and smoke foul cigars. They went out to find people whom they might love and who might love them back. They went out knowing that at the midnight hour they might have to prove their manhood in some brutal fight in the street. They might start the evening in the cheap seats at the theater and end up at a dance hall or a brothel. It didn't matter. Shakespeare or dancing girls: They were better than rooming houses.

On the Bowery, the young men found myths that might make the world more understandable. Or at least more fun. One was the myth of Big Mose, who rose out of the slums as the Paul Bunyan of nineteenth-century New York. As described by Ned Buntline in 1848 and then as seen on the various stages of the Bowery, Mose was a volunteer fireman, as were so many of the young men in the audience, but he was the epitome of all firemen, and a bit more. The myth said that Big Mose was eight feet tall, used lampposts as clubs, could hurl horses halfway across the North River, was fearless and just. He was loosely based on a real volunteer fireman named Moses Humphrey, a printer who worked for the *New York Sun* and belonged to Engine Company 40. In life, Humphrey was the most fearsome street fighter in New York, right up until the day in 1838 when he was beaten senseless by a tougher fireman, Henry Chanfrau of Engine 15. Within weeks the real Mose disappeared in shame from the city and was said to have died in Honolulu.

The facts didn't matter. The myth was born. In some ways, Big Mose was a precursor of the superheroes of twentieth-century comic books, presenting images of power to people who had no power at all. But he was also an example of the way the popular imagination works with the materials at hand. If there had been no Five Points, with its wretchedness and dangers, if there had been no culture of toughness and honor, there would have been no fictional Mose. On those streets, the young needed myth, and the myth of Big Mose would last for decades.

One foggy spring night, crossing Forsyth Street, I saw a huge figure moving through shreds of fog. Here he comes, I thought, out of the nineteenth century fog: Big Mose. As the figure drew closer I saw that he was a black man carrying a bass fiddle in a leathery case. He nodded and moved on. Fearless. Just.

Theater was also a business, then as now, and the impresarios knew that one way to sell tickets was to offer the forbidden. This wasn't easy, since the official culture was in the grip of an imported, heartless Victorianism.

Preachers and editorial writers were always on beady-eyed alert to the presence of temptation and sin. But the impresarios came up with a variety of dodges: Adam and Eve tableaux, "statue girls" with bare legs, or dramas of seduction made acceptable by tacked-on sermons. Sometimes the cops closed the shows. The young men lined up for the next one the following Saturday night.

Then, on September 12, 1866, with audiences longing for escape from the lingering horror of the Civil War and the assassination of Abraham Lincoln, along came a show that really was something new. For the first time all the Bowery specialties were assembled in one extravaganza: a melodramatic story line, torrents of music, many jugglers, about eighty dancing girls, continuous suggestions of sins of the flesh. *The Black Crook* did not open on the Bowery, but it was a Bowery child. The actual theater was Niblo's Garden, in the Metropolitan Hotel at Broadway and Prince Street. The producer was an Irish immigrant named William Niblo, and his theater offered three thousand seats. The primary author of the show was Charles M. Barras, and it would run for a then-astonishing 475 performances and earn a million dollars.

Everybody, it seems, went to see it, including a thirty-one-year-old Samuel L. Clemens. He was then rising to immense popularity as Mark Twain. Clemens wrote about the show: "When they put beautiful clipper-built girls on the stage in this new fashion, with only just barely clothes enough on to be tantalizing, it is a shrewd invention of the devil." He summed up: "The scenery and the legs are everything."

The Broadway musical was born. More than a century

later, the critic Hollis Alpert elaborated: "Barras' melo-drama, originally designed as an opera libretto and con-taining noticeable echoes of *Faust* and von Weber's *Der Freischutz*, allowed for many scenic effects: a mountain storm, a flaming chasm, a grotto of golden stalactites, gilded chariots and angels descending through mist and clouds, and, not the least, a grand masquerade ball." The convoluted plot was full of preposterous characters, and the show's music is never heard anymore. But *The Black Crook* was to be revived again and again for the rest of the century. I wish it could be revived one final time, so I could get to see it.

One of its revelations was about the attitude of the New York audience. They simply refused to be lectured about sin, and that refusal remains part of the New York char-acter to this day. For generations, severe Protestant preachers continued railing at the theater as a kind of vestibule of Hell. For generations, New Yorkers ignored them, as they generally ignore such jeremiads today. There were church steeples everywhere at the time, but New York was becoming a triumphantly secular city. Even today, New Yorkers prefer dancing girls to jeremiads.

There was, to be sure, some substance behind the rhet-oric of the preachers. According to historian Edward K. Spann, in *The New Metropolis: New York City, 1840–1857*, sin was widespread. In the 1850s, there were an estimated ten thousand prostitutes in the city, some of them part-timers, some desperate streetwalkers trying to pay rent, others re-siding in brothels of various levels of elegance or degrada-tion. There were probably seventy-five thousand residents with some form of venereal disease. But there was little that most ordinary citizens could do about such evidence of human weakness or desperation, except murmur a few prayers or offer simple acts of kindness.

On the Bowery, other stage inventions were not as endearing as *The Black Crook* was on Broadway. The most important was the creation of racial and ethnic stereotypes. The Stage Irishman made his appearance, often to the secret, conspiratorial delight of Irish audiences. On stage, the Irishman was a version of the Victorian-era cartoons and caricatures that showed him with simian features, a fringe of whiskers, a hat that didn't fit his head, patchy clothes, smoking a clay pipe. His speech was full of bejase and begorra interjections, his apparent genetic stupidity deepened by drink. But the best of these performers added another level to the act: a sly, smart, sometimes witty subversion of the stereotype itself. The performer often spoke a certain barbed wisdom, directed at the people who wanted to believe the stereotype, and the Irish in the audience knew exactly what he meant. They laughed *with* the Stage Irishman, not at him.

With some exceptions, the African Americans did not collaborate with stereotypes in the way that Irish performers did. When the first African American theater was opened by William Brown off Duane Street in 1821, the troupe performed *Richard III*. Brown was a serious man, a former ship's steward and free man of color (as noted, slavery endured in New York until 1827). In an extraordinary career, Brown opened a series of theaters, including one in Greenwich Village, encouraged integrated audiences (often to his regret when white hooligans showed up to heckle), and promoted an honorable African American presence in the theatrical version of the New York alloy.

The stereotype of the shuffling, ignorant black man — first called Jim Crow, later joined by Zip Coon — was, of course, the creation of white men. They donned blackface and performed in minstrel shows, those bizarre entertainments that were invented outside New York but soon became a basic moneymaking genre in the theaters of the Bowery and Broadway. Since the principals were white versions of black people, there was clearly a secret fear at the heart of the shows. In New York, as in Ireland itself, Stage Irishmen made jokes of themselves to keep themselves safe from people with power. If the ruling parties were laughing, they wouldn't hurt you. But white performers in blackface were helping white audiences believe that blacks (particularly black men) were harmless. The vast majority of New Yorkers were white. The underlying idiocies of even the best minstrel shows helped them feel better about the continued degradation of actual living and breathing African Americans. Nobody wanted to face the fact that the great tides of European immigration were good for the Europeans but not good at all for the descendants of Africans. They lost many jobs, began to sink into poverty, and endured many small humiliations. A few exploded into sudden violence. Better to believe they were harmless.

Minstrel shows began losing their mass appeal after the Civil War, as other forms of competition came to the theaters. But in various forms, they lasted for a very long time. There were, of course, modifications, with a reduction in the most blatant racism and a greater emphasis on the music (leading to ragtime). But such huge stars as Al Jolson and Eddie Cantor worked in blackface in the early twentieth century. The blacks in D. W. Griffith's *The Birth of a Nation* (1915) were a vile mixture of sinister, sex-obsessed black males and the harmless figures of the minstrel shows. That movie was the greatest recruiting device for a renascent Ku Klux Klan. In the 1930s, blacks were routinely presented on screen as shuffling, harmless, eye-rolling fools, particularly in B movies. But with a few exceptions, such as Jolson, they were no longer portrayed by white men in blackface. The best known of those later black performers was Stepin Fetchit. Alas, there were others.

After the Civil War, the Bowery went into steady decline and then suffered a fatal blow. As happens frequently in New York, the blow fell in the name of progress. This sudden event was the coming of the elevated railroads. The earliest versions, in 1867–70, were crude, using mechanical cable equipment to pull the wooden cars. At first, they were limited to the lower West Side and seldom used. Then the New York Elevated Railway Company took over, added steam locomotives and more stations, and was soon running along Ninth Avenue all the way to Sixty-first Street. In the late summer of 1878, they rammed a line down Third Avenue, right through the Bowery. Suddenly, the old street had an iron roof. With the sun blocked by the steel structure, the street went into a permanent twilight. Cinders often fell upon pedestrians on the street, igniting women's dresses, spoiling men's hats and overcoats. Smoke poisoned the air. Even the Saturday night toffs started going elsewhere for laughter and music. The Bowery was claimed by the most squalid saloons, the cheapest bordellos. By 1892, the songwriters Percy Gaunt and Charles Hoyt had written the street's sad anthem. The chorus goes:

> *The Bow'ry! The Bow'ry!*
> *They say such things,*
> *And they do strange things*
> *On the Bow'ry! The Bow'ry!*
> *I'll never go there anymore.*

That songwriters' evocation of New York nostalgia would endure through most of the coming century. But it was not the end of the story, of course. After the el was taken down in 1955–57, and sunlight returned, and the old bums blinked at the sight of the sky, the Bowery remained squalid. Then one of those mysterious New York shifts took place. In the 1970s, the rummies and winos began wandering out into the wider city. They became known by the politer name of "the homeless," and New Yorkers could not avoid them as they did when they were confined to the alcoholic ghetto of the Bowery. Many New Yorkers were contemptuous of ruined men, but others, charged with compassion, responded to their presence by creating all over the city a system of shelters and kitchens. Many of the damaged men never went back to the doorways and flophouses of the Bowery.

Instead, artists arrived, moving into many of the high-ceilinged apartments on the great wide street. Some were bohemian pioneers. Some had been displaced by the escalating costs of living in Soho to the west, a neighborhood that itself had been rescued from oblivion by artists in the 1970s. The new residents could walk to Chinatown and Little Italy, and then small new restaurants began to open on the Bowery. From the Canal Street end, Chinese merchants, grocers, and fishmongers began taking over abandoned stores and apartments, and the street began to erupt with color and life. The once decaying 1874 cast-iron bank building at 330 Bowery is now gleaming with white paint, calls itself the Bouwerie Lane Theater, and houses the Jean Cocteau Repertory Theater. Directly across the street is CBGB, still lively and dark and theatrically (or comically) nasty, the place where punk rock blossomed almost thirty years ago. Here performed the Ramones, Blondie, the Police, Talking Heads, and the B-52s, among many others. Who then could have imagined that in 2003 there'd be a sign renaming Second Street and the Bowery as Joey Ramone Place?

Not far from CBGB is the place that used to house a rowdy club called Sammy's Bowery Follies. In 1946, during a three-month visit to New York, the thirty-three-year-old French novelist, philosopher, and editor Albert Camus visited the sawdust joint several times in the company of *New Yorker* writer A. J. Liebling. They often dined first in Little Italy and then walked east on Grand Street, past the block in which every store sold wedding dresses. Camus was impressed (the larger city filled him with "an impatient nostalgia") and wrote about it later:

> I knew what was waiting for me, these nights on the Bowery, where at a few steps from those splendid shops

with wedding dresses (not one of the wax brides was smiling), some five hundred yards of such shops, live forgotten men, men who let themselves be poor in the city of bankers. It is the city's most sinister neighborhood, where one doesn't meet any women, where one man in three is drunk, and where in a curious café, seemingly out of a western movie, one can see fat old actresses who sing of ruined lives and maternal love, stamping their feet at the refrain, and shaking spasmodically, to the roaring of the audience, the packets of shapeless flesh with which age had covered them. Another old woman plays the drums, and she resembles an owl, and some evenings one feels like knowing her life story, at one of those rare moments when geography disappears, and when solitude becomes a somewhat disordered truth.

Camus would not recognize the new Bowery. There at 308 Bowery is the Bowery Poetry Club, the sidewalk crowded with desperate cigarette smokers (smoking now banned within), the interior loud with "poetry slams" and readings of great vitality by unknown poets. They all have the confidence of youth. And yet there is an undercurrent of insecurity too. These people have helped revive one of Downtown's lost avenues. But pause, listen, talk: There are complaints now that new housing developments, driven by the cardinals of real estate, are about to ruin the Bowery. *I didn't move here to live on the tenth floor, man.*

Walk on to the corner of Grand Street, and there before you is the old Bowery Savings Bank. Like so many other New York architectural masterpieces, this was designed by Stanford White. Construction began in 1893, the year of a great financial panic and a subsequent depression that was filled with terror. The mainly working-class depositors in the bank needed reassurance, a building that provided at least the illusion of security in an uncertain time. White gave them what they needed. The plot was oddly shaped, a large U with one entrance on the Bowery, another on Grand, and a third facade on Elizabeth Street. Like any great architect, White designed within the limitations of the plot and still presented a sense of grandeur and permanence. Just inside the columned Bowery entrance is a triumphal arch leading to the banking room. The interior columns (some merely painted) are elegantly placed. The light is glowing. When it was finished in 1895, White must have felt one frustration: The el was already rattling along the Bowery, blocking the full rays of the sun from falling on the white Bedford limestone of the exterior. Today, the visitor can see it in ways that even eluded its architect.

Now in the evenings taxis pull up to the curb and discharge passengers who walk through the columned entrance into an elegant restaurant. Years of graffiti and greasy crud are gone. Columns have been repaired. The old battered steps seem new. Ten years ago, White's creation appeared to be destined for the architectural graveyard. But in New York, even impending death can sometimes turn out to be a false alarm, as new forms of velocity come rushing from nowhere, carrying life.

Chapter Six

PARK ROW

IN THE SUMMER of 1960, I was working nights at the *New York Post,* an afternoon tabloid, trying to learn my imperfect craft. I started each shift at one a.m. and finished, most mornings, at eight. Then, if I had a few dollars in my pocket, I would go to the Page One, a saloon on Greenwich Street, and wait for the first edition, which arrived fresh off the presses at nine. At the bar, in the company of older professionals, I received a good part of my professional education. They examined headlines, often with a bilious eye. They scrutinized stories, including my own. They issued fierce criticisms, savage, often hilarious indictments. They told me what I should never do again, and I tried hard not to repeat my latest published barbarism. I was never happier.

On mornings when I had little money, or worked past the deadlines on other stories, I would leave the *Post* through the Washington Street exit and head for Broadway. The great street at that hour was usually thick with frantic people, bumping one another, dodging 'round one another, grumbling their apologies, then dashing across the paths of careening taxicabs. I loved plunging into the tumult, knowing that I was on my own while almost everyone else was going to work. My treks took me past Trinity and the Equitable Building, where I had lounged away so many lunch hours, then into the rushing infantry rising from the subways at Fulton Street. In a coffee shop with a street counter, I'd buy a cardboard cup of coffee and a cheese Danish. I had the morning papers with me, but usually I also had a book. On days of decent weather, I'd head for City Hall Park. There I'd bow my head in reverence to the Woolworth Building (often humming some lines from the tune "Million Dollar Baby"), find a bench, sip the coffee, and gaze at the vanished majesties of Park Row.

In a way, this was another form of my newspaper education, for Park Row was once the center for all the great newspapers of Manhattan. From my bench, I could see the void where Joseph Pulitzer built a skyscraper to house his newspaper, the *World*. Both the newspaper and the building long ago had been smashed into memory. But the building erected by Henry Raymond and his partners for the *New York Times* was still there. The newspaper had departed for Longacre Square in 1904, where publisher Adolph S. Ochs had that crossroads renamed Times Square in its honor, but the newspaper's downtown origins could never be denied. The old *Times* building is now part of Pace University and is beautiful to look at. Down on the right stood the headquarters of the old *New York Herald,* a paper now long vanished, along with the building from which it was published. Other newspapers made Park Row their homes. They're gone too.

The area itself was dense with history. The point where Broadway intersected with Ann Street, Vesey Street, and Park Row was a place where many strands of our character collided, erupted, or merged. It was not the city's first plaza, but it was certainly the first New York crossroads. Clustered around the foot of the nineteenth-century City Hall Park were St. Paul's Chapel, the Astor Hotel, the Park Theater, and P. T. Barnum's insanely wonderful museum. The American Museum was crucial to the emerging human alloy of the city, drawing spectators from every part of the city's life, including freshly arrived immigrants. They had never seen anything like it in the stony west of Ireland or the forests of Germany. In an 1866 guide to New York there's an advertisement for the museum, which opened at "sunrise" and closed at ten at night, with tickets costing thirty cents, half price for children under ten. The advertisement read:

The management of this STOREHOUSE OF EARTH'S NOVELTIES, for the STUDY AND ENLIGHTEN-MENT OF ALL, has sought to make it an ATTRACTIVE MEDIUM OF POPULAR DIVERSION. There has been a sedulous desire to combine all the EXCITABLE ELEMENTS OF ENJOYMENT, with the total absence of an impure suggestion. All that is NOVEL AND CURI-OUS, comprising *FOREIGN ODDITIES AND NATIVE WONDERS,* are here exhibited for the purpose of collect-ing curiosities being established in America, Europe, Asia, and Africa. In addition to the list of **A Million Curiosities**, is a collection of ZOOLOGICAL RARITIES, which is constantly receiving additions of singular and curious species, forming a splendid Menagerie of Living Animals. The exquisitely interesting GRAND AQUARIA, OCEAN AND RIVER GARDENS, containing the finest specimens of fish, truly pronounced the EIGHTH WONDER OF THE WORLD. The life-like MOVING WAX FIGURES—ENORMOUS GIANTS—DIMINUTIVE DWARFS—LIVING OTTERS—THE MAMMOTH WHALE TANK, containing Splendid Specimens of LIVING WHALES—THE LIGHTNING CALCULATOR—GLASS BLOWERS—MAMMOTH FAT WOMAN—LIVING SEALS, etc. may be seen at all hours. Refined and pleasing entertainments are given THREE TIMES DAILY. . . .

Barnum was the most successful showman of his day, his theater offering three thousand seats to all comers except African Americans. But his ad in the 1866 guide was wasted, and demonstrated the hazards of lead time, the gap between submission of copy and actual publication; the theater burned down near the end of 1865. It was rebuilt, and again burned down in 1868, and Barnum shifted his talents to the circus. How I wish I'd been able to see those moving wax figures and the mammoth whale tank. They were certainly seen by the editors and reporters who worked in the area, along with all the other oddities. Barnum's gifts for showmanship, promotion, and novelty surely affected the newspapers they made each day. Barnum, after all, spoke in banner headlines.

The content of newspapers was also affected by the hokum and hoopla that came from Barnum's fertile mind. A unique human blend was forming in that first major New York crossroads, combining God, politics, commerce, sin, and spectacle. These were all essential components of the emerging city and became the fundamental table of contents for the more than twenty daily newspapers. The combination remained part of the city's 1960s tabloids and exists in its own variations to this day, made even more vivid (or brainless) by the advent of cable television. Around the crossroads near Barnum's American Museum, the nineteenth-century side streets bustled with restaurants, bookstores, bordellos, drinking establishments, "day" gambling joints, cigar stores, tailors, printers, and other, less prosperous newspapers, including my own *New York Post,* which was housed after 1902 at 20 Vesey Street, just off Church.

As the South Tower collapsed on the morning of September 11, 2001, and the great fierce cloud came rushing at me, my wife, Fukiko, and some cops and firemen where we stood at the corner of Vesey and Church streets, I was separated from Fukiko, unable to see through the opaque cloud that had engulfed us. The horizon vanished. The impact of all that falling glass and steel had emptied the world of sound. I was coughing and stumbling and calling my wife's name and then was shoved to safety into the lobby of that same former New York Evening Post Building. That is, into the place where the journalistic heirs of William Cullen Bryant once directed reporters in the name of civilization. Later that terrible morning, walking away from the disaster into a world covered with the fine white talcumlike dust of mass death, I saw that all of City Hall Park was white too, and all the surrounding buildings, and I remembered for a moment sitting in the park when it was green and so was I. After a while, in the changed white world, I found my wife eight blocks away and we hugged each other with the joy of the living.

In those innocent days when I was learning my trade, I often wondered what it would have been like to work for Horace Greeley or James Gordon Bennett in a time when there were no electric lights, no typewriters, no telephones, and no telegraph. In imagination, I saw myself scribble in candlelight. I saw myself rushing to the Bowery with pencil and paper, in search of some story, and finding that Stephen Crane had arrived before me. I saw Richard Harding Davis emerging from a hansom cab on a morning thick with harbor fog, as handsome as the drawings by Charles Dana Gibson that used him as an American male archetype, and striding into the World Building. Or I was working at the *World* for the most sadistically brilliant of all city editors, a man named Charles Chapin. By all accounts, he had a gift for anticipating breaking news, drove his staff hard, treated them like swine, and fired them for minor infractions (in those dreadful days before the creation of the Newspaper Guild). In my lurid young man's imagination, I was two minutes late one morning, and Chapin fired me, and I beat him senseless and went down the block to work for the *Sun*. Then I exulted, in a shameful way, after Chapin admitted shooting his aging wife, Nellie, in the head in a 1918 "murder-suicide pact" (that later tabloid staple). Chapin, alas, couldn't find the nerve to kill himself. In my mind, I went to cover his trial and saw him plead guilty. Later, with some pity and more compassion than Chapin ever showed his subjects or his staff, I wrote about his death in Sing Sing in 1930 and how the warden said he had become gentler and had created a rose garden for his fellow cons. In my youthful imaginings, newspapermen always had the last word.

I was reading about all of them, trying to fill in the blanks of my education, a task I now know I will never complete. In an imaginary 1858, I went drinking in the dark smoky cellar of Pfaff's on Broadway at Bleecker Street, the first true outpost of the city's underground bohemia, and met all the newspapermen and bad poets and hungry painters, and their women too, and even talked one afternoon with Walt Whitman, over for the day from Brooklyn. I was summoned to Paris by James Gordon Bennett Jr., the bizarre son of the man who created modern journalism. He was, of course, drunk and abusive and insisted that I shave my beard in his presence, and I left his office and sent him a variation of the famous Hemingway cable to another press baron: UPSTICK JOB ASSWARDS.

For a while, I worked in my mind at the *New York Tribune* for Horace Greeley, whose statue is now to the east of City Hall, looking pensive and tired, a newspaper drooping in his hand. In that 1890 bronze by sculptor John Quincy Adams Ward, Greeley doesn't look up at Park Row or the place where his newspaper once stood until it was demolished to widen the approaches to the Brooklyn Bridge. He appears to be thinking about his time on earth in the amazing city (he died in 1872, and the tranquil, melancholy statue was a long time coming). In life, Greeley was small and brave, a country boy with a reedy voice. His often fleeting enthusiasms charged his newspaper with a sense of surprise. Greeley never encountered an ism that he didn't like. He embraced socialism (even hiring Karl Marx to send a column from Europe, a weekly letter that was probably written by Friedrich Engels and continued for more than a decade). He championed abolitionism. He celebrated vegetarianism. Late in life, he even dabbled in table-rapping spiritualism. But he put out a very good newspaper. He fought valiantly in print against slavery and saw clearly that the fate of the conquered Mexican territories could lead to a great, heartbreaking American civil war. His reporters returned again and again to the miseries of the New York poor, even though Greeley knew that his middle-class audience preferred a moralizing indifference. He was erratic, an imperfect husband, a self-deluded player in professional politics (even running for president against U. S. Grant in 1872, after abandoning the Republican party he'd helped create). But he was a superb newspaperman.

The man who deserved a statue and never got one was James Gordon Bennett. He was tall, gaunt, cross-eyed, sardonic, sober, intense; Dickens, that old court reporter, would have loved him. Even now, I wish I'd been around when he was inventing the kind of newspaper that I was working for in 1960 and will always cherish. Bennett published a tabloid before there were tabloids. He was born a Catholic in Scotland and started the *New York Herald* in 1835 in a cellar in Ann Street with, as he said, "five hundred dollars, two chairs, and a dry-goods box." He sold his new four-page newspaper for a penny, directly competing in price with the three-year-old *New York Sun.* He started finding an audience. The following year, he discovered a crucial part of the newspaper formula: the endless New York appetite for murder.

The occasion was the brutal killing of a twenty-three-year-old prostitute who called herself Helen Jewett. On the Saturday night of April 9, 1836, her body was found smoldering on the bed of a bordello at 41 Thomas Street. This was three blocks north of Chambers Street, between Church Street and Chapel (now West Broadway). The young woman had been hit on the head with a small ax and then set on fire. As the news spread the following morning, Bennett did something revolutionary: He went to the scene of the crime. Until then, crime news was generally buried inside the newspapers, if covered at all, and the reporters were satisfied with secondhand versions from the police. What the hell: Bad things do happen on Saturday nights. Bennett's Sunday morning visit revealed details that made the crime a sensation. It was one of those accidents of timing that change everything.

To begin with, Bennett noticed a portrait of Lord Byron on the wall. He saw books on a shelf by Walter Scott, Washington Irving, Edward Bulwer-Lytton, Alexander Pope, Homer, Dryden, and others. Clearly this was no ordinary prostitute. Beyond the furnishings, he saw the young woman's body, uncovered for him by a friendly policeman. Bennett was then forty-one. His description of the young woman's corpse, as several feminist scholars have since pointed out, borders on the pornographic:

> I could scarcely look at it for a second or two. Slowly I
> began to discover the lineaments of the corpse as one

would the beauties of a statue of marble. It was the most remarkable sight I ever beheld—I never have, and never expect to see such another. "My God," exclaimed I, "how like a statue! I can scarcely conceive that form to be a corpse." Not a vein was to be seen. The body looked as white, as full, as polished as the purest Parian marble. The perfect figure, the exquisite limbs, the fine face, the full arms, the beautiful bust, all, all surpassed in every respect the Venus de Medici according to the casts generally given of her.

The helpful policeman told Bennett that Jewett had assumed her present appearance in less than an hour. Bennett wrote on:

It was the first process of dust returning to dust. The countenance was calm and passionless. Not the slightest appearance of emotion was there. One arm lay over her bosom—the other was inverted and hanging over her head. The left side down to the waist, where the fire had touched, was bronzed like an antique statue. For a few moments I was lost in admiration at this extraordinary sight—a beautiful female corpse, that surpassed the finest statue of antiquity. I was recalled to her horrid destiny by seeing the dreadful bloody gashes on the right temple, which must have caused instantaneous dissolution.

Bennett went on and on in that first day's story, proving that even editors need editors, but he had found something that shook the genteel world of the business-oriented newspapers of the day. In the expanding, unruly city, violent crime was now a critical newspaper subject. Murder was the best subject of all. For days, Bennett followed up his first-day story on the Helen Jewett case, describing in detail her life before New York and her true identity, along with many details about the man who was quickly charged with her murder, a well-off young bachelor named Richard P. Robinson. The *Herald*'s crude presses broke down trying to service the audience. At one point, Bennett was selling thirty-five thousand copies a day while the respectable sheets were averaging eight thousand. He followed the trial of the accused (young Robinson eventually got off with the help of expensive lawyers). Bennett shifted and turned in his own judgment of the man's guilt, first convinced Robinson was the killer, then wondering in print how such a well-brought-up young American could have committed such a heinous crime. The readers didn't care about his inconsistencies; they kept reading. As he grew older and richer, Bennett never forgot the lesson taught by the case of Helen Jewett. Details, clearly presented, were everything. In the future, the *Herald* would always be the home of vivid writing. Most other newspapers learned from Bennett and by the time I was learning the craft, 125 years later, murder remained part of the daily package. Because of Bennett, crime had become a permanent part of the New York imagination.

But Bennett didn't limit his newspaper to crime. He created the first cadre of foreign correspondents. He accelerated the velocity of news, using carrier pigeons, fast harbor boats, pony express, and eventually the telegraph to get the news while it was new. He insisted that the stock market, society, sports, and religion were worthy subjects of sustained scrutiny too. In those decades before photoreproduction, he illustrated his stories with woodcuts, if necessary, or cartoons, or charts and maps. He demanded live interviews with people in the news, written in words that made pictures in the minds of the readers. He invented the weather report and the women's section, and sent his reporters off to the Bowery theaters and the surging district of the new Broadway to deal with what came to be known as popular culture. Bennett didn't get moralistic about certain facts of New York life. He created what is now known as a personals column, where lovers could make appointments and ladies of the sporting life could offer their services.

His rivals tried to destroy him. They said he was a vulgarian, a crude sensationalist, a man coarsening the life of New York. Bennett fought back, modified some of his stridency, and survived. To be sure, he had immense flaws. In his own writings, he was too quick to cast aspersions. He libeled his competitors with fierce abandon (earning at least one public horsewhipping). He was often blatantly racist and supported slavery in the South, where he had many readers. He sneered at all abolitionists, starting with Greeley. But he published a newspaper that many thousands wanted to read, even when they were furious with its editorials. The *Herald* was alive. It was bright and audacious. It was driven by reporting. The editorials were often frantic, but the news was new. Or as new as Bennett could make it.

As a young reporter, reading about the men who made the newspapers in the nineteenth century, I had few grand illusions. I never thought that I was entering the greatest center of communications in the United States and therefore the world. I just wanted to work at a trade I loved. I also had no illusions about the moral superiority of my colleagues, neither those I worked with at the *Post* nor those I worked against from the other papers. Most lived with the wisdom taught by human folly. They'd all have laughed at such pretensions. I was also instructed about human frailty by the history of the trade itself, as practiced in New York.

One great case history was the story of James Gordon Bennett Jr. His father died in 1872, leaving the *Herald* in the hands of his spoiled lout of a son, who was then twenty-six. In spite of his great flaws as a human being, his impulsiveness, his invincibly self-indulgent ways, Junior turned out to be a surprisingly good newspaperman. He spent most of his time after 1877 in Europe because of a personal scandal in which he was the key figure. The script was unintentionally hilarious. On New Year's Eve 1876, he was engaged to marry a young society woman. He arrived late at the young woman's home, where friends and family were gathered for a party. Young Bennett proceeded to urinate in front of fiancée and guests. One report said he used the fireplace as his receptacle. Another insisted that it was a grand piano. Whatever the prop, the drama erupted, and the appalled men of the family threw Bennett into the night.

The aggrieved young woman broke the engagement. And a few days later, the woman's brother horsewhipped Bennett Jr. in front of the Union Club, making blood run in the snow. This was great stuff. The upper orders of society, which had accepted Bennett when they wouldn't accept his father, immediately blackballed him. He received no further invitations to New York events where women would be present. Off he went to Paris, where he had been raised, and stayed for almost four decades. He built the grandest yacht of the day. He created the *Paris Herald* (dismissed as a rich boy's whim, it remains alive today, owned by the *Herald*'s old rival the *New York Times*). Bennett sent Stanley in search of Livingston, ordered up hundreds of other stories. He maintained control of the New York paper through a network of office spies called the White Mice. Under his long-distance command, the paper maintained high standards of reporting and continued to break story after story.

In New York, however, everything was changing in the newspaper business. Joseph Pulitzer arrived in 1883, an immigrant from Hungary who had been a Union soldier in the last year of the Civil War and gone on to make a great success of the *St. Louis Post-Dispatch*. He was thirty-six, his eyesight already failing, but he was burning with a passion for newspapers. He bought the failing *World* for $346,000 from the notorious stock speculator Jay Gould, a huge price for a paper that was losing $40,000 a year. Almost immediately, Pulitzer transformed it into the most profitable newspaper of its time. The key to success, as usual, was solid reporting. The reporters were the front line of Pulitzer's crusades against desperate living conditions, poor schools, inadequate water and transportation. The politics of the editorial page were liberal, in contrast to the conservative politics of almost every other New York newspaper. As an immigrant, Pulitzer also insisted that his reporters cover the new arrivals from Italy and Eastern Europe, even if they could not read the *World*. "Their children will," he said. And they did.

One person closely watching Pulitzer's achievement was William Randolph Hearst, a rich young man from the West whose father had become a millionaire with a piece of the Comstock Lode. For a brief time, after leaving Harvard in 1886, young Hearst worked as a reporter for Pulitzer, studying the formula as Pulitzer was practicing it. Then he went west, took over his father's *San Francisco Examiner,* and made it a huge success with a kick-the-door-down brand of aggressive reporting. Hearst perfected a cruder version of what Pulitzer was doing in New York. The vision was simple: Life in an American city was made of white hats and black hats, and Hearst, the roaring populist, was on the side of the white hats in crusades against vice, corruption, and crime. Within a few years the circulation of his newspaper doubled, and Hearst made a small fortune. At the same time, he was dreaming larger dreams. He began casting a covetous eye on New York.

The chance came in 1895. That year, he bought the failing *Morning Journal,* which had been founded by Pulitzer's estranged brother, Albert, years before Joseph took over the *World*. Armed with an enormous fortune ($7.5 million) given to him by his widowed mother, Hearst set out to transform a loser into a winner. The battle that followed is familiar to many people now, if only through the fictional version of Hearst shown in *Citizen Kane*. He and Pulitzer fought with competing crusades. They fought with cartoons and comic strips. The first regular cartoon was a weekly panel called "Hogan's Alley," written and drawn for Pulitzer by Richard F. Outcault about a wisecracking slum kid in a yellow nightshirt. Yellow ink held fast better than other colors on the newer high-speed presses, and from that cartoon panel came the phrase "yellow journalism." Pulitzer and Hearst raided each other's staffs, with Hearst stealing editors, reporters, and even Outcault for the *Journal.* They fought with highly paid freelancers, including Richard Harding Davis, who covered the Yale-Princeton football game for Hearst and was paid an amazing (for the time) $500 as his fee.

The competition reached its fevered climax with the run-up to the war against Spain in 1898. Hearst beat the war drums. Pulitzer rose to the jingoistic challenge. Every morning brought fresh tales of Spanish atrocities against their local rebel opponents in Cuba, Spanish use of torture, Spanish contempt for the United States. The popular "yellow" press was driving a president toward armed conflict with a country that had done nothing to the United States. Then the USS *Maine* blew up in Havana harbor under circumstances that remain unclear. In the end, Hearst and Pulitzer got their splendid little war.

When it was over, both newspapers were losers. Daily circulation at the peak of the war reached more than a million each for the *World* and the *Journal.* But their expenses had been enormous. Each paper lost money, Pulitzer for the first time since arriving in New York. There were also signs that Pulitzer was ashamed of the way he had succumbed to the war fever. The true winners were Adolph S. Ochs, who had taken over the *New York Times* in 1896, and Bennett's *Herald.* Ochs had no money to send fleets of correspondents to Cuba and so reported the basic war news while concentrating on the local and adding such cultural features as book reviews. He also dropped the price of his paper from three cents to one. His circulation tripled. From distant Paris, Bennett also seemed to gaze at the war with a cooler, more European eye. The *Herald*, which under his father had introduced the sensational to New York newspapers, was much more restrained than its competitors. Both the *Herald* and the *Times* presented news — particularly foreign news — in a more sober style. Their comparative gravity suited a number of readers who were embarrassed by the ranting jingoism of the "yellow" sheets. And then all of them, including Pulitzer, got lucky. Hearst managed to go too far.

In the run-up to the war with Spain, Hearst had vilified President William McKinley, a Republican, for his cautious refusal to go to war when Hearst told him to go to war. His enduring contempt for McKinley was expressed in a 1901 *Journal* editorial: "If bad institutions and bad men cannot be got rid of except by killing, then the killing must be done." That September, a psychopathic anarchist shot McKinley at the Pan-American Exposition in Buffalo. McKinley died eight days later of gangrene. The other New York newspapers hauled out the old Hearst editorial and a column by Hearst's Arthur Brisbane, who asserted that Lincoln's assassination had brought many Americans together. The competitors lashed out at Hearst with high moral indignation. The circulation of the *Journal* started falling.

Then Hearst went into active politics. He was elected twice to Congress as a Democrat. But he lusted for the presidency. The Democrats turned him aside at the convention in 1904. He lost out in bids for the governorship of New York and lost, through Tammany swindling, in his campaign to become mayor of New York, then failed again. In the end, he had spent $1,750,000 on a political career that was almost entirely a failure. Worse, the credibility of his newspaper eroded even more. Its crusades and its editorial positions seemed calculated only to endorse the dreams of political glory of its publisher.

Meanwhile, Park Row was changing. Bennett was the first to move, in 1893, building a new plant at Thirty-fifth Street and Broadway, designed by Stanford White. His grateful new neighbors changed the name of the crossroads to Herald Square. Then, in 1904, Ochs moved the *Times* uptown to Longacre Square, where Broadway reached Forty-second Street. He arranged with Tammany friends to change the name of Longacre Square in honor of his newspaper. In April, Manhattan had a new name to remember: Times Square. Away to the south, in the old part of town, Park Row was beginning to look abandoned, if not yet forlorn.

And so my present as a newspaperman was always accompanied by the past. Bennett and Greeley, Pulitzer and Hearst hovered near me as I was taught my craft. There was one other immense ghost in the room: Joseph Medill Patterson, who had started the tabloid *New York Daily News* on Park Place in 1919, moved it to a new Raymond Hood skyscraper on Forty-second Street in 1929, and built it into the largest-circulation newspaper in the United States. For one major reason, the tabloid was made for New York: It was easy to read on subways by men and women in a hurry. In the booming 1920s, almost everybody was in a hurry. Patterson's tabloid was bright, accurate, funny, thorough, and lively about sports, filled with a variety of service features, along with heavy emphasis on show business. It featured the best photography in the city and called itself "New York's Picture Newspaper." Like Greeley, Patterson had once been a socialist, even managed a campaign for Eugene V. Debs, and after socialism faded as a personal passion, he still insisted on making a newspaper for the common man. That often meant making a newspaper for the immigrants to New York and for their American children. Certainly my father was not alone in becoming an American through the *Daily News* sports pages. He never did get to read *The Federalist Papers*.

Patterson died in 1946, but the *News* was still the largest game in town, even though some newspapermen detected a weakening of its energy and stylishness. My own *New York Post* had become a tabloid in 1943, with Dorothy Schiff, a proud liberal, as the publisher, but remained in 1960 the seventh in circulation among the seven New York dailies. It made up for lack of funds with literary style and a brave liberalism (in particular during the dark days of McCarthyism). The sports section was aggressive and well-written. The columnists included Murray Kempton, which was like having Henry James sitting across the city room banging on an old Remington typewriter. My own instructors included a brilliant, hardboiled editor named Paul Sann, a young editor named Ed Kosner, a sour copy editor (and superb writer) named Fred McMorrow. The staff was small, so there were few specialists. On the same night you could write a murder, a labor dispute, and a fire. Everybody took part in the process, cracking jokes, making remarks, showing a kid how to fix a lead. Most nights, I never wanted to go home.

I quickly realized that newspapers were among the institutions that bound together the many different people of the city. In their own way, they were as important as baseball teams, public schools, and the subways. Television was, of course, everywhere now in the New York night, and its stars were known to millions. But many New Yorkers, after viewing the news on television, still needed a newspaper to make it feel real. And in those newspapers, the basic formula hadn't changed since the days of the giants of Park Row. Except in time of war, foreign news was generally left to the *New York Times* or the *New York Herald-Tribune* (the two former rivals had merged in the 1920s). But the rest of the papers knew that all news, like all politics, was local. They covered power, particularly the nexus of New York wealth and New York politics. They were heavy on sports, and added great dollops of Broadway and Hollywood gossip in imitation of Walter Winchell, of Hearst's *New York Mirror*. A few even began covering television. There were society columns too, and advice columns, and comics, and puzzles.

Above all, there was crime. Big bank robberies, huge cases of corruption, drug busts: All were given attention according to the flow of other news. New Yorkers love calamity, so a swindle or a drug bust could never compete on page one with a war, a paralyzing blizzard, the explosion of a power plant, or a fatal crash in a subway. But from the time of Bennett, crime had been a beat for every newspaper. With the arrival in the early 1960s of the dreadful combination of guns and heroin, New York was becoming more dangerous. The annual murder statistics would climb from around three hundred a year to more than two thousand by the 1990s. A sense of menace began to pervade the city, staining the night, making each citizen—reading about the latest outrage on the way to work—feel uncertain and vulnerable.

From the nineteenth century on, most New Yorkers knew that there were only a few basic scripts for murder. Some desperate fool with a rented gun would try a stickup, panic, and shoot the owner of the delicatessen, who was invariably the father of three young children. Another fool would try a mugging on a dark street and get gunned down himself when the victim turned out to be an off-duty cop. A busted-out gambler would be drinking in an after-hours club when a tall gunman and a shorter partner walked in with guns blazing. The cops, and the tabloids, would then send out an alarm for a Mutt-and-Jeff bandit team. The felons were always caught.

Occasionally some hoodlum would be found in an alley with an ice pick in his ear. He had done something terrible inside the Mob, and his corpse was proof of the existence in the city of the ultimate secret society. Some reporters concentrated exclusively on the Mob, revealing its connections to unions, real estate, gambling coups, fixed fights, and, increasingly, to heroin. They made charts of the powers in the different Mafia families, traced their connections to Las Vegas or to other American mobs that were set up as intricately as the Federal Reserve system. Some became immense newspaper stars: Lucky Luciano, Bugsy Siegel, Frank Costello, Meyer Lansky. Most of the time, the dead were from the lower ranks, not the high command. Siegel was murdered in Los Angeles in 1947, but Luciano, Costello, and Lansky died in bed.

Mob murders were almost all in the name of business, but their numbers were tiny when placed among the statistics. An equally small number of murders were driven by avarice, particularly among those poor souls with large insurance policies. The truth was that human passion drove most homicides. One night in the early 1960s, a sad-eyed detective named Ray Martin told me: "The biggest killer in New York? It's not drugs. It's not robbery. It's not greed. It's jealousy." That seemed true then and remains true now. Month after month, faithless husbands were killed by enraged wives. Faithless wives were killed by enraged husbands. The lovers of each were killed too, but less frequently. Often, the romantic logic of such murders—"I can't live without you!"—commanded the killers to then kill themselves, leaving a one-day story without a mystery, a pursuit, an exercise in detection, a trial, or a final journey to the electric chair, labeled in its day by tabloid reporters as the "hot squat."

There were so many of these crimes of passion that not all of them made the newspapers, unless they fit into a special category: Murder at a Good Address. A murder driven by jealousy on Park Avenue was bigger news than a similar murder in Brooklyn. If the slain husband, wife, or lover came from the community of the rich, the headlines shouted. If they came from a slum, they were lucky to produce a three-paragraph story deep in the newspaper.

Because murders had become so common in New York life, editors demanded those details that would make familiar scripts seem new. "Concrete nouns, active verbs, and *details*," Paul Sann said to me one morning in the *Post* city room. "That's all you need. Starting with the goddamned details."

The details never lost their horror. Human beings killed other human beings with guns, knives, poisons, axes large and small. They strangled them with ropes, neckties, and belts. They caved in their skulls with ashtrays, lamps, hammers, lead pipes, baseball bats, bricks, and frying pans. They shoved them under subway trains. They ran them over with automobiles. They heaved them off rooftops. Sometimes the corpses were naked. More often, they were clothed. The victims never had pictures of Lord Byron on the wall. But the accounts of their final hours went all the way back to James Gordon Bennett and his visit to 41 Thomas Street in 1836. His spirit was in the city room one hot summer night in the 1960s when nothing seemed to be happening anywhere on the planet. A few of us were standing around the city desk with little to do.

"Man," I said, "what we need around here is a good murder."

"At a good address," said the city editor.

Chapter Seven

THE FIFTH AVENUE

FROM THE BEGINNING, Fifth Avenue was a very good address, although it seldom had any murders. It did, alas, contain murderers. The social and geographical foundation of what was called "the" Fifth Avenue for most of the nineteenth century was Washington Square. And before its six and a half acres were laid out as the city's first *planned* square, it was the potter's field. Starting in 1797, the impoverished were buried here, many of them women who had ended their days in the city's almshouse. Buried here too were the thousands of victims of the many yellow fever epidemics, along with hundreds of African Americans stacked on top of one another in fifty square feet allotted to the African Zion Methodist Church, whose church crypts were overflowing. But in the center of today's square—at approximately where the fountain was built in the 1960s—stood the gallows.

Here, in the early years of the young republic, before crowds of the curious, the vengeful, and even some relatives of victims, the city's murderers were hanged for their crimes. When they were safely dead, they were buried deep in the weeds of the spongy field with the luckless innocent. The field would eventually hold the bones of twenty thousand human beings. Public hangings were ended in 1820, and the last person executed was a black woman named Rose Butler, who was hanged for setting fire to the house where she almost certainly was a slave. All became part of the permanent alloy of the graveyard. The potter's field was finally closed in 1826, filled to its capacity. But even in the late 1950s, when I was living in the East Village and spending time around the square, old residents were telling me tales about how on certain foggy nights you could see the dead rising from below the grass and the footpaths. Some wore the yellow shrouds in which they were buried, identifying them as victims of the fever. Some had distended necks. Many were women. I didn't believe a word of these tales, of course, but knew they must be true.

The first settlers in the area, at the time of the Dutch, were several hundred freed Africans, who were granted the right to live and farm in exchange for annual tribute that included at least one pig. That was all canceled when the British took the colony, confiscated the African land, re-enslaved some of the freedmen, and went into the slavery business in a major way. The remaining free Africans — some too old to work — settled in shanties in the marsh around Minetta Brook, which still courses under parts of the area, specifically under the southeast corner of Washington Square.

But in the years after the Revolution, it was yellow fever that drove the first well-off New Yorkers to the edge of the ghastly potter's field. Crowded, humid downtown, filthy with the leavings of pigs and horses, dense with mosquitoes, was the fever zone. The village of Greenwich, with its open land and steady breezes, seemed much safer from disease, particularly in summer, when the epidemics arrived to kill so many people (nobody was yet aware that the disease came from mosquitoes and the epidemics usually ended with the arrival of cold weather). The first summer houses, hastily built of wood, rose along the North River, where boats could carry workers to their downtown jobs.

But after the opening of the Erie Canal, and the flood of profits that came to the expanding city, the Knickerbocker merchants began looking for permanent homes in those parts of Greenwich that were not inhabited by commoners. They bought empty properties along the edges of the closed potter's field while Mayor Philip Hone led the drive to transform that field into a park. The political cover for Hone and his associates was very American: military defense. The city's Seventh Regiment needed a place to drill. A drill field had to be reserved before more and more speculators occupied the theoretical rectangles of the grid. In a fine political stroke, the patriotic Hone told the Common Council that he wanted the field ready for the fiftieth anniversary of the Declaration of Independence and that it would be named the Washington Military Parade Ground. The planners got their way in 1827. On July 4, the new ground, still lumpy and weedy, its borders an erratic mess, was opened with a huge celebration. Governor De Witt Clinton led the parade from the Battery to what newspapers were already calling Washington Square. Famous Knickerbockers were of course in the entourage, Van Rensselaers, Van Courtlands, the Fish and Bogardus clans. But so were the enthusiasts of Jacksonian democracy, all cheering at the right moments, all helping themselves to the food, which included two roasted oxen. Presumably, since they were New Yorkers, many were drinking and smoking. Presumably, the Seventh Regiment musicians played stirring tunes, including "Yankee Doodle." Presumably, too, the real estate speculators looked on with immense visions in their heads, not only for the square but for what lay to the north: the Fifth Avenue.

Quickly, the borders of the field were expanded and clarified; they would eventually encompass thirteen and three-quarters acres. Bodies too close to the surface were exhumed and buried elsewhere. The general lumpiness of the surface was leveled. Grass was planted. Paths were created. A wooden fence was constructed to keep wandering pigs (and other animals) from grazing too freely. Soon, the amateur militia soldiers were drilling in Washington Square, the weight of their artillery pieces sometimes uncovering the crushed coffins and muddy skeletons of the nameless dead. There were more patriotic assemblies, with bands playing and small boys cheering. And the grand houses along the edges of the square began rising. The first were built along the south side, all of them now gone. A number of those along the north side, larger and grander in a Greek Revival style, have survived to the present day, with their front yards, fine brick, welcoming stoops, and evocations of Henry James.

❧   ❧   ❧

When I first started wandering on Lower Fifth Avenue, from Washington Square to about Thirteenth Street, I felt like a visitor to pre-Colombian Palenque. When I paused and looked, the architecture suggested a lost civilization. Unknowable. Gone.

I would always start at the arch, because the Avenue started its long journey uptown at the arch, and because it was a wonderful thing to look at. Once again, as with so many things I loved in Manhattan, it was designed by Stanford White. His world was now gone too, but it did not end as abruptly as his life. I knew the tale of the arch; it was in all the guidebooks and the biographies of White. How the first arch was made of wood in 1889 to celebrate the 100th anniversary of the inauguration of George Washington; and how some prominent citizens wanted it made permanent and were actually willing to pay for it; and how White then designed it for marble and hired Alexander Stirling Calder (father of the later modernist maker of mobiles) to make the "civilian" statue of Washington and Frederick MacMonnies to carve the relief work. Henry James hated it, describing it as "the lamentable little Arch of Triumph which bestrides these beginnings of Washington Square—lamentable because of its lonely and unsupported and unaffiliated state."

But it was loved by others, evoked in a few fine paintings and many more bad ones, transformed in 1916 into a symbol of liberated bohemia when the painter John Sloan, the dadaist Marcel Duchamp, and three friends forced passage into an interior staircase, climbed to the top of the arch, cooked food in a bean pot, lit Japanese lanterns, fired cap pistols, launched balloons, and declared the independent republic of New Bohemia. The very correct residents of the square were not pleased. And though there is no evidence of cause and effect, that year, in distant London, Henry James became a British subject. The interior door of the arch was sealed. Life went on and so did the bohemian spirit. And I would look at the arch when young and make a connection to the arch in Grand Army Plaza in Brooklyn, and feel as if I owned them both.

Lower Fifth Avenue itself seemed oddly alien to me in those years and yet beautiful in some whispering, guarded way. Across the decades, I've gazed through the plate glass window of 2 Fifth Avenue at the small domed fountain rising from the buried Minetta Brook, where Dutchmen, Lenape Indians, and freed Africans once came to drink. Young Henry James, who lived a few blocks away on Washington Place, often visited his grandmother at number 18 Washington Square North and used it as the setting for his 1881 novel *Washington Square*. That building and several others were demolished in 1950 and replaced with this clumsy apartment house. The fountain remains as a liquid symbol of the invincible flow of time itself and the futility of the human desire for permanence. Flowing water is one of the hoariest of clichés for time, but here, still living in this glass cage, it seems perfect for the place; if all around it is ravaged by some natural or man-made calamity, the Minetta Brook will flow.

I was about fifteen when I first looked from this spot across the avenue at the Brevoort Hotel, rising five stories on the northeast corner of Eighth Street, all of it painted white, with elegant awnings for each window. Somehow

(from newspaper stories or books) I had learned that beginning in 1854, when the hotel was opened, it had provided rooms for many writers and painters, along with
businessmen and assorted transient peddlers of dreams
and desires. The famous basement café, with its French
menu, drew to its tables, at different times, Eugene
O'Neill and Theodore Dreiser, Edna St. Vincent Millay
and Edmund Wilson, John Dos Passos and Isadora
Duncan, and many others, including, on his rare trips to
New York, Ernest Hemingway. I wanted to lunch there
too and never did. I could never afford to stay at the
Brevoort in those years, or in any other hotel, but I wanted
to curl into one of its beds on a snowy January night with
a girl who loved me. In 1952, I went away to the navy.
When I came back, the white hotel was gone. By then, I
had read Irwin Shaw's splendid short story "The Girls in
Their Summer Dresses," and its first sentence would rise
in my mind until I sought release by reading it still again:
*Fifth Avenue was shining in the sun when they left the Brevoort and
started walking toward Washington Square. . . .*

Those words and that story described Manhattan in a
time I didn't know, when many young New Yorkers were
trembling fatalistically on the eve of the Second World
War. The characters in Shaw's story are aching with a
need for permanence and the certainties of love while
knowing that neither is possible. I knew that Shaw was
from Brooklyn too, and thought I recognized in the story,
buried between its lines, the same kind of wonder that I
found in my own passages through Manhattan. Years
later, when I knew Shaw, I asked him about Manhattan of

that time: "Did you think it was Oz?" He pondered the question, then said, "Listen, it was more beautiful than Oz." And paused. "And a hell of a lot more wonderful."

Sometimes, charged with something like wonder, I would look at the Church of the Ascension on the northwest corner of Tenth Street, designed in 1841 by the same Richard Upjohn who did the final version of Trinity Church. It was the first church erected on Fifth Avenue, and the interior brims with warmth and mystery in the late-Episcopalian manner. But the church I saw wasn't entirely the one Upjohn made. In the late 1880s it was redesigned by (of course) Stanford White, who added the stained glass windows and the mural of the Ascension, both by his friend John La Farge. Willa Cather, during her New York years, loved the church and the work of La Farge. But Henry James was even more enthusiastic, describing in 1905 his first view, one summer afternoon, of the interior of the church:

> Wonderful enough, in New York, to find oneself, in a charming and considerably dim "old" church, hushed to admiration before a great religious picture; the sensation, for the moment, upset so all the facts ... the important work of art itself, a thing of the highest distinction, spoke, as soon as one had taken it in, with that authority which makes the difference, ever afterwards, between the remembered and the forgotten quest.

Through the dense thicket of his prose, James was hesitant in his praise, because he was certain that the church would succumb to "the possibility of doom," that it would be torn down, as had so many buildings he cherished, and replaced with a skyscraper. That is why, for James, the Church of the Ascension "upset so all the facts." After two decades away from America, the facts of the new Manhattan had made James ache with unacceptable losses. His own stammering form of New York nostalgia permeates his report as he mourns those buildings of his childhood that had been replaced, for vulgar commercial reasons, by structures of inferior quality. The Church of the Ascension was beautiful; therefore, he reasoned, it must die. He hopes timidly that his fears for the future are misplaced. They were. A century later, the Church of the Ascension is still there, with its glorious windows and its masterful painting by John La Farge.

When I first saw them, so were many other buildings on Lower Fifth, living evidence of the New York past that was not my own. None were as easily entered as a church. All were objects of my own remembered quest. Their interiors, like those in Gramercy Park, were beyond knowing until I started reading Edith Wharton. Sometimes I would stand before 47 Fifth Avenue, the Salmagundi Club, on the east side of the street between Eleventh and Twelfth streets, my eyes taking in its full-length French doors, wide stoop, overhanging eaves. I came to know that La Farge and White were members, and William Merritt Chase (who had painted the landscapes of Brooklyn), and the master illustrators N. C. Wyeth and Howard Pyle, whose images of pirates and Treasure Island had filled my childhood. I would imagine these men in the final decades of the nineteenth century, well-dressed, mustached, all glowing from brandy and gaslight. They valued wit and irony. They were beyond envy or petty jealousies. They might enjoy practical jokes, the company of loose women, gossip about various upper-class fools, but they would never behave the way James Gordon Bennett Jr. did in sight of his fiancée's fireplace. They were the boys from *Trilby* who had come home.

Or so I thought. And how I envied those fictional creatures of my imagination. As a young man, staring at 47 Fifth Avenue, I wanted to be part of the same kind of confraternity, without the tuxedoes or the gaslight. I wanted the company of others who had absurd dreams. I didn't find that confraternity until the night I first walked into the city room of the *New York Post*.

Within a few years, the Knickerbockers had created on Fifth Avenue what by the time of the Civil War would be known as Old New York. There were branches of this mysterious region in Gramercy Park after 1845, and in enclaves to the east. But the Avenue was the capital. The memory of the simpler pleasures of downtown faded while a new sense of possession took hold and a new hope for permanence. St. John's Park was forever behind them, and so was that much simpler Broadway. Their later nostalgias would include the way Lower Fifth was in the early years, when there were still houses standing without neighbors on Twelfth Street, and how the Avenue remained muddy in spring and how there were almost no gas lamps in the streets.

But there was space. The Fifth Avenue was one hundred feet wide, as were all avenues sketched in the Commissioners' Plan of 1811. The roadway was sixty feet wide, the sidewalks twenty. As the first houses were built, they adapted aspects of the houses on Fourth Street, today's Washington Square South. Some were built in clusters, becoming the city's first row houses, each of similar design, with front gardens in homage to the houses in London's West End. The city fathers allowed the Fifth Avenue builders to take part of the twenty-foot sidewalks for their own gardens, usually filled with tough, colorful geraniums. Most houses were three or four stories high, with an entry to the basement underneath a stoop (and a backyard beyond). The stoops had handsome iron banisters. The servants, black or Irish, lived on the low-ceilinged top floors. There were outside privies, their functions disguised by trellises and bowers of flowers.

Life in these houses was comfortable but not always luxurious; the age of conspicuous ostentation did not arrive in Manhattan until the decade after the Civil War. Men came home for a leisurely dinner about two, the day's main meal, and then made the return journey to the downtown countinghouses. Or they stayed home for a day and received their business associates in the new houses, with the young women safely out of sight. At night, they ate lightly and had tea. As time passed, and horse-drawn traffic clogged the streets, more dined downtown in the flourishing restaurants. Their women and children (usually tutored at home) dined together. Or the women visited with other women, or walked west to Broadway and examined the latest wares in the new shops. They all went "visiting" on New Year's Day, following the old custom. As paving arrived on the streets, and the spaces between houses were filled, and trees sprouted from the sidewalks, the families also strolled together on Sunday afternoons. Here, five-year-old Edith Jones walked with her father long before she became Edith Wharton.

In their tight little world, privacy was all. The scandals of their lives were hidden behind veils of secrecy and discretion. Unmarried women suddenly departed for Europe, to return in a year. Some were seen leaving the home of Madame Restell, the city's most notorious abortionist, but their names never appeared in the newspapers. Proposed new marriages were subjected to deep scrutiny, of bloodlines, social credentials, and bank accounts. The codes were precise. There were Things That Were Not Done. Cads were ostracized. For a long time, the public mood of the street was a combination of Presbyterian rigor and Episcopalian belief in redemption. A few older men and women surely yearned for the village of their lost downtown. But most seemed to believe that all of that was the past. This was the present, and also the future.

And so Fifth Avenue became the third major avenue in the emerging city. While Broadway was melding into a combination of commercial stores, fine hotels, and the best entertainment, and the Bowery was established as the main promenade of blue-collar Manhattan, Fifth Avenue became the street of social power.

The early notion of a powerful native aristocracy was gone—they would not rule democratic New York—but there were more indirect forms of power. The Knickerbockers set social rules that would last for decades, even if the most brutal cruelties could often be expressed, as in James, with a raised eyebrow. They insisted that wealth itself was not a virtue. It was all a question of property versus trade. Wealth derived from the ownership of property, they insisted, was far superior to wealth earned from trade. They were people with property—real estate, distant farmlands—and property was a sign of long residence, of bloodlines that antedated the Revolution, of comfortable, essentially passive security. Trade was grubby, vulgar, active. Trade was forever hungry and voracious. It destroyed all permanence. It devoured the old to make way for the new. Trade must be resisted. Tradesmen must be kept at an immunizing distance.

With their hard belief in property, the Knickerbockers tried to defend themselves from all change, from the arrival of so many immigrants, from municipal disorder. None was truly affected by the Astor Place riot, the draft riots, or the Orange riots of 1870–71 that took place near Eighth Avenue and Twenty-third Street, and cost the lives of almost seventy Irish Catholics and Protestants in a replay of the dreary religious struggles of the Old Country. For the Knickerbockers, the Old Country was made of the streets and abandoned homes of downtown Manhattan. They would not allow its disintegration to happen again. Or so they believed.

They had learned that social prestige and money were levers that could bring them better street lighting, better policing, early access to running water from the Croton Reservoir, and lush trees for their sidewalks. What politician could refuse an invitation to dinner behind the closed doors of Fifth Avenue? Their needs were expressed to the representatives of the masses around roaring fireplaces, all whispered urgings, probably maddeningly vague but still unmistakable. They did have friends, after all, that politicians needed: editors and publishers of newspapers, businessmen who could alert them to potential profits from the countinghouses of South Street, real estate speculators, stockbrokers. But there were certain things that must be understood. The first was simple: This was their part of the city. They wanted to stay here forever.

The mansions kept moving up Fifth Avenue, and so did the cobblestones for the horses, and the gardens and the churches. By 1850, the mansions had reached Twenty-third Street and were pushing toward distant Forty-second Street. None lasted. Lower Fifth remained reasonably stable, but the mansions and private residences beyond Fourteenth Street endured for a few decades and then were erased to make way for taller, more profitable office buildings (just as lower Broadway was giving way to loft buildings for the dry goods trade). After the Civil War, the velocity of change was extraordinary.

On the corner of Sixteenth Street, there once stood the Atheneum Club, where men from the brownstones gathered before going home, drinking too much, smoking too many cigars, making deals. In 1888, the club gave way to the present building, designed by Stanford White for *Judge* magazine, its ground floor now occupied by Emporio Armani. At Seventeenth Street stood the home of Ambrose Kingsland, a sperm oil merchant who became mayor. The office building that replaced it now houses a Banana Republic store. There at the corner of Eighteenth Street is the site of the old Chickering Hall, where Alexander Graham Bell in 1877 made the first telephone call to another state, neighboring New Jersey, and where

Oscar Wilde and Matthew Arnold (among many others) did readings and lectures.

Across the street was the opulent mansion of a man named August Belmont, who was to change the character of Fifth Avenue above Fourteenth Street. He was an extraordinary New Yorker: born of Jewish parents in Germany in 1816, working as an unpaid office boy for the Rothschilds at thirteen, a confidential clerk at eighteen. In 1837, he was sent by the Rothschilds to Cuba to investigate financial possibilities. He never made it to Havana. He stopped in New York, saw the empty docks, and heard the moans on Wall Street caused by the great Panic of 1837. Some men's miseries are always another man's opportunity. The young man started August Belmont and Company, working closely with the Rothschilds in London, buying currency, notes, securities, and property at prices as low as 10 percent of their value before the collapse. Within three years he was an important city banker, and rich. He became an American citizen, was active at the top levels of the Democratic Party, and by 1846, during the Mexican War, he was acting as a financial agent for the American government. In 1849, he got married. The bride was Caroline Slidell Perry, whose father, Commodore Matthew Perry, was a naval hero of the campaign to take California from Mexico (and who would open Japan to trade in 1854). The couple was married in the Church of the Ascension. Their children were raised as Episcopalians.

After a time in residence at a mansion on Twelfth Street and Fifth (and diplomatic service in Austria and the Hague), Belmont moved six blocks uptown into a new family mansion at 111 Fifth Avenue, the grandest yet seen on the Avenue. It was the first mansion in the city to have its own ballroom, capable of holding four hundred guests. Belmont loved good food and wine, and the house served both. He even owned his own red carpet, rather than renting one for special occasions from a caterer, and unrolled it to welcome his party guests. The house had its own art gallery, with paintings by Rosa Bonheur, Bouguereau, and Meissonier, and books that Belmont actually seemed to have read. He loved horse racing, soon had one of the finest stables in the nation, and his name lives on today through the Belmont Stakes, part of racing's Triple Crown. It was first held in 1867 at Jerome Park in the Bronx.

The Knickerbockers were uncertain about how to measure Belmont, which is to say, how to judge him. He was not exactly in trade, nor was he part of the old landed aristocracy. They could not easily dismiss him with an anti-Semitic remark, and of course their manners were too refined for them to make such remarks to his face. In truth, he was practicing the art of the possible. The combination of intelligence, political connections, and money was essential to the growth of the city. August Belmont looked at the city with an immigrant's cool eye and saw the future.

The native Knickerbockers were increasingly imprisoned by the certainties of the past and their inevitable loss. As the wealthy part of the city moved into the Gilded Age, with its dreadful, occasionally disgusting excesses, it was perhaps no accident that some of them took to spiritualism in vain attempts to reach into the past. Nor was it an accident that so many of them read ghost stories, in which all of the houses were haunted.

Chapter Eight

ON THE RIALTO

ON THE DAY after the long night of September 11, after we had called our families to say that we were alive, after we had walked the midnight streets and filed our newspaper stories, after we had watched television until four in the morning, after some broken hours of jagged sleep, my wife and I went out together to see the changed world. Everything ordinary was suspended. The newsstand was closed, and the only store still functioning was the Korean deli four blocks away, packed now with begrimed rescue workers. The ruins of the World Trade Center were still burning, and the air was filled with an odor new to all of us, some vile combination of pulverized concrete, melting steel, and burning carpets, desks, paper, and human flesh. At that point, the numbers of the dead and missing were still unknown but were, as Mayor Giuliani said, "more than any of us can bear."

We had to show passports to get beyond the police and National Guard barriers on Canal Street. Nearby Chinatown was shut down. Many Chinese women, blocked from the sweatshops in which they labored, stood a block beyond the barriers. Many of them were probably illegal, with no passports from the country in which they worked so hard. The streets were loud with the sounds of alarm: sirens from fire trucks, ambulances, police cars. We found some food. We found some newspapers. We made many notes. We wrote our stories, substituting work for sorrow or fear. And that evening we found our way to Union Square.

I still don't know exactly why Union Square became the center for our Downtown collective mourning. Location had something to do with it, I suppose. For thirty years, you could see the Twin Towers from Union Square, the smallish park between Fourteenth and Seventeenth streets, Park Avenue South and Broadway. Now you could see only smoke and emptiness. And the equestrian statue of George Washington, high on his plinth just above Fourteenth Street, was facing south, to where those ruins were burning. There was, of course, no plan, no pre-arranged agreement that in the event of a monstrous calamity, we would all converge on Union Square. But Times Square was out; it was a place for mass celebration, not grief, its most enduring image being Alfred Eisenstaedt's famous photograph of that sailor kissing that girl on the day the war ended in 1945. For whatever reason, my wife and I and thousands of others went together to Union Square.

There we saw the candles at the base of the Washington

statue, guttering in the breeze, forming congealed puddles of wax on the sidewalks. We saw posters, with their messages of anger or sorrow, some written in Spanish. We saw the first leaflets inquiring about those still missing, with their names printed in boldface, the places in each tower where they had worked, home telephone numbers, and, of course, photographs. In the photographs, every person was smiling. They were photographs taken at office parties or vacations or weddings, frozen moments of amusement or happiness.

And all around us were people from the Downtown tribes, all races and classes, all ages, living versions of the people on those leaflets, most of whom would be among the missing forever. Some wept alone. Some prayed. Strangers whispered for a while, then burst into tears and embraced. Fukiko and I walked over to the edge of the park, and I stared in both directions at Fourteenth Street, for so long a kind of discarded, shabby monument to decay. Somehow, it now had a kind of tough majesty. "Goddamn these bastards," I said to her. "They've ruined the world." She shook her head and said, "Not yet." Off to the side, under the trees, people talked in bursts and then surrendered to the sound of a saxophone player who was, of course, playing a blues. We walked back into the crowd, and I noticed small yellow leaves falling around the man with the horn. The blues, full of melancholy, filled the New York night. I held my wife tighter than ever, staring at the flames of the candles.

For a while in the early nineteenth century, some optimistic Knickerbockers took to Fourteenth Street. The geography of Fifth Avenue, after all, was never absolutely strict. Grace Church, at Tenth Street and Broadway, was an adjunct of Fifth Avenue, its clergymen full of certainties as they collected the pew rents and enforced the iron codes of social exclusion. So it was no surprise in the emerging city of right angles that a number of well-off people made a turn and moved into Fourteenth Street. Some of their money came from the traditional sources — whale oil, shipping, insurance, and banking, along with rented property — and if they had waited too long to inhabit Washington Square or Lower Fifth, well, Fourteenth Street would be fine. Some of the money was "new," its possessors dismissed by the Knickerbockers as parvenus. The distinctions didn't matter to the sellers of plots.

The first mansion on Fourteenth Street was erected in 1847, and many followed. The exteriors were the familiar reticent brownstone. The interiors gleamed with satin, rosewood, immense mirrors, glistening porcelains stacked in cabinets, a variety of mediocre works of art. Each household averaged eight servants, and some had more, most of them Irish. The new arrivals were also filling University Place, which extended north from the growing New York University, founded in 1831. For all the residents, the social codes remained the same, no matter how often they were violated in secret. They also shared an urban vision. Together, they would establish the first of Manhattan's great crosstown streets, moving from river to river, with ferries at each end to bring them downtown or across to New Jersey or Brooklyn. They would indeed establish Fourteenth Street, but it was not to be the wide, genteel, tree-lined street of their visions.

Crucial to the early vision was the presence of Union Square. At midcentury, the square was still poorly designed and landscaped, and it would go through many renovations in the century to come. But it was open space in a city becoming more crowded by the day, a "ventilator," as the press called it, reasonably safe, a pleasant place for strolling, showing off Sunday clothes, and flirting. Changes in Fourteenth Street would come sooner than anyone could have predicted, and the Knickerbockers would turn out to be the architects of their own later exodus.

The most powerful agent of change was culture. In 1854, the lavish Academy of Music opened on the northeast corner of Fourteenth Street and Irving Place, presenting opera, symphonic music, and traditional theater to upper-class patrons from the mansions. In the early 1850s, the New York economy was booming, and there was money to spend and invest. And so the Academy of Music was financed by the same people who would become its patrons, those who still yearned for a European-based musical culture in spite of the violent riot that had doomed the Astor Place Opera House. Most of the audience could walk to the glorious new opera house from their brownstones, and if there weren't enough of them to fill all four thousand velvet-covered seats, those in the less-expensive seats were generally well-behaved, and there were no disturbances.

Not even in 1860. That year the nineteen-year-old Prince of Wales arrived in New York on an official visit and was given a grand ball at the Academy by his adoring Anglophile admirers. The hall was transformed into a daz-

zling vision of gaslight and flowers. A platform for dancing had been built over the seats on the main floor for the
ball. As the prince walked in, the orchestra played "God
Save the Queen," followed by "Hail, Columbia." On the
receiving line, there were curtsies, bows, and other forms
of upper-class genuflection. New York had come a long
way from 1783. Then there was a huge crashing noise.
Under the weight of the groveling aristocrats, two sections
of the platform collapsed. A number of tuxedoed gents
vanished into the darkness of the orchestra seats. None
were badly injured, but the reception line was stopped and
the prince hurried off to supper in another part of the
Academy. While he chose among heaping platters of
turkey, suckling pig, grouse, and pheasant, a team of car-
penters worked feverishly on the collapsed part of the
platform. They knew what they were doing, made the repairs, and the dancing started at midnight. The embarrassed New York aristocrats declared the event an
immense triumph. The prince said little. About a week
later, after a prolonged round of other social events, the
prince accepted the offer of James Gordon Bennett Jr. to
see something beyond formality and painfully tedious dinner parties. Bennett arranged for firemen to place a ladder
at the window of his suite in the Fifth Avenue Hotel on
Madison Square. The prince then went off to do what
young princes usually do: He spent the night in a brothel.

Meanwhile, a familiar process was under way on
Fourteenth Street. The brownstones started changing
hands with increasing velocity. Familiar faces abruptly
vanished, leaving no farewell notes. Some were men so set
in their ways that they could not adjust to new technology.

Others presided over exhausted businesses that could no longer sustain the money-draining combination of leisure and domestic opulence. Some were those parvenus who had their moments in the New York firmament and then vanished like shooting stars. Some were ruined in the Panic of 1857, when almost five thousand New York businesses collapsed forever. Some evaded personal disgrace by fleeing to Europe. Some went west. They all disappeared from the New York narrative.

The brownstones found new inhabitants, and they owed their presence to what was becoming known as the Rialto. Its most powerful castle, its source of energy and authority, was the Academy of Music. "What news on the Rialto?" said Shylock in *The Merchant of Venice*. "Who is he comes here?"

He and she who came to the Rialto of Fourteenth Street included some inevitable stock characters in the evolving New York show: brothel keepers, operators of boarding-houses, con men, men without history. But many came from show business. The Academy of Music attracted hundreds of musicians, piano makers, sellers of sheet music, and teachers. Other theaters were being built in the neighborhood. In 1861, Wallack's on Thirteenth Street became the finest "legitimate" theater of its day, a successor to the much-mourned Park. It specialized in what were considered sophisticated comedies of manners, many written by an Irish immigrant (and actor) named Dion Boucicault. Steinway Hall, operated by the great piano-making firm started in 1853 by another immigrant, Henry Steinweg of Germany, was built on the corner of Union Square five years after Wallack's opened its doors. Along the way, the Steinweg family had changed its name to Steinway, and their hall was designed to show off the excellence of their pianos. They booked superb artists from Europe for public recitals while accomplishing their commercial goal: selling many pianos. The hall had room for three thousand people and would be an ornament of the square for decades.

Actors, musicians, and writers began taking rooms in the Fourteenth Street boardinghouses, gossiping in tiny new cafés, waging small feuds, and competing for roles or lovers or both. If to the brownstoners Fourteenth Street was a branch of Fifth Avenue, to the actors, musicians, and writers it was a branch of Broadway. They were sometimes volatile, almost always transient, devoid of any instinct to live safe, predictable lives. They were renters, not owners. And they were often in the company of newspapermen, whose editors knew that readers wanted the latest news about this vibrant world. Newspapermen, drawing on Shakespeare and the language of the London theatrical world, almost certainly labeled the entire neighborhood the Rialto.

In 1861, while the country moved more rapidly toward civil war, a restaurant named the Maison Dorée opened in the largest house on Fourteenth Street, the 1845 Italianate mansion of a departing whale oil baron. The address was 44. The chef was a man named Charles Ranhofer, who had previously catered grand Parisian balls for Napoleon III and the Empress Eugénie. The most stubborn brownstoners jammed its tables, as did the visiting European musicians, the employed actors, and even an occasional journalist.

Surely there must have been much table talk about the approaching calamity of war, and predictions that grass would grow on the New York docks as the crucial trade in southern cotton came to an end. As in many places on the brink of war, there must also have been a kind of forced gaiety or a defiant fatalism. But to some of the visiting journalists, there was another story right there in the Maison Dorée: It was the first Manhattan restaurant to challenge the long supremacy of Delmonico's.

By 1861, Delmonico's was a New York institution, featured in all the guidebooks of the day as the finest in the city, patronized by the American rich and visitors from the rest of the wealthy world. It had started as a wine and pastry shop in 1827, operated by two brothers from Switzerland. Three years later, they opened their first restaurant at 25 William Street, and because of the quality of the cuisine and the perfect service, it was a huge success. The brothers soon had to call for help from their nephew Lorenzo, who proved to be a genius at the new (to Manhattan) business of providing food for strangers. The restaurant burned down in the Great Fire of 1835, but a temporary version opened the following year on Broad Street, and two years later it moved into 2 South William Street, where it remained until 1890. Delmonico's menus became famous, listing more than one hundred items, including specialties of Lorenzo's own invention, such as lobster Newberg, eggs Benedict, and baked Alaska. Lorenzo Delmonico catered to the rich, pampered them, memorized their names and birthdays and wedding anniversaries, provided private space for their special celebrations and grand parties, and charged them handsomely for the service. Early on, he understood that fashionable New York was moving uptown, and in 1856 opened a second restaurant on Chambers Street that drew customers from the new hotels, shops, and theaters of Broadway, and the well-off women who came to shop at Stewart's. It would not be the last.

Maison Dorée suddenly rose as a threat, and Lorenzo fought back. He took over the Grinnell mansion at Fifth Avenue and Fourteenth Street, and transformed it into a third elegant restaurant. Then he hired away the rival's chef, M. Ranhofer, who would stay with Delmonico's for thirty-four years. The Civil War came, and the faithful remained loyal to Delmonico's even as the exodus continued from the brownstones of Fourteenth Street. For a while, the city itself had a haunted feeling. Then slowly, a day at a time, the city adjusted to the war, to the loss of the southern trade. There was even, in places like Delmonico's, a certain gaiety. To be sure, too many of the rich diners at Delmonico's were happy to pay three hundred dollars to save their sons from the draft. They would let the Irish poor do the dying. And after the draft riots, too many rich children were sent for the duration to European safety, where they could ponder the works of the Renaissance or the genius of Francis I, far from Gettysburg or the Wilderness. In New York, ruthless new merchants prospered in the manufacture of uniforms for the Union army, goods of such poor quality that the word *shoddy* entered the language to stay. They were not welcome in Delmonico's. As the dying continued on the distant battlefields, most of New York wanted the war to end, even if that meant the secession of the

South and the continuation of slavery. But in general, the brownstoners remained loyal to the Union. They raised money, headed committees to improve sanitation among battlefield troops, and gave financial support to a regiment of black volunteers. Not all of their sons bought their way out of the draft. The cemeteries of New York and the South hold the bones of those rich young men who died in the war, along with the bones of the valiant poor who made up the infantry. In the 1864 election, Abraham Lincoln won only one Manhattan ward, the Fifteenth, which, in those brownstones, housed most of the old Knickerbocker families.

On the local level, other changes were already under way before the killing started at Fort Sumter. The human turnover on the Fourteenth Street of the Knickerbockers was dramatic. In 1858, a man named Rowland Hussey Macy opened a small dry goods store on Sixth Avenue, just below Fourteenth. He was born in New England, went to sea at fifteen (coming home with a tattoo of a red star that later became a symbol of his store), and tried various businesses in the Midwest before settling in Manhattan. His little dry goods store quickly expanded into a little department store. Building on the merchandising ideas of A. T. Stewart, and using advertising to promote himself and his wares, Macy made the store a huge success, including the introduction of ready-made clothing. He put trade on Fourteenth Street. The success of Macy's would tempt many others to move to the street, drawing thousands of customers from other parts of the city. Through the most terrible of the war years, the process went on. Some young men went off to the killing fields. Others shopped. Or dined at Delmonico's. And actors strolled the Rialto, dreaming of playing Hamlet.

The war ended, Lincoln was assassinated, mourning was general, and then a boom began that was to prove that the United States could prosper without the use of four million slaves. In 1867, under the direction of Boss William M. Tweed, Tammany Hall opened its muscular new headquarters next door to the Academy of Music. The building was large and grand. On the ground floor, it even had its own theater. If the snooty Whig patrons of the Academy of Music objected, they said very little in public, not even when the new Tammany Hall was host to the 1868 Democratic Convention. But some residents of Fifth Avenue must have seen this as a sign of the changing times. If so, they were right. The working-class masses—the "lower one million," in contrast to the "upper ten thousand"—had this peculiar belief that in a republic no streets could be owned by an elite. Fourteenth Street was theirs to traverse too, its shops and restaurants and theaters theirs to patronize, if they had the money. Union Square, after all, was named because of the planned union of Broadway with the Bowery, not as an homage to that union for which so many New Yorkers had died. The working class might not be able to afford Delmonico's or the Academy of Music, but they could come up from the Bowery or cross Fourteenth Street from the North River docks and stroll in Union Square on a Sunday afternoon. It was part of their city too. Among them were some writers, actors, and musicians who brought their own robust genius to the Rialto—and then to the world.

With the exception of Lower Fifth Avenue and

Gramercy Park, the brownstoners were soon in full retreat. Grander, more imposing mansions were offering better, presumably safer lives as far north as Forty-second
Street and Fifth. All you needed was a good sale of the old
house and a bit more to buy and furnish the new one. The
old families, with their useless children and their aversion
to trade, sniffed at the possessors of "new" money, all those
railroad people and oil people and steel people. Why, there
were even *Irishmen* possessed of fortunes! And it seemed
for a while in the 1870s and 1880s that the robber barons,
as the press would label them, were arriving in New York
every month, almost all of them passing through
Pittsburgh on the way to Upper Fifth Avenue. The Gilded
Age had begun. Old New York sniffed. The new people,
to Knickerbocker noses, smelled crude, ill-mannered, ignorant about the refinements of life. They showed far too
much, uh, energy. They bought art by the crate. They
failed to distinguish between forks at dinner. They preferred fat slabs of beef and mashed potatoes to the intri-
cate delicacies of Delmonico's.

But the old Knickerbockers could count. Their own fortunes were dwindling. They had given their faith to the
monotheistic god of property, and that god was now failing them. They would buy houses of summer refuge in
Saratoga or Newport, if only they could afford them. Why
should some robber baron peddle his homely daughter to
an impoverished English duke? There were, after all,
many beautiful young Knickerbocker women who could
begin the process of civilizing these rich new American
men. Slowly, an exchange was made. The Knickerbockers
began to merge with the new money, exchanging blood-

lines and manners for a share of the new wealth. Their own names were often lost in the process.

And yet something of Old New York survived among those dispossessed downtown people. It was impossible simply to move away from the old houses, built with such certainty, and forget them forever. Husbands had died in those houses, and wives, and, alas, too many children, and those dead lived vividly in memory. The books and furniture and paintings were packed into the moving vans, and the pilgrimage resumed to the north, but in memory, the discarded houses still glittered with life. It was no surprise that as the years passed, more and more women (and a few men) sought contact with the past through mediums and clairvoyants. They wanted to speak again to the dead, to hear one final admission of love or happiness, and various charlatans were glad to provide the voices. Literature, high and low, memoirs, and some journals underline their permanent sense of regret. Regret for the thing unsaid. Regret for the cruel remark that *was* said. In some ways, that emotion was the only permanence they ever attained.

Along the Rialto of Fourteenth Street, an aching nostalgia always had its place too. The scholar Jon W. Finson reminds us that much of popular song in those days was about death. So many men had died in the Civil War. So many men, women, and children had died of tuberculosis or cholera or smallpox. Such songs can be dismissed too easily today, in our age of glib ironies, but in nineteenth-century New York, they helped thousands of people to express deep emotions. There were many songs directed at the Irish immigrant market, too many of them calculated

Tin Pan Alley rubbish in the "Mother Machree" vein. But even the junk had power, a kind of acknowledgment that from the 1840s to the Gilded Age, Irish women had held families together against terrible odds. A few songs combined immigrant nostalgia for the Old Country with the finality of an American death. One example was "I'll Take You Home Again, Kathleen," written in 1876 by an Indiana schoolteacher named Thomas P. Westendorf. It was swiftly embraced by many of the Irish of the day. The song is clearly a man's address to a dying wife. It makes no direct reference to Ireland, or the wasted Irish countryside that a million of them had left behind in the 1840s. But the name of the wife was all the Irish needed to embrace it:

I'll take you home again, Kathleen,
Across the ocean wild and wide,
To where your heart has ever been,
Since first you were my bonny bride.

My father was the singer in our family, but my mother had her own songs, and this was one of them. I can hear her singing it in her light contralto voice in the immigrant parlors of Brooklyn before television, that lost time and place, as my sister Kathleen toddled among the guests. Anne Devlin Hamill, of 32 Madrid Street, the Short Strand, Belfast, Northern Ireland, was still singing it in the 1960s, when we, her American children, asked her to sing. I suspect she also heard it sung by others down near the old Rialto. As noted, she met my father at an Irish dance in the early 1930s at Webster Hall, three blocks below Fourteenth Street. The lyrics of the song went on:

185

"The roses all have left your cheek, / I've watched them fade away and die ..." The roses left my mother's cheeks, of course, and my father's, and they are buried beside each other in Staten Island. They died as they had lived most of their lives, as Americans. But as was true of so many other American millions, the Old Country never completely left them. On some nights now, I pass Webster Hall, at 125 East Eleventh Street, loud with hip-hop and DJs and crowds of the young. I hope that at least a few frantic young New Yorkers will find one another in the way my parents did. Someday, if they have long lives, they might even ache for the simplicities of Webster Hall.

On Fourteenth Street in its heyday, nostalgia was not the only expression of the new city. Many other emotions were expressed on those stages too, provoking astonishment and laughter. The man who put most of them together was a New Yorker named Tony Pastor, who had been born Antonio Pastore, the son of Italian immigrants. He did his first turn as a singer when he was six, at a temperance meeting. In 1846, at age twelve, he started his career as a clown at P. T. Barnum's Museum, moved in and out of blackface minstrelsy, and soon became a regular at the "free-and-easies" on the Bowery. But Tony Pastor had wider ambitions. He ran several of his own concert saloons, trying hard, with limited success, to keep the acts decent in order to attract respectable women. By his midforties, he was possessed of a brilliant idea: What if you could take the vitality of Bowery culture and cleanse it of its most vulgar surfaces? What if you completely transformed entertainment for blue-collar males into entertainment for the entire family? And what if this form of entertainment could find its place on the Rialto?

In 1881, Pastor rented the theater in Tammany Hall, right next to the Academy of Music, and put his concept on stage. The format was familiar: the variety show that by 1875 had grown out of minstrelsy. Pastor enriched the format with the best available talent, including the brashest, most clever young performers. There were sad singers and comic singers, comedians, jugglers, and dancers, all moving at a slam-bang pace, with a lively orchestra backing them up from the pit. Among the dancers were young men who had learned from other men who had learned from dancers who once saw Master Juba. In the house itself, Pastor established strict rules. No cursing. No double entendre jokes. No politics. No drinking. No cigars. Just fun. For the whole family. The place was a roaring success. Middle-class women came to the shows, and so did orphaned newsboys and Tammany politicians and the remnants of the brownstoners. The format was soon named vaudeville.

Until the triumph of motion pictures around 1920, vaudeville was the dominant form of American entertainment, with the performers traveling on "circuits" all over the country. In New York, Tony Pastor was king. The Academy of Music had sealed its own doom as a venue for opera when it refused to sell boxes to the new men of wealth; they responded by building the Metropolitan Opera House on Broadway and Thirty-ninth. Its first season was 1883. Three years later, the Academy was finished as a venue for opera and other upper-class entertainments. Tony Pastor was not finished. Rival houses opened on the

Rialto, along with more theaters, but the great attraction was Tony Pastor's, where he introduced such stars as Lillian Russell, Weber & Fields, and George M. Cohan. His presence even helped keep the raunchier competition away from the Rialto. Most of the newer low-life shows set up for business to the north and west, from Twenty-sixth Street to Forty-second Street, west of Sixth Avenue. The district became known as the Tenderloin. Pastor made no moralizing speeches. He just presented the best entertainment he could find and went on living his life. By all accounts, he was a generous man who did not forget where he came from. He stayed in business until 1908, when he closed the theater and retired. He died the same year, leaving only about $45,000 in the bank. His friends explained that over the years of his great success, he had given away more than a million dollars. Not all New Yorkers, then or now, do it only for the money.

Across the street from Pastor's, a new restaurant opened in 1882, and among the investors was William Steinway, who presided over Steinway Hall. The restaurant was called Luchow's. The food was German, and there were "oompah" bands playing each night and waiters moving around in lederhosen. The musicians and performers from Pastor's often came through its doors after their last show. So did other performers, actors, and songwriters (the American Society of Composers, Authors and Publishers — ASCAP — was founded there by an Irish immigrant named Victor Herbert in 1913 to protect the copyrights of those who made the music). Stars came too, including the upscale performers from Steinway Hall such as Paderewski and Caruso. Across the coming years, others would be seen there: Cole Porter, Leonard Bernstein, Larry Hart. You might even see H. L. Mencken dining with Theodore Dreiser, the two of them discussing literature or politics over Wiener schnitzel.

When I was getting to know Fourteenth Street in the late 1950s, the street was a mess of cheap shoe and clothing stores. The old Academy of Music had been hammered into dust in 1926 to make way for the massive headquarters of Con Edison. Its once-powerful neighbor, Tammany Hall, had vanished too, taking the remains of Tony Pastor's stage with it. In 1929, the politicians opened their new headquarters on Union Square and East Seventeenth Street, where this last Tammany Hall would remain until 1943 (it's now a small, elegant Off-Broadway theater and the location of the New York Film School). In the 1950s, almost everything of the Rialto was gone, with the immense exception of Luchow's. In those days, I could never afford to eat in the place, bringing my custom across the street to the Automat. I did pass it four or five days a week on my way to the Gramercy Gym, a few doors down, where I hung out with the professional fighters, including my friend Jose Torres, who was on his way to becoming the light-heavyweight champion of the world. The great trainer Cus D'Amato ran the gym and was often on the premises, pointing out to me the great lessons for boxers to be learned from the memoirs of Ulysses S. Grant. "Read this part," he said one afternoon in the small office where he sometimes spent the night. "Read how Grant understands that the other guy is just as afraid as you are, and so the only way to make him *more* afraid, the way to *win*, is to *attack!*"

One autumn evening, as I was leaving the Gramercy, a

bit of the ancient, mindless glamour of the lost Rialto made an appearance. A black limousine pulled up at Luchow's, the heavy, glistening doors opened, and there by herself, so white-blond she could hurt your eyes, was Zsa Zsa Gabor. I laughed out loud, for Zsa Zsa was one of the great symbols of unearned celebrity, more famous for her many rich boyfriends than for her performances. But I stood there anyway, along with about a dozen other people, and watched her arrival. She looked exactly like the woman she had played in John Huston's 1952 film *Moulin Rouge*, with the creamy skin and the too-perfect nose and the rustling silken clothes. She smiled, bowed to show a bit of cleavage, blew us kisses, said, "Good evening, darlings," and went in. I hoped that Henri Toulouse-Lautrec was waiting at a good table.

As the years passed, nobody except derelicts sat at the stone tables in Union Square. It declined swiftly, as had its counterparts south of Fourteenth Street. The pattern was now familiar. Degradation always preceded menace, and Union Square was for many years a scary place. And then in the 1990s, it too changed. Landscapers and policemen did their jobs. The junkies went somewhere else. So did the knife artists and the peddlers of handguns. A green market opened and was a major success. Barnes & Noble opened its flagship store. Excellent restaurants opened on the edge of the square and on its side streets. Once more, the square was a "ventilator," a good green place where New Yorkers could loll in the sun or read on benches or order ice-cream cones. It belonged to all of us again, and on September 12, 2001, it was there when we needed it.

Chapter Nine

SOME VILLAGES

THE CENTER OF my old Manhattan neighborhood was Second Avenue and Ninth Street. In 1958, after one year in Mexico and another in Brooklyn going to art school, both on the GI Bill, I felt it was time to try living, as we said, "over New York."

The agent for the move was an ex-marine named Barney Leggett, who had a day job on Wall Street and, to make a few extra dollars, served as the superintendent of three buildings around what would become the center of a new life. With two friends from Brooklyn, I moved into the third floor right at 307 East Ninth Street. The rent was fifty-four dollars a month. Sometimes I still wake up in the dark, thinking I'm there.

The railroad flat had the classic tenement design: a kitchen, two doorless bedrooms, a living room, and a bath- room. I was working then as a commercial artist and designer, and set up my drawing table against a window in the kitchen, with a view of the weed trees in the backyard. Sometimes I worked all night, with the radio pitched low to Symphony Sid on WEVD, the only radio station in America named for a socialist (Eugene V. Debs). With three of us in the flat, someone had to take the couch in the living room. It didn't matter. We were having more laughs than any human beings deserved.

There was, of course, much drinking. In the 1950s, there was a lot of drinking all over New York, a leftover from the days of Prohibition and the celebrations of the end of the war. It was a time of big parties, bathtubs full of canned beer and ice, as many young women as we could lure to the flat, dancing to Ray Charles, Sinatra, the Penguins, and the Orquesta Aragon. There were also too many cigarettes, dirty glasses, spilled drinks, and some fistfights and visits from the cops. Some of the hangovers were moral.

But the five years I spent in that neighborhood were full of excitement. To begin with, I was living, at last, in Oz, and not just passing through.

Like most human beings, we explored this new fraction of the world in expanding concentric circles. The northern border of our little village was Fourteenth Street, only five blocks away, but the main drag was Second Avenue. From about 1880, this had been the center of what became known as the Jewish Rialto, where Yiddish variations of the Fourteenth Street formulas were staged for Jewish immigrant audiences. But its great days were long over, for a variety of reasons, but primarily because of the erosion of the Yiddish language. The Holocaust had cut savagely into the flow of Yiddish-speaking immigrants from Europe, since the dead cannot leave for a new world. Increasingly, the Yiddish speakers were old, and eventually there would be more readers of the *Jewish Daily Forward*—the robust and beloved *Forvetz*—in Miami than in New York. In the 1920s, it sold 250,000 copies a day. Today, it's a weekly, with a circulation of about 15,000, published almost entirely in English.

But along Second Avenue there were still traces of what had passed. You'd see a "delicatessen store" here (where you ordered a "glass tea" with the goodies) and the Gem Spa there (offering the finest egg creams in Manhattan). There too was Ratner's, the dairy restaurant near East Sixth Street where so many learned to love cheese blintzes, latkes, and kreplachs, in spite of the calculated rudeness of the waiters. And down toward Houston Street, there was Moskowitz and Lupowitz, with a menu more varied than Ratner's, better-mannered waiters, and higher prices. There were Yiddish newspapers on the newsstands, and on weekends, you would see cars from the United Jewish Appeal roaming the side streets, its young drivers and passengers visiting old people who had been left behind by children and grandchildren, and lived in tenements that had imperfect heat or too many flights of stairs. Most of them were women, and when I spent a day following the young volunteers around, the old women turned out to be widows, at once cranky and grateful.

When I walk those streets today, I often think of those women, and how they held on so long to their small pieces of New York. Old photographs of the Lower East

Side show how that world once looked, but those solitary old women added another level of resonance. They are like characters in the final chapters in a long elegiac novel. The early American chapters can be seen in photographs of the immigrants arriving in the port of New York. From the far side of the ship's railing, we can see that most of them were small. Their faces were still, the eyes wary. Ahead of them was America. Behind them were all those heart-chilling experiences that had urged them into exile: pogroms after the assassination of Czar Alexander II in 1881; the permanent, sleep-killing possibility of sudden violence; more anti-Semitic violence after 1905. Behind them were the packing of goods at midnight, the movement along frozen roads heading west, the confusions at the piers of Hamburg, then the long voyage across the Atlantic.

Ahead lay life in many of the streets where I roamed in the late 1950s. A century earlier, some Jews took up residence for a while in the Five Points. Most wandered into Kleindeutschland, on the East River side of the Bowery, where many people understood Yiddish. The emigration from Russia, Poland, and Eastern Europe did not abate. Between 1881 and 1914, two million Jews left Europe and sailed into New York. By 1905, most of the Germans were gone, seeking the consolation of distance after the *General Slocum* disaster, when more than a thousand German children died in the sinking of that excursion ship in the East River. They moved uptown, to Yorkville and other places. The entire area from the Bowery to the East River, from Houston Street to the Brooklyn Bridge, was then called the Lower East Side, and it was overwhelmingly Jewish and poor. For some of those abandoned old women, it was the only America they ever knew.

Here was their American life: the stench of tenements, the streets jammed with pushcarts, endless temptations for the young. Most flats shared toilets in the hall. The few bathtubs were located in the kitchen. The streets were worse. Those temptations could be very real. Some of the young became gangsters. According to historian Albert Fried, some of the young women were lured into prostitution, seduced by Jewish pimps called "cadets"; some of the women were drugged and shipped off to the mining camps of the West. The favored targets of the cadets were red-haired Polish girls.

For most of the immigrants, the Lower East Side was a place of grueling work and invincible hope. Many of the men had no professions or came from country places like the Irish before them and the Italians who arrived later. Suddenly cast into a large, teeming, indifferent city, they took whatever work they could find, primarily in sweat-shops, while their wives did piecework in the crowded kitchens. Like the Irish and Germans before them, few envisioned anything as extravagant as a career. That would be for their American children. The hope for many was to own a pushcart and then possibly a small shop. The pattern lasted for a long time.

I remember wandering the area once with a friend from the navy named Nick Ochlan. His father owned a small grocery store on East Fifth Street, where the lights were dim to save money, and the halls leading to the upstairs apartments were gloomy with twenty-watt bulbs. Nick's father had a distended jaw, broken by Nazi goons. The family, as did the families of many shopkeepers, lived in a tiny apartment at the rear of the store. "It's a horror," Nick said, "but it's better than where they came from."

That was a second-generation version of the mantra that must have kept so many of the immigrants going. And in the Lower East Side there were things that they simply didn't have in the shtetls they left behind. There was, to begin with, free education. The public schools were free. They were then, as now, imperfect, the teachers often impatient with the slowness of children trying to become American. But it turned out that they weren't the only institutions for learning. New, privately financed places began to emerge, where the failures of the public schools could be repaired. Their aim was to accelerate the process of Americanization.

The impetus behind these alternative places of learning was an uneasiness rooted in class. Many of the so-called uptown Jews, those who had been more easily assimilated earlier in tolerant New York, were sniffy about the immense flood of Eastern European Jews jamming the tenements of the Lower East Side. The new arrivals spoke Yiddish, not German. They had (or so the uptown crowd thought) bad manners. To the uptown Jews, the new arrivals were locked into medieval orthodoxy, untouched by the secular influence of the Enlightenment. They would look like stereotypes to their own friends, the haughty Knickerbockers and their descendants. They could cause anti-Semitism in America.

Those who lived uptown were not, by any means, all rich. But they were all now Americans, and most were educated. The earliest arrivals, the Sephardim that included the family of Emma Lazarus, were initially uneasy with the Ashkenazi who came in the mid-nineteenth century. But in the final decades of the nineteenth century, both assimilated Sephardim and Ashkenazi looked down upon Jews from the provinces of Eastern Europe or Russia. Or, to be more precise, many did.

There were extraordinary exceptions. Some, like Emma Lazarus, accepted the duty to try to help their fellow Jews. As just one example: In 1889, wealthy German Jews created the Educational Alliance on East Broadway, one of the great glories of the city for all the years that followed. The youngest children of the Lower East Side could attend kindergarten to prepare for the public schools. Poor children could go there to use the gym or to take their first showers. They could drink pasteurized milk. They could go away to summer camp. More important, they could learn. The sculptors Louise Nevelson, Jacob Epstein, and Chaim Gross, and the painters Raphael and Moses Soyer took their first lessons in art at the Educational Alliance. David Sarnoff received his first instruction in English there, before moving on to a career that would take him to the Radio Corporation of America, where he created the National Broadcasting Company, the first radio network, in 1926. There were classes in dance. There were classes in theater. Some of the children had gifts for laughter too, and one of them, Eddie Cantor, from Eldridge Street, went on to a long career in vaudeville, radio, and movies. The Educational Alliance gave many impoverished kids the chance to dream. It still does, although the kids now are Latino or Asian or African American.

By the end of the century, the Lower East Side was

dense with self-help societies, with educational centers, many of them built upon older structures left behind by the German Jews. By the turn of the century, Lillian Wald had established the Henry Street Settlement, and others were blossoming.

At the same time, two related streams were converging on the area. One was political, the other cultural. The first was a combination of socialism and European-style anarchism, which shaped a generation and helped establish the trade union movement among exploited Jews. The last of that generation could be seen in Union Square in the 1950s, grizzled soapbox orators still proclaiming the true faith of their youth. They believed in the class struggle, the iniquity of bosses, the need to organize. The world of working people had changed drastically, but they still found much evidence to fuel their anger. For them, the 1911 fire at the Triangle Shirtwaist Company, which killed 146 workers, almost all young women, had happened the previous Saturday morning. When young, they studied the texts of Marx, Engels, and Lenin, or Bakunin and Kropotkin as if they were the new Talmud. Some of them insisted they were a new kind of Jew, secular, rational, materialist, intent on making the brave new world here in New York. Some of them angrily discarded religious beliefs held in their families for a millennium, blaming them for the passive condition of too many Jews. A small number embraced the new creed of Zionism. For many of those young American Jews, the Lower East Side was always a place of manifestos, leaflets, demonstrations, marches, and, eventually, strikes. It was as if they had adopted the Irish proverb "Contention is better than loneliness."

At the same time, a great cultural tide was rising from the immigration, and its vanguard was the Yiddish theater. It first appeared in the early 1880s and lasted until the 1930s. Some of its theaters were still on Second Avenue in the late 1950s, but except for an occasional revival starring Menasha Skulnik or Molly Picon, the surviving theaters had been absorbed by a new phenomenon called Off-Broadway. The Café Royal was gone, the place on the corner of Twelfth Street and Second Avenue where the great Yiddish actors, playwrights, directors, and impresarios once gathered, along with the finest Yiddish newspapermen, a few brilliant critics, and those who wanted to emulate them. In 1958, there were still many people alive who could talk about the departed stars, Jacob Adler, Boris Thomashefsky, Ludwig Satz, and others whose names are now engraved in the sidewalk in front of the Second Avenue Deli on the corner of Tenth Street. But there weren't enough such people to fill theaters six days a week. In 1958, the Jewish Rialto was as dead as the Rialto on Fourteenth Street.

After almost a half century of vitality and triumph, the Yiddish theater had passed into the country of permanent New York nostalgia. Somehow, in the years after World War II, its moment had passed, the musicians had departed, there was dust on the orchestra seats and the balconies. Alas and farewell. The affection for the vanished theaters was genuine, of course, and for good reason: By all accounts, the Yiddish theater had given the city many amazements. The artists among the Yiddish performers reveled in the freedom of New York. Here, no secret policemen would descend upon them for making fun of the czar.

Nobody would come knocking at their doors at midnight, and if they did, some tough Jews would throw them down the stairs. *This is America, boychick! No more crap!* Or so they believed, so they hoped. They looked at the city and were inspired by almost everything they saw. They must have sensed the permanent New York nostalgia, that pervasive urban emotion caused by the imaginary presence of the Old Country and the velocity of change in New York itself. That emotion, after all, was in their work. In the early days, after 1885, Yiddish playwrights hacked out sentimental dramas about loss and separation and heroic mothers and hardworking children. The dramas provoked cleansing tears. They gave consolation to these strangers in a strange land. Most of this work was dismissed by the Yiddish intellectuals as *shund*, or trash. Their judgments didn't matter to the people jammed in the seats on Saturday nights.

But all was not *shund*. The creators of the American Yiddish theater also provided what earlier entertainers had given to the Irish and the Germans: the immense gift of laughter. They used gags, skits, slapstick, and wit to make fun of one another. Romanians made fun of Hungarians. Both made fun of Poles. All made fun of Russians. They skewered the greenhorns, the pompous nouveau rich, the greedy landlords, the humorless goyim, the corrupt politicians; and they added something else, an attitude that forever shifted the New York mind: irony.

That is, they made jokes out of the difference between what America promised and what America actually delivered. Irony remains the essence of American humor to this day. They were also triumphantly eclectic. The creators of the Yiddish theater made their own versions of what they saw the Irish doing in the rowdy theaters of the nearby Bowery. They attended shows on the Rialto of Fourteenth Street and took what they thought would work on Second Avenue, peppering it with wit imported from the cafés of Vienna or Berlin, the whole enlivened by the energy of the new immigrants. They adapted Shakespeare for their blue-collar audiences, giving them a Jewish *Hamlet,* a Jewish *King Lear* (with a happy ending added), and even a Jewish version of *The Merchant of Venice.* There were few pretensions about making high art; this was entertainment, for people who needed a respite from the grind of work and life on the margin of prosperity. Eventually, high art would emerge in the Yiddish language, in the same evolution that led from the Bowery theaters to Eugene O'Neill. It just took a while. But in their own way, the downtown Jews were repeating the pattern established by the poor Irish and Germans, and thus were becoming part of the New York alloy.

On our little piece of Second Avenue in the 1950s, there remained some monuments of that past. Across the avenue from us, between St. Mark's Place and Ninth Street, was the Ottendorfer Branch of the New York Public Library. It's still there, in its rich terra-cotta glory, still opening its doors to the people of the neighborhood. Those doors were first opened in 1884. The man who built the library was a wealthy German American named Oswald Ottendorfer, one of those New Yorkers who truly used his wealth to help others. He hired a German immigrant architect named William Schickel, who had worked for the

famous Richard Morris Hunt, and, like Hunt, Schickel
drew upon the Renaissance for his design. The entrance is
an arcade, and above it are the words "Freie Bibliothek u.
Leschalle" (Free Library and Reading Room). The crucial
word was *Freie.* Oswald Ottendorfer's purpose was simple:
to provide books, newspapers, and periodicals in German
and English for the poorer residents of what was then
Kleindeutschland. At first the cast-iron stacks were closed,
with visitors required to ask for titles. By 1890 that had
changed, and the stacks were open for anyone's scrutiny.
This was America, after all, and you should be able to
choose your books and find your way to surprise or even
astonishment. Sometimes you might find Goethe or
Schiller. Sometimes, in translation, there was Dickens,
Victor Hugo, or, with any luck, Mark Twain.

Eventually, as the Eastern European Jews began to
move into Kleindeutschland in larger numbers, they too
found their way to the Ottendorfer. Few of them lived on
Second Avenue. But they could walk uptown from the
miserable tenements to the south and east, the way they
walked to the Yiddish theaters. At the Ottendorfer, they
discovered what all New York generations have discovered: Every library is a temple of human wisdom.

When I first visited the Ottendorfer (it was, by the way,
the first branch of the New York Public Library), there
were many men from the Bowery at the tables, seeking
refuge from brutal New York winters. Most of them were
reading. A few of them were, as New Yorkers would say,
"a little ripe." No matter. There were also Latinos who
were settling in the tenements to the east and some old-
fashioned bohemians. There were very few Eastern

European Jews. Their children had gone to the City College of New York, had fought in two American wars, had taken full advantage of the GI Bill; they could afford to buy their own books now. But when I visited not long ago, there were computers in the main room past the arcades, all busy with seekers of information, and on a shelf near the door, pink leaflets from the library offered "Free English Classes for Speakers of Other Languages." In a city where about two hundred languages are now spoken by the largest number of immigrants to live among us in a century, the New York Public Library is still doing its job.

Next door to the library on Second Avenue stands another building that Oswald Ottendorfer financed and William Schickel designed. It was once called simply the German Dispensary (Deutsches Dispensary), and what it dispensed was free medical care to the poor. The building is twice the size of the library, and an earlier version was built there in 1857. Those who came for its services were the same as those who used the library: Germans at first (including German Jews), and later the Eastern European Jews, and then Latinos and Bowery types and the beatniks and hippies who came to the neighborhood in the late 1950s and early 1960s. The German Dispensary was forced to change its name during the anti-German hysteria that accompanied American entry into World War I. The new name was the Stuyvesant Polyclinic. So it remains, as part of the Cabrini Medical Center. Hurting human beings still enter in search of help. Few notice the adornments of the building, the portrait busts of Hippocrates and Aesculap flanking the doors. Aesculap is surely better known as Asclepius, the son of Apollo who was the Greek and Roman god of medicine. Nor do casual passersby, or even patients, glance at the sculpted heads near the roof, properly heroic images of the English physiologist William Harvey, the Swedish botanist Carolus Linnaeus, and others, once honored on Second Avenue, now part of New York memory too.

And part of mine. Above the cell phone store to the left of the library there was once a theater called the St. Mark's where I saw Jean Genet's *The Balcony.* Across the street, on the corner of Ninth Street, there was a small Ukrainian coffee shop where I often ate breakfast and joked with the old white-mustached man who ran the place (his name now lost in memory). It's now three times the size of that old shop and is called the Veselka and serves a lot more than eggs and coffee. Beside it is the large building that houses the Ukrainian National Home. It once was a dance hall called the Stuyvesant Casino, which on weekends in the 1950s was used by Dixieland bands. There were many Ukrainians in the immediate neighborhood in the 1950s. Most were still called DPs, for Displaced Persons, those refugees from the horrors of Europe who were granted the right to come to America in spite of the stupid immigration laws. Some were Christians, some were Jews, all could speak to one another in the old language. They worked and they worked and they worked, and made a purchase of their own small piece of America. A Starbucks now occupies the southwest corner of Ninth and Second, but who would go there if you could find a seat at Veselka?

Down the east side of Second Avenue, just across St. Mark's Place, is the Orpheum, once the finest of all

Yiddish theaters, then a thriving Off-Broadway venue where I saw *Little Mary Sunshine* in some lost year and where *Stomp* has been running since the second Reagan administration (or so it seemed on my last visit). Across the street, just below Seventh Street, Ratner's Dairy Restaurant is now a Met Foods supermarket. The building rising above it is NYU's Tisch School of the Arts. Somewhere in that building was the Central Plaza, where a trombone player (and actor) named Conrad Janis led the Dixieland revival in the 1950s (of which the Stuyvesant Casino was a part), the music a kind of anti-bebop retro movement. There were usually big fights at least once a night and hurled beer pitchers and overturned tables and some very efficient bouncers, but on two visits I saw the great drummer Sid Catlett sit in with the group, like Michael Jordan playing in a schoolyard.

There was a movie house here too, called Loew's Commodore, that became the Fillmore East, where Jefferson Airplane and the Doors and Janis Joplin came to perform, and where the Who premiered the rock opera *Tommy*. A passionate man named Bill Graham ran the place, and many aging fans believe that it was the greatest of all rock and roll venues. Another block away, at 91 Second Avenue, George Gershwin lived as an infant, right next door to where the "dairy" restaurant Rappoport's once thrived. Neither Gershwin nor most of the old clientele of Rappoport's lived to see Jefferson Airplane.

Before reaching those places, a visitor can take a right on East Seventh Street and come to McSorley's Old Ale House, said to be the oldest drinking establishment in the city (the claim is subject to some dispute, since New

Yorkers dispute almost everything). This saloon was the subject of a fine 1912 painting called *McSorley's Back Room*, by John Sloan, showing a white-haired mustached man sitting in the late-morning light of a side window, his hands loosely enlaced. He wears a full dark blue overcoat, so we know it is winter. He has neither book nor newspaper on the table before him. Only a stein of ale. He seems lost in a pool of solitude and nostalgia. To the side, two other men lean toward each other, obviously murmuring but suggesting neither dark conspiracies nor sullen angers. Behind them a fire burns red in a fireplace while one of the saloon's collection of clocks ticks away the minutes of their lives.

Sloan did another McSorley's painting the same year (*McSorley's Bar*) and years later returned to the place for *McSorley's at Home* (1928), *McSorley's Cats* (1929), and *McSorley's Saturday Night* (1930). The five paintings have the same urban warmth that infuses Joseph Mitchell's *New Yorker* portrait of the place. But I never felt anything like their obvious attraction to McSorley's. The sense of the nineteenth century (epitomized in some way by the pot-bellied stove) stirred my curiosity and urged me to imagine the men who once came to drink there. And visiting the premises put me in closer touch with John Sloan and Joe Mitchell, two artists I revered. But I didn't like the taste of ale, and there was nothing else on tap. And I was also young: The place barred women, and I wasn't passionate about saloons where I couldn't meet women. Youth needs the possibility of romance. In the 1970s, during the most vehement time of a revived feminism, McSorley's finally admitted women to its dark embrace, but it was too late for me, and probably too late for the women.

McSorley's is still open, but there is nothing else on the block that connects the saloon to the distant New York Irish past. East Seventh Street is a Ukrainian center now. Down on the corner of Third Avenue, west of McSorley's, is the First Ukrainian Evangelical Church and a Ukrainian crafts shop. Across Seventh Street, on the corner of Shevchenko Place, is the St. George Ukrainian Catholic Church, which was once smaller and more charming. The old church was torn down in the 1970s and replaced with this one, which, like so much modern ecclesiastical architecture, seems inspired by Howard Johnson's roadside restaurants rather than the mysteries of time and faith. Most younger Ukrainian Americans have left the neighborhood for the larger city and the suburbs, but you still see giant gatherings for weddings and funerals. And once, long before he was murdered in 1996, I saw the Second Avenue Deli's Abe Lebewohl, from Kilykiv, near Lviv, walking down this block with a Catholic priest, the two of them talking in Ukrainian and laughing.

When I walk uptown, and pass the churchyard of St. Mark's-in-the-Bowery, I flash on A. T. Stewart and the way his corpse was kidnapped, or imagine old Peter Stuyvesant hobbling on his peg leg, raging at Jews and other strangers, or remember my friend Joel Oppenheimer, a proud, tough Jew, bearded, exuberant, filled with love of the world below Fourteenth Street, obsessed with the New York Mets, and leading a poetry workshop in Stuyvesant's church. Around the corner at

110 East Tenth Street, Stanford White was born in 1853. And in the block between Third and Fourth avenues in the 1950s, there were about a dozen art galleries: the Brata, the Tanager, the Camino, the Grimand, the March, and others. The critic Harold Rosenberg, who invented the term "action painting" to describe the work that others called abstract expressionism, lived on the block. So did the painter Willem de Kooning. I would see them from time to time, walking together, heading west. Rosenberg was more than six feet tall, with a fierce Zapata mustache. De Kooning had the mellow look of a Dutchman who was living in a town that the Dutch founded. On some nights in autumn or spring, you could walk into a gallery opening, with bold paintings on the walls and wine served in plastic cups and women in leotards and sweaters, drinking hard, and Charlie Parker on a turntable.

On the corner of East Twelfth Street and Second was the Phoenix Theater, where many New Yorkers saw Ann Corio's wonderful tribute to a dying art, *This Was Burlesque*, and later *Oh! Calcutta!* and *The Best Little Whorehouse in Texas* and *Grease*. Originally, it was the Yiddish Art Theater, which is why the Star of David was on the ceiling. The driving force behind the 1,300-seat theater was Maurice Schwartz, also from the Ukraine, who was in turn heavily influenced by the charisma and intelligence of Abraham Cahan, the journalist and novelist who was the editor of the *Forward*. Across the street, on the southeast corner, was the Café Royal, where the menu was basically Hungarian but where artistic contention was the main dish. In 1953, the Café Royal closed forever and is now a Japanese restaurant, filled with the New York young. I suspect that nobody there discusses the plays of Arthur Schnitzler or the work of Abraham Cahan.

I still go to Abe Lebewohl's Second Avenue Deli, where I used to sit over blintzes or kasha varnishkes with Paul O'Dwyer, the tough, laughing, white-haired defender of almost everybody who needed defense. He was one of the last in a line of passionate Irish lawyers that started with Thomas Addis Emmet in the early nineteenth century. Every time he walked into the Second Avenue Deli he was embraced by the owner, the waiters, and half the customers. The other half were from out of town.

After a few years at 307 East Ninth, I moved next door to 309, where I lived on the first floor right, just up the stoop. The reason was simple: One of the guys from the apartment at 307 got married and was granted the apartment by common consent. The bathtub at 309 was in the kitchen, with a chipped ceramic cover, and sometimes, in desperation, I walked up to the Gramercy Gym on Fourteenth Street to take a shower. I was working nights at the newspaper, trying fitfully to sleep days, but in that small place I first read the great Brazilian novelist Machado de Assis, hosted a few jammed and sweaty parties, and sometimes wore my press card to bed. Down the block lived Edward Hoagland, whose novel *The Circle Home* showed me many things about writing, and I would see Allen Ginsberg ambling along in poetic (I thought) solitude on sunny afternoons. Around the corner on St. Mark's Place was the latest version of the Five Spot, where Thelonious Monk seemed to play every night and all the customers dressed like Miles Davis. On that same block lived W. H. Auden, and I would see him, with his gullied face, walking alone toward Second Avenue, but I never had the nerve to speak to him.

Sometimes I would walk east to Tompkins Square Park and sit on a bench reading and look at all the fine young women and the kids in the playground and the old men reading the Yiddish newspapers. At first, I didn't know who Tompkins was (Daniel Tompkins was New York governor from 1807 to 1816 and led the fight to abolish slavery in the state), but I loved the park that bore his name. Only a few people, most of them real estate hustlers, were then calling this the East Village. The blocks on the far side of the square were not yet part of the degraded, dangerous place the cops called Alphabet City. Nor was the park a free range for junkies and predators. After five years (and one final flat at 150 Second Avenue), I moved on from the neighborhood, returning usually as a newspaperman, covering what the arson squad called "successful fires" and double homicides. In the sixties, many middle-class kids started coming to the neighborhood, to play for a while at poverty and rebellion. The truly poor resented them, because if they got into any real trouble they could always call Daddy for a check. Most of them were sweet and naive, playing Dylan and the Stones at top volume, cursing the war in Vietnam, Lyndon Johnson, and then Richard Nixon. But too many of them found permanent trouble. As a newspaperman, I covered at least three cases of kids wrecked on acid who walked off tenement rooftops.

There was a band shell then in Tompkins Square Park, and I once watched Jimi Hendrix play there, full of power as he pushed the blues back into rock and roll. It was his neighborhood too, since he lived for a while at 321 East Ninth Street, a few doors east of where I lived, a building where La Mama had its first experimental theater in the basement. The Grateful Dead played that band shell too, with thousands of Deadheads staring at the sky while the cops looked on in wonder and unease. A few of the cops even knew the tunes, humming along with Jerry Garcia.

But as years passed, life went terribly wrong in Tompkins Square Park. In the 1980s, armies of homeless men moved throughout the city, and many of them found their way to the park. They began to transform it into a permanent encampment, their billets hammered together from wood and canvas and tin. Heroin was everywhere, and, later, crack cocaine, along with every variety of alcohol. The stench of excrement filled the air. Flowers were trampled. Men urinated on the pink marble of the monument to the victims of the *General Slocum* disaster. The grass wore away and the ground turned to gluey mud in the rain. Trash baskets were used for fires. Parents retreated with their children. Very few old men sat on benches reading books or newspapers. Such public human squalor hadn't been seen since the Hoovervilles of the Great Depression.

In 1988, after many complaints from those who paid rent in the neighborhood, an attempt was made to clear the encampment, using the police. The subsequent riot should have been predictable. Young cops, many of them from the suburbs, few of them veterans of the armed forces, lost all discipline. Many covered their badges with tape to hide their identities. Heads were beaten. Rocks and bottles arced through the air. When it was over, forty-four people were injured. And the men were still in the park. Now they were supported by others: old hippies, squatters in abandoned houses, middle-aged people possessed of the romance of poverty. They blamed evil landlords, capitalism, gentrification, for all the trouble. To be sure, they didn't speak for the entire neighborhood. The Latino poets, painters, and writers who had started calling the area "Loisaida" (a latinization of Lower East Side) in the 1970s generally stayed aloof from the quarrel. Those people who had already begun the slow process of gentrifying the neighborhood wanted the park cleaned out, so they and their children could actually use it.

After a smaller riot in 1991, Mayor David Dinkins closed the park for "renovations." The homeless men were evicted. A fence went up around the ruins. The band shell was demolished. And then something miraculous happened. The park was brought back from the dead, and the grateful were the living. After fourteen months, Tompkins Square Park was opened to everybody. The damaged paths were repaired. The lawns were reseeded. The trash baskets were used for trash, not fires. Mayor Giuliani's policy of "zero tolerance" for minor offenses took hold. I wander there now, and in good weather the benches are full and children are laughing and running and the dog people are leading their canine charges to the dog run. A few homeless men wander through the park, but they keep moving. At midnight, the new gates to the park are locked.

Our neighborhood eased into other neighborhoods, and there were no clear borders of separation, no requirements

to show a passport to gain admission. Sometimes we wandered down the Bowery and took a right at Spring Street
and entered the top of Little Italy. It seemed changeless
then, with its restaurants that stayed in the same locations
for decades, its old women in black heading to church, its
tough longshoremen and artisans arriving home each
evening in varied states of exhaustion. To be sure, there
were Mob guys still around then, dressed in car coats and
creased trousers and glistening shoes, practicing hard
looks, stealing admiring glances at themselves in the store
windows. But they didn't bother visitors. You saw them at
tables in Luna's on Mulberry Street or standing in front of
social clubs or piling into Cadillacs.

There were a lot of teenagers around too, many with nothing to do except blunder into trouble. As late as the end of
the 1960s, the dropout rate of Italian American youngsters
was higher than the rate for the poorest blacks and Latinos.
There were various reasons for this. Many of the original immigrant parents had contempt for education, and that attitude survived into the second generation of Americans. The
cliché in Little Italy was the same one I heard in my neighborhood in Brooklyn: *I knew a guy went to college and he's working on
the docks.* At sixteen, too many of them dropped out and went
directly to the docks or a year or so later to the army. But
there was a pervasive, generally unconscious bigotry among
their teachers too, an attitude that for too long considered
the Italian American kids as hopeless cases who with the
best of luck might pass the civil service test for the Sanitation
Department. Although Frank Sinatra and Joe DiMaggio
had attained great popular fame (along with other Italian
American athletes and entertainers), there were few political

or intellectual models for the kids to emulate. Fiorello La
Guardia was the greatest mayor in New York history, but he
died in 1945, and although a number of Italian Americans
entered politics or became judges by the early 1960s, the
Little Flower had no true successors as charismatic figures.
Mario Cuomo had yet to emerge as a public figure of elo-
quence and passion. Martin Scorsese and Francis Coppola
were still in the dreaming stages of their careers as movie
directors. Gay Talese was just beginning his extraordinary
career as a journalist, the writer Pietro di Donato (*Christ in
Concrete*) was already forgotten, and Mario Puzo had not yet
written *The Godfather.*

The tale of the Italian Americans was certainly worth
telling. The Italian migration began in the 1880s, around
the same time as the movement of the Eastern European
Jews. But there were some major differences. Many of
the Jews were literate in their own languages, as was fitting for the People of the Book. A healthy number had
skills that could be used in New York. Most Italian immigrants were from Sicily or the south. They were *contadini,*
people who worked the land, often in semifeudal societies.
Most were illiterate in Italian. In addition, most of the
Italians (certainly not all) were young men. They came to
America to earn money and then return to Italy. At one
point, for every one hundred Italians who arrived in New
York, seventy-three went home. After the turn of the century, this was made easier by advances in the technology
of steamships. A journey from New York to Naples could
be done in ten days. Some of the Italian men made a number of such journeys: to New York for a year or two,
where they hoarded money, and then a return for a few

years until the money ran out, and then back to New York.

Still, many Italians settled in New York, and their first stop was often the Five Points and its neighboring streets. Eventually, most of them moved above Canal Street. Their community became known as Little Italy. When I started going there in a serious way, Nick Pileggi of the Associated Press (and later *New York* magazine) was my occasional guide. From him, and a few others, I learned that I was looking at a world without truly seeing it. Elizabeth Street, for example, was a street of Sicilians. Up near Greenwich Village lived the Italians from the north, Tuscans and Genoese. As it did for the Jews, after 1904, the expanding subway system made other places possible. Italians settled in East Harlem, the Bronx, and South Brooklyn, while Jews found new places from Brownsville to Washington Heights. But Little Italy remained the primary Old Neighborhood. Some families stayed in the same tenements for decades. Others could not bear the thought of leaving behind the coffee and pastry at Ferraro's or the Café Roma, the cheese, bread, and pastries in a dozen beloved groceries.

And yet that too all changed. In the 1980s, the third generation of Italian Americans began to leave. They were Americans, after all, and many had now gone through high school to the City University, and then on to medical school or law school. They moved to Staten Island or New Jersey or Long Island, where they could own homes, have American driveways where they could park American automobiles, and have American barbecues on Sunday afternoons in summer. They found no raffish charm in the myths of the Mafia and the dumb stereotypes that came with those myths. Some of the old tenements were sold. Most were rehabbed and rented for sums beyond the imagination of the older residents. As in other parts of New York, some people fell into a new longing for the past: rent nostalgia. "See that place? My aunt used to pay sixty-two dollars a month there; now it's eighteen hundred!" And then, in the 1990s, the latest downtown immigration wave began to arrive in large numbers.

The Chinese were bursting out of the old Chinatown, thanks to changes in immigration laws in 1965 that allowed women to come at last to America and help Chinese men form families. The Chinese had American children now, many of them forging ahead in the New York City school system. By 1995, at Stuyvesant High School, one of the city's elite public high schools, 60 percent of the students were Asian. There were now Chinatowns in Queens and Brooklyn too, connected through the subway system to the old Chinatown, which had been on the downtown side of Canal Street since the 1880s. There were still poor Chinese, still too many sweatshops, still too many Chinese controlled by gangs. But many of the new Chinese had money to invest, in businesses and in real estate, some of it in flight from Hong Kong after 1997 as it moved into unhappy union with mainland China. The Chinese moved north and east, and Little Italy began to shrink. By 2002, the San Gennaro Festival on Mulberry Street had begun to look like a theme park, with *Sopranos* T-shirts, *Sopranos* posters, and *Sopranos* cookbooks. Tourists bought "Fuhgeddaboutit" T-shirts and ordered ravioli in the restaurants. In the parking lots, there were many cars with

Jersey plates. In a shrunken Little Italy, there were more tourists than Italians.

This was not surprising. On the Lower East Side, as I write, Katz's Deli is still open on Houston Street, as is the Yonah Shimmel Knish Bakery, the store that has been there since 1910. There are kosher bakeries along Grand Street near the East River. But when I took an evening stroll recently along the length of Hester Street, one of the legendary streets of the New York Jewish past, every single store bore a sign in Chinese.

Eventually, all our village roads led to the Village. If you lived in Manhattan, as we did, you never said, "Let's go to Greenwich Village." The Village was simply the Village, and there was not yet an East Village. If you walked west along Ninth Street and turned left for a block on Broadway, you found yourself at Eighth Street, the main stem of the Village.

On a summer evening, it was a marvelous show. The sidewalks were dense with people: artists in paint-spattered jeans and T-shirts; bearded poets or bohemian poseurs; gay young men in twos and threes, some of them transvestites; tourists with startled eyes; careening groups of drunken college boys in corduroy trousers and desert boots; black men with white women, and white men with black women; young Holden Caulfields, who would tell you everything if you really wanted to hear about it (and you didn't); sailors on liberty from ships tied up at the Navy Yard; knots of Ukrainian women free for the evening from the rules of Second Avenue; strollers chatting in French, Italian, Greek, and Spanish from Spain (with a lisp); cops looking casual; panhandlers; con men; Latinos from uptown or the East Side, eating ice-cream cones; motorcycle riders in leathery armor; kids with a basketball, heading for the playground on Sixth Avenue; professors from NYU with the *Village Voice* tucked under their arms; Irish longshoremen from the West Side piers; delivery boys; sidewalk artists; kids up from Little Italy, full of mockery; young women from the Ivy League schools trying to find University Place and the Cedar Street Tavern, where the poets and the painters did their drinking; musicians heading for gigs, their horns in cases, wearing sunglasses at midnight; peddlers of pot or smack or shaved ice in six flavors.

On weekend nights, Eighth Street was a sensual festival of unlimited possibility. The sixties lay ahead, but until about 1964, Eighth Street was that era's first draft. Drinking was the fuel of its existence, and many of the strollers were heading to bars scattered through the Village: Jack Delaney's on Sheridan Square, or Louis' Tavern (where you might spot James Dean among the other actors and poets), the Cedars, of course, or the place a few blocks uptown called the Stirrup, where Billie Holiday ruled the jukebox. The smoky, boozy destinations included the Kettle of Fish, the San Remo, the White Horse, and Chumley's; or the Riviera at Seventh Avenue and West Fourth Street, where a lot of the old seagoing communists from the National Maritime Union stood at the bar with poets and cops.

The binding music of our village was jazz, which was played at the Café Bohemia on Barrow Street and the Village Gate and the Village Vanguard (where I saw Art

Tatum for the only time) and many other joints, some operated by Mob guys. Charlie Parker was dead, but you
saw "Bird Lives" scribbled on the men's room walls of all
these places and in the subway stations and on the walls of
parking lots. I saw John Coltrane play with Miles Davis
in one of those places, and Charlie Mingus in many of
them. Coltrane was in the era of his prolonged solos, and
one night, the legend went, Miles finally said, in his growl
of a voice, "John, you gotta end them goddamn endless
solos." And Coltrane explained, "Miles, I don't know,
Miles, I get so deep into the solos, I don't know how to get
out of them, man . . ." To which Miles replied, "John, just
take your mouth away from the motherfuckin' horn."

Mingus was playing the Gate one night (the owner Art
D'lugoff told me) when a group of black middle-class folks
at the brink of the stage kept talking through his solo.
Mingus lifted his bass fiddle, walked off the stage and into
the men's room, and finished the solo in its tiled solitude.
These were serious musicians. To them *tom* was a verb,
and they were not going to tom for anyone.

Big-time rock and roll had not yet happened; the
Beatles and the Rolling Stones were still learning their
craft in Hamburg or Liverpool or London. But there were
things happening, many things happening. Some were political and social: the election of John F. Kennedy in 1960,
along with the emergence of the civil rights movement.
Both were about the new, about the gathering power of
the young. Some were musical. In 1961, Bob Dylan
started to play Village gigs, still a folkie, breaking out at
Gerde's Folk City. He stayed for a while at the Hotel Earle
on Waverly Place, just off the northwest corner of

Washington Square, a hotel erected in part in 1902 that had degenerated into a semi-fleabag. Many musicians stayed there. But so did others. Every time some reporter or rewriteman from my newspaper was tossed out by an obviously intelligent wife, he ended up, at least for a while, at the Hotel Earle. For Dylan, residence at the Earle must have been a seminar in the consequences of loss.

My guide through part of this world was Al Aronowitz, a brilliant colleague from the *New York Post*. He had written much about the Beats, and knew Jack Kerouac and Allen Ginsberg and Gregory Corso. He took Dylan to meet Ginsberg in 1964. The Beats (particularly Corso and Lawrence Ferlinghetti) had heavily influenced Dylan's earliest work, the freedom of its language and imagery, the vision of other ways to lead American lives. Around the same time, Aronowitz introduced the Beatles to Dylan, an encounter that in turn influenced all rock and roll. *Sgt. Pepper's Lonely Hearts Club Band* played, in its way, the music of Eighth Street.

But there were antecedents to much of the ferment. With Aronowitz in 1961, I went to a crowded party at the apartment of LeRoi Jones and his wife, Hettie, to celebrate the publication of a magazine called *Yugen*. In memory, the party was on the top floor and spilled into the hallways, with much drinking and much reefer. Jones was a sweet man that night, and we talked about a poem he had written about *Krazy Kat*, the amazing comic strip by George Herriman. Miles was playing on the phonograph, alternating with blues singers. Jones turned to speak with Jack Kerouac, who seemed shy and oddly sullen, and I heard him say, "Cheer up, frère Jacques." Kerouac smiled and sipped from a bottle of Budweiser. Soon, LeRoi Jones was gone from the Village, and gone from Hettie, and had returned to Harlem, where he became Amiri Baraka and embraced black nationalism; in 1964, we all went to see his fierce play *Dutchman* at the Cherry Lane. He would end up in Newark as a polemicist and a spokesman for black rage, which, alas, often contained a nasty strain of anti-Semitism. Something was indeed happening.

Or, to be more precise, many things were happening. Some were literary. There were bookstores here, including an outlet of the old Marboro chain near Sixth Avenue. In the 1950s, one of the clerks was Jasper Johns, who would become one of the great American painters in the 1960s. On Cornelia Street there was the Phoenix, with great collections of poetry and European literature. But the Eighth Street Bookshop at the southeast corner of MacDougal Street was one of the ornaments of the Village—and of Manhattan. Writers, poets, and readers came there from all over the city. Norman Mailer was a regular. We met while covering the Floyd Patterson–Sonny Liston fight in Chicago in 1961 and are still friends. One winter evening I saw James Baldwin reading Goethe's *Faust* in solitude against a wall of books, his large eyes squinting. We'd met at that same prizefight in Chicago, but to interrupt him would have been to break a spell, and I moved to the history section. Another time, I saw Auden leaving with a bag of books, and Ginsberg joking with Eli Wilentz, who owned the store with his brother Ted. In that glorious store, I found my way to the rest of the Beats and to those writers who seemed to be their allies. Barney Rosset of Grove Press and the *Evergreen Review* (another regular) was an immense force in liberating publishing from the old restrictions, fighting legally to bring out his edition of *Lady Chatterley's Lover* by D. H. Lawrence and the major works of Henry Miller. We were all reading Miller and his friend Lawrence Durrell, along with William Burroughs and John Rechy and Alexander Trocchi. Some of the work was extraordinary; much of it was narcissistic rubbish; but all of it was part of its New York era in a way that writing has never been since they all faded away. Within a few years, the hippies had replaced the Beats, creating a culture of bohemianism without art, where the sacred texts were all contained in rock and roll. Psychedelic drugs replaced wine and vodka and bourbon. These children of television didn't read much, and overvalued the few books they did read. Their poet was Dylan, who was very good indeed, but they absorbed his lyrics with no knowledge of Dylan Thomas, whose name Bobby Zimmerman had adopted as his own. In 1965, the Eighth Street Bookshop moved across the street to number 17, where it remained an institution until one day in the 1980s, when the owners cleared out the stock and locked the doors for good.

At the same time that the Beats were having their moment, the urgencies and power of Off-Broadway were pulling us to the theater. The conventional Broadway theater was taking few chances in those years, placing itself in the service of what the Prohibition saloon keeper Texas Guinan once called "big butter and egg men." Broadway was for shows; the new, imperfect, sometimes amateurish downtown venues specialized in true theater. In the early 1950s, there was a downtown revival of the great Irish playwrights, Sean O'Casey and John Millington Synge among them, with several of the Clancy Brothers playing important acting roles (and on Monday nights reviving traditional Irish music in a war against the concocted Irish tunes of Tin Pan Alley). Suddenly, in tiny theaters below Fourteenth Street, in storefronts, in the archipelago of Off-Broadway, the names Samuel Beckett and Antonin Artaud and Eugène Ionesco were in the air, along with the first works of Harold Pinter. The *Village Voice,* founded by Norman Mailer, Edwin Fancher, and Dan Wolf, and published for a while after 1955 upstairs from Sutter's Bakery on Greenwich Avenue, was central to what was suddenly happening all around us. The *Voice* drama critic was Jerry Tallmer, a gifted writer and an intelligent man of passionate tastes who was able to express enthusiasm without sounding like a publicist. Like any good journalist, he saw what was new in the event he was watching, and for many of us, he became the essential guide. Some of the work that Tallmer embraced left me indifferent or doubting my own intelligence. I wasn't alone in thinking that novelty just wasn't enough. But often we went back to the work that had most moved us. I saw *The Iceman Cometh* (starring Jason Robards Jr.) three times at Circle in the Square and mourned when the theater was torn down in 1972 for another ugly apartment house. *The Threepenny Opera* played for seven years at the Theater de Lys on Christopher Street, pulling me in four times. In the Village, theater was part of the psychic geography.

Movies were part of the Village too. On Eighth Street there were the Art (now part of NYU) and the Eighth Street theaters, both small, both featuring movies that could not be seen in the gaudy palaces of Times Square. If you missed the Kurosawa at the Thalia, you learned to wait for its arrival at the Eighth Street or the Art. There we saw Fellini, Bergman, and Kurosawa, Truffaut and Godard and Jacques Tati, all of them somehow meshing with the books we were reading and the theater we were seeing and the music we were hearing. There was a sense in the air itself that the world was brand-new, and it wasn't only because we were young and therefore new too. The election of Kennedy had released a sense of optimistic possibility that seldom came from politics; there truly was a feeling that the torch had passed to a new generation. The right-wing orthodoxies of Joe McCarthy had been defeated; so too, we thought, had the pressure to conform to some standardized notion of what it meant to call yourself an American. The civil rights movement was gathering power and clarity, as the Freedom Rides kept moving into the South and we began, more and more, to hear the name Martin Luther King. It seemed possible, as Camus once said, that you could love your country and justice too.

In the Village, as in the larger city and the country beyond, it was a time of much excellence. Or the ambition to be excellent. The word *hip* was used in those days to mean "knowing," not to describe what was fashionable. We wanted the writing and the music and the art to be hip *and* new, to jolt us into new ways of seeing, feeling, and thinking, but at the same time to be more than simple novelty. Some of those naive desires actually survived the assassination of John F. Kennedy on November 22, 1963, the day the sixties actually began. Looking back now, many of the novels and poems of the time don't hold up. But the music does, and so do those movies we saw in the darkness of the

Eighth Street and the Art. Two out of three, as the cliché goes, ain't bad.

But even in the music, there were few happy endings. At some point around 1968, Jimi Hendrix, a young man from Seattle, was in the first flush of his stardom, with a fat new recording contract. This must have been around the same time that I saw him perform in Tompkins Square Park. He decided to build his own studio in the basement of the Eighth Street Theater. This space had once been a kind of yee-haw joint called the Village Barn, where New Jersey kids took girls after the senior prom. The studio's construction ran into many delays. The ceiling, for example, had to be three layers thick to insulate the movie house from the sound of rock and roll. Hendrix and his architects also discovered the existence of the Minetta Brook flowing toward Washington Square below the old foundations of the theater. In August 1969, Hendrix played at the immense festival at Woodstock, where he caused a sensation with his deconstructed version of "The Star-Spangled Banner." On August 27, 1970, the day after the official opening of his Electric Lady Studios, he left for England. Hendrix played an erratic set at the Isle of Wight festival, then went on to Denmark and Germany, where fans booed his slovenly, semistupefied performances. Back in London, he died on September 18, 1970, after choking on his own vomit because of an overdose of sleeping pills. He was twenty-seven and never got to make an album in the studio he had built.

The Electric Lady Studios was still there when last I strolled Eighth Street. The number on the entrance is 52, and in the window beside it there are large photographs of

Jimi Hendrix from the final years of his life. He is dressed in a kind of white Elvis glitter suit. He looks like a man in his fifties.

The movie house is gone, of course, boarded over and shabby, as is much of this block of Eighth Street. The decline was at once swift and gradual. A Gray's Papaya hot dog restaurant opened on the corner of Sixth Avenue, crowded with young men in shades who ate very little, and the street slowly became part of the retail end of the drug trade. Dealers made their way from Washington Square as part of a nightly route, peddling pot, heroin, acid, meth, and eventually crack. On the stoops across the street from the Eighth Street Theater, stoned kids clustered at midnight with warring boom boxes, and people who had been residents for years began to move away (in 1990 my brother Tom and his wife, Nin, who had lived two doors from Electric Lady Studios since the early 1970s, were part of the exodus). The police seemed incapable of bringing any sort of order to the street. For a long time, the movie house itself drew crowds to midnight showings of *The Rocky Horror Picture Show*, and afterward the young attendees would retreat noisily to the cellar clubs that opened and closed on the block with exhausting regularity. Shoe stores opened along the north side of the block, one of them taking over the last home of the Eighth Street Bookshop.

Across the decades since the early 1960s, I've lived on Bank Street, and Waverly Place, and upstairs from O. Henry's steak house at the corner of West Fourth Street and Sixth Avenue. I've paid rent on Patchin Place (where the ghosts of E. E. Cummings, John Reed, and Anaïs Nin drifted around the courtyard), on Horatio Street, on Church Street near Chambers, and have lived for two extended stays in the Chelsea Hotel on Twenty-third Street. The Chelsea was an outpost of the Village, full of painters, writers, jazz musicians, and rockers, and I'd often take walks to Madison Square, to see where Stanford White's magnificent Garden once stood, or the Metropolitan Life Building, where my mother worked for a decade, or the glorious Flatiron Building, that tall ocean liner steaming due north without moving an inch.

Almost always, I was working for newspapers or magazines based in Manhattan. But often my true destination was a marvelous saloon called the Lion's Head, at 59 Christopher Street. On the corner was the latest office of the *Village Voice,* and the Seventh Avenue subway brought newspapermen uptown from the *Post* and downtown from the *Times* and the *Herald-Tribune.* But it was not just a newspaperman's bar. There were stockbrokers in the crowd, and off-duty cops and firemen, and ballplayers, and old communists, and folksingers, seamen, priests, and nuns. Musicians came in late; so did bartenders from other Village joints. Some husbands showed up with their wives, but it was also a place of consolation for those whose wives had departed for good. There was much drinking, much singing, an occasional fistfight (usually with someone strange to the bar), much laughter. I loved talking to Joel Oppenheimer, about baseball and politics and the art of typesetting (to which he had been apprenticed years before becoming a poet). My friends included the novelist David Markson; each of the Clancy Brothers; the newspapermen Larry Merchant, Vic Ziegel, Dennis Duggan,

and Joe Flaherty; a tough little veteran of the Abraham
Lincoln Brigade named Curly Mende; the actor Val
Avery; a political junkie (and fine writer) named Doug
Ireland; a stockbroker and ex-marine named Tom Quinn;
and the novelist and essayist Edward Hoagland. In its special way, the Head was true to the historic Village ethos in
that all sins were forgiven except cruelty.

More and more, Vietnam was part of the texture of the
talk in the Head, but if the tone of the discourse was sometimes angry, it was never hysterical. Usually the poets
were talking about money while the stockbrokers talked
about art. But all over the country, including the Village
outside the door, the sixties were getting more frantic. In
the Lion's Head we were all a little too old for flower
power or the Weathermen. None of us went to
Woodstock. Only a few did drugs, and with even fewer
exceptions, none in a serious way. Our drugs were all liquid. In short, the Head (as we called it) was part of the sixties and yet outside its main currents. It was more rooted
in older notions of bohemia than in what was being called
the counterculture. But even bohemia was changing. By
1968, that most terrible year, the year of the Tet offensive,
the murders of Martin Luther King and Robert Kennedy,
and the chaos of the Democratic Convention in Mayor
Daley's Chicago, all the old Village assumptions were
ebbing away and most artistic rebellions seemed minor.
Who cared about art when young men were dying? The
most important poet in that America was, of course, Bob
Dylan, and for a long time the Head had no jukebox.

There was a curious tendency to neutrality among many
citizens of the older Village. Yes, they would vote against

the war. Yes, they might send a few dollars to those cam-
paigning against it. But many had nostalgia for the Village
that was disappearing in the sound and fury of the era.
They wanted to go back to a time when they could argue
about poets or painters or the stars of the Theater of the
Absurd. They saw signs on the separate roads: Jack
Kerouac reduced to blubbering irrelevance only ten years
after the publication of *On the Road* while his friend Allen
Ginsberg enlisted with the guitar armies and chanted at
most major demonstrations, including the Chicago convention. Who had chosen the correct road? There were no
true answers in the coffee houses of MacDougal Street or
the Eighth Street Bookshop or the Lion's Head. There
were opinions, and harsh judgments, but no answers. And
the war was only one issue; every other assumption of
American life was under challenge. Or so it seemed. Race,
class, work, education, gender: All were being shaken by
the italicized demands for change. When the Stonewall
riots erupted on June 27, 1969, a few doors from the
Head, and went on for three days, the regulars from the
Head watched, offered verbal encouragement, but took no
part in the demonstrations that gave birth to the Gay
Liberation movement. There were too many journalists
among us, trained to the codes of detachment, and too
many who had donned the armor of irony. Timothy Leary,
from Harvard, was urging the young to turn on, tune in,
and drop out. In a different way, some of the older drinking class was doing the same thing. Many would think
back on their choices later with a kind of regret.

Eventually, all of that ended too, including the regret.
I stopped drinking on January 1, 1973, and though I still

visited my friends in the Head, it wasn't the same. Oppenheimer had stopped drinking and so had Flaherty, the three of us costing the Head about a thousand dollars a week. In August 1974, Richard Nixon resigned as president, enmeshed in the Watergate scandals, and that was the true end of the sixties. On April 30, 1975, the war ended too, with the last Americans being lifted by helicopters off the roof of the embassy in Saigon. For a long while, the mood in the Head was diffuse, sometimes dark, particularly if you were looking with sober eyes. Some of the regulars walked out one midnight and were never seen again. Flaherty died. Oppenheimer died. Out in Queens, Kerouac died. Ginsberg died. Finally, the Head died too.

And after each death, after the mourning was over, life continued. We didn't just go to funerals; we went to weddings and christenings and seders, to graduations and birthday parties. We feasted. We danced. My friends all knew that we had shared a long hard time in our city, but it hadn't hardened us. If anything, the bad times had given us a sense of proportion. Each of us refused to be trapped in the seductive mists of the past, where the endings were already known. We owned that past, but we lived in the present and still had visions of the future. On the day after my mother died, my first grandson was born.

Yes: I work every day. I find time to visit art galleries and museums with my wife, to breakfast with my oldest friends, to walk alone through the streets of my native city. I love seeing the latest versions of Shaw's girls in their summer dresses. I get emotional over the contests of the Knicks and the Mets. The phone rings and I absorb the latest gossip, and even believe about 10 percent of it. I see my brothers and collapse with them in laughter over the absurdities of politicians and other scoundrels. I read books I thought I'd read when young, and they are even better to me now, after having lived a life.

I can be dazzled by the new, or repelled. But as a native New Yorker, I am also a citizen of the country of nostalgia. On days of gray rain, part of me wants to cross Broadway into Eighth Street on a summer evening and plunge into the carnival. I want to eat a lemon ice and stare into the window of a bookshop and see some volume that I cannot live without. I want to hear Tito Puente from a passing car and see two Latinas break into steps of amazing intricacy before walking on to the west, giggling. I want to bump into Joel Oppenheimer and see him light up a Gauloises and walk with him to the Lion's Head on Sheridan Square, where the bar is full, and Paddy and Tom Clancy are in the back room and we all start singing "Eileen Aroon." There is no clock on the wall. There is no time. We laugh, all of us, and everything seems possible. Later, I walk across town to a tiny flat on Second Avenue and Ninth Street and fall into a long dreamless sleep.

Chapter Ten

CROSSROADS OF THE WORLD

THE SUMMER I was sixteen I got a job in Times Square. I worked with a man named Butler, who was heavy, growly, with a whiskey-hurt Hell's Kitchen face. He said he was fifty-one, but he looked seventy. Our job was to change the show cards in the lobbies of movie houses. Together we would pry out staples and take down the old show cards, which were five or six feet high, four feet wide, all in color. *Good-bye, Joel McCrea; so long, Yvonne De Carlo....* Then I would hold the new show cards steady while Butler stapled them into place. *Hello, Rita Hayworth; enjoy the run, Glenn Ford.* Then Butler would have a nice long cigarette break before we moved to the next theater.

I loved that job. There I was, at the crossroads of the world, with the breaking news moving around the face of the Times Tower and the waterfall flowing between the giant nude statues of the spectacular Bond Clothes display and smoke rings floating perfectly out of the mouth of the guy on the Camels sign. The sidewalks were jammed with sailors, pimps, cops, streetwalkers, dancers, actors, musicians, and tourists. Where Broadway crossed Seventh Avenue, traffic was a raucous, noisy show, big yellow taxis honking their horns like staccato punctuation from Gershwin, trucks and buses bullying their way downtown, and big New York voices coming out of the din: *Whyncha watch where ya goin', ya dope! Dis ain't Joisey!*

One morning, Butler and I were standing under the marquee of the Victoria Theater while he pulled deep drags on a Lucky Strike. Coming down the street was a blind man, complete with dark glasses and tin cup, but no Seeing Eye dog. People dropped coins in the cup and hurried on, too busy for thanks. Then Butler flipped his butt into the street and gestured with his head toward the blind man.

"Ya see dis guy?" he said. "Ya see him wit' da cup and all? Well," he said, the voice suddenly brimming with outrage, "I happen to know for a fact dat *he's got five percent vision in one eye!*"

I thought: This life business is not going to be easy.

Even at sixteen, I was no stranger to Times Square. How could I be a stranger? I was a New Yorker, and this was the city's central plaza. I'd been coming through here since 1942, when I was seven, on Saturday journeys with my mother and brother Tom. On my eleventh birthday, I was taken to see Maurice Evans in *Hamlet*, the first play I ever saw anywhere. I couldn't understand the glorious Shakespearean language, but I was filled with confused, turbulent emotions put into me by the power of art. Those feelings stayed with me when the play was over as we walked through the dramatic tumult of the streets: limousines with heavy thumping doors, and cops on horses, and yellow Checker cabs, and thousands of men and women moving across honking traffic into bars and restaurants, and street musicians playing fiddles or drumming with spoons, and men with scary faces, and women in rouge. And there on the corner, the street sign carrying one word: Broadway.

Later that year, I started going to Times Square from Brooklyn without an adult beside me, usually with Tom, the two of us standing like sea captains in the lead car of the subway train, plunging together into the eerie tunnels, racing under the streets and the East River, then emerging into the hard light of the stations, making the transfers to the IRT train, emerging at last in the tumult of Times Square. We were perfect targets for predators, naive and very young, but I never felt a sense of menace. The prevailing emotion was wonder. We'd gaze at the amazing blocklong signs rising ten stories above the crossroads of Broadway and Seventh as if they were structures imported from ancient Egypt or the hills of Rome. They were called "spectaculars," and that's what they were. We saw immediately that the Great White Way was more of a neon rainbow, the spectaculars never at rest, blinking, moving, changing color and shape with the speed of magic. We'd watch the sketch artists drawing sailors. We'd listen to barkers calling to the crowds. *Right inside, folks, stuff ya never saw before, oney a quarter, come on and try it and . . .* We'd look at the eight-by-ten glossies of the girls in the glass cases, girls who worked in the upstairs dance halls, their faces not as perfect as movie stars', which made them seem even more dangerous in their bare-shouldered dresses. Sin was becoming the obscure object of our desires, or at least of mine. Once, we saw Willie Pep, the great featherweight champion, walking with a blond woman who was a head taller than Willie. He was my father's favorite prizefighter, and we followed him uptown from the Paramount Building until he vanished into the Hotel Taft, the blond woman's angular arm draped maternally across his shoulders. As good Catholic boys, we were disappointed that Willie was about to drop a decision to Satan here in the capital of sin, and we worried about his chances against Sandy Saddler. Years later, I interviewed Pep when his great days were over and told him the tale and asked if he had been disappointed too. He smiled like a witness before a grand jury and said he didn't remember.

Through my adolescence, Times Square kept calling. On summer nights in my teens, jazz lured me to West Fifty-second Street. This wasn't precisely Times Square but was definitely one of its major tributaries, feeding into the square and pulling people from its vivid lights. The jazz clubs were almost all Mob joints, the owners too cheap to provide air conditioning, which meant that on humid nights in July and August, when the doors were open to the hope of a summer breeze, I could just stand around on the sidewalks and listen. That's how I first heard Dizzy Gillespie, Ben Webster, Roy Eldridge, Carmen MacRae, and Lennie Tristano. Live. Outside one club, on a warm, drizzly night, a doorman, dressed in a royal blue coat adorned with gold braids, like someone from the court of the Austro-Hungarian Empire, said to me in a menacing New York accent, "*Don't lean on ∂a cabs, ki∂.*" To this day, every time I see a doorman, I think of that man in his glittery uniform. I've never again leaned on a parked car.

Later, when I was home on leave from the navy, the same impulse toward jazz put me into Birdland, where Miles often played, and Dizzy and Max Roach. A tiny man named Pee Wee Marquette was the MC. If a musician did not tip him properly, his introduction would tail off before the mention of the player's name. "Ladies and gentlemen, Birdland is proud to present the great mummadamummadà mum . . ." The club was named, of course, for Charlie Parker, who opened it in December 1949, when every jazz buff knew him as Bird. At first (or so the story goes), there were a number of caged parakeets on the premises, but they all died within a few months from the cigarette smoke. Dizzy Gillespie once told me he thought they died because they didn't tip Pee Wee Marquette. Bird played Birdland for the last time on March 4, 1955, and eight days later he was dead. The club lived on until 1965, but it had already played a part in the story of the New York alloy.

Down the block from Birdland was the Palladium, where the greatest Latin bands all played: Machito and His Afro-Cubans, Tito Puente, Tito Rodriguez. Mambo, pachanga, rumba, charanga, cha-cha: All threw Caribbean heat into the New York night. The subway carried men and women here from Spanish Harlem and the Puerto Rican enclaves in the South Bronx and from the streets along the Brooklyn waterfront. Many first saw the astonishments of Times Square while heading for the Palladium.

The old dance hall was up a flight of stairs, and I arrived one night to see the singer Alan Dale tumbling head over heels down the stairs. I noticed that he was wearing what were then called elevator heels. He pulled himself up, holding on to a railing like a drowning man who'd found the edge of a lifeboat, wiped at a bloody nose with a paper napkin, and walked on wobbling legs into the night. I never saw him again. I have no way of knowing what sin Alan Dale had committed, but the bouncers looked down at him as he disappeared with looks that said, We have done our duty. Then they turned and stepped into the Palladium. I went up the stairs after them.

The Palladium and its bands drew the most amazing dancers in the city, better (to my taste) than any of the professionals in the Broadway theaters, far better than the Rockettes, who were thought of as an act for midwestern tourists. In memory, all the women at the Palladium had golden skin, white teeth, amazing hips, narrow waists, and bosoms encased in black silky dresses with straps as thin as the straps of slips. They wore three- and four-inch high heels, with which they hammered the hardwood floors while never losing the beat. Their skin glistened with a fine spray of perspiration. They gave off the aroma of gardenias. I'm sure these images are the result of some youthful defect in my vision. Hormone overload can distort the objects of anyone's scrutiny. But in truth I don't remember any women at the Palladium who were not beautiful. As for the men, I don't remember them at all.

I do remember Dizzy Gillespie walking into the

Palladium one night, carrying his horn, goateed and smiling. He was appearing that night at Birdland and was obviously on a break. He nodded at many of the beautiful
women, smiling in a devilish way, and made his way to the
bandstand, where Machito awaited him, beaming. After a
few minutes, Dizzy began to play, the bell of his trumpet
aimed at the ceiling, the roof, the unseen New York sky.
The Latin musicians played with ferocious precision, em-
bracing the great musician from that other world right up
the block. Together, for a few long minutes, they drove
loneliness and anguish out of the night. Together they
were making something new, welding New York to
Havana and San Juan and Ponce, downtown to uptown,
America to all the outposts of Africa. When I listen now to
the recordings that Dizzy later made with Machito, I'm always thrown back to that thrilling night, and I wonder
what happened to all the high-heeled women, who are
grandmothers now, and most certainly still beautiful.

In late 1955 I was working in the art department of a small
advertising agency on Forty-seventh Street between Fifth
and Sixth avenues. This street was the great midtown center of the diamond trade. I got to know some of the merchants, who tried in vain to explain the differences
between Orthodox Jews and the Hasidim. They were patient with me, the curious goy, even though I never once
had the money to purchase anything they offered for sale.
At all hours of the day, even in rain and snow, the merchants would cluster on the street in small knots, examining some precious stone with a loupe, not trusting the
artificial lights of the shops. Every month or so, there

would be a moment of heart-stopping panic as some tiny gem slipped from the hands of a customer and fell through the subway ventilation grate to the muddy floor ten feet below. Then from some secret place would come a man with a long pole—its tip gummy with some mysterious substance—and a special flashlight, and they would peer into the darkness until he found the stone. The men would exhale and, in at least one case I witnessed, cheer.

Some had moved uptown from Canal Street and the Bowery, and a few older men remembered when the trade was practiced on Exchange Place, near Wall Street, before the rising skyscrapers made the street too dark for the examination of precious stones. There were men among them, too, who had survived the death camps of Europe, and on summer afternoons, you could see their bluish tattooed numbers. I tried in a muted, stumbling way to talk to such men about what had happened to them. Not one of them would say a thing. They would shrug, exhale, change the subject, working hard at being New Yorkers, residents of a city where self-pity was still one of the cardinal sins.

In the middle of Forty-seventh Street there was a bookshop of uncommon excellence called the Gotham Book Mart (it moved to 16 East Forty-sixth Street in August 2004). The store's founder in 1920 was a woman named Frances Steloff, and she was still there when I started visiting, small, white-haired, with focused eyes behind her glasses. She was to New York what Sylvia Beach had been to Paris between the wars, a person who loved and celebrated literature, and did what she could to keep people reading works of talented unknowns and the century's finest artists. Outside her store was a sign designed by

John Held Jr., the man who during Prohibition made all those drawings for *Life* and *Judge* of flappers and Fitzgerald sophomores. The sign's motto said, "Wise Men Fish Here." And in its spirit, I often went fishing there. The rare books were beyond my bankroll, but there were little magazines for sale and inexpensive monographs on artists and obscure writers (obscure, that is, to me, but not to Frances Steloff). At the Gotham, I bought the first issue of the *Paris Review* and a few pamphlets by Beat poets like Ray Bremser and Jack Micheline that I hadn't seen downtown on Eighth Street. But on the shelves of the Gotham I could also find out-of-print William Saroyan and James T. Farrell and, yes, Damon Runyon too. In the dusk of winter evenings, leaving the advertising agency or the Gotham while the diamond merchants shuttered their stores, I'd look to the west and see the glorious, garish lights of Times Square. They all seemed connected by more than simple geography.

Then, for almost a year, I adopted a new routine. I'd leave the art department of that agency on Forty-seventh Street and hurry up Fifth Avenue to Forty-ninth Street, pushing through crowded streets at the end of the workday, and into the building in Rockefeller Center that housed the National Broadcasting Company. To save money for a year in Mexico, I was now working two jobs: the ad agency until five in the afternoon, and then NBC, where I worked as a page, a kind of glorified usher, until midnight. I worked on Sid Caesar's show (". . . next aisle on your right, ma'am, next aisle on your right . . ."); on a failed tryout of a quiz show for which Mike Wallace was to have been the MC; a fifteen-minute musical show starring Matt Dennis; and, the culmination of my long day's journey into night, on *The Tonight Show*, starring Steve Allen.

Steve Allen, like so many others in those years, was helping to invent television. He was an okay piano player but not great. He was an okay songwriter but not great. And yet he had a loose, hip, relaxed style that was perfect for the emerging medium. He was what hipsters, and later Marshall McLuhan, called cool. He helped Skitch Henderson to create a fine band made up of solid studio musicians who were happy with the steady money and thankful that they did not have to play in saloons. He hired singers who later became stars: Steve Lawrence; Lawrence's future wife, Eydie Gorme; Andy Williams. The show was one hour and forty-five minutes long, and it was live.

The Tonight Show took place each night at the old Hudson Theater on the uptown side of West Forty-fourth Street between Sixth and Seventh avenues. The theater dates back to 1902, and Allen seemed delighted to be there, playing piano himself or watching other talented people from his desk. Sometimes, on steaming New York summer nights, he would open the back doors behind the stage and aim cameras into Forty-fifth Street. The inevitable New York characters would come by, peering into the brightness while Allen made wisecracks for the television audience. On any such night, you could see older women who sold flowers, dumb kids pulling faces, pretty young women in tight T-shirts, tourists with alarmed eyes. I'm sure the cops were watching too, looking for some dope who was wanted in four states. One night an immense hairy guy in a sleeveless undershirt came to the back door and stopped. Hair covered his chest and his arms and his back and bloomed from his ears and nose. He peered into the harsh lights, unable to see what was on the other side. He bared his teeth. He flared his amazing clogged nostrils. He scratched his hairy back. Allen called him King Kong, just arrived from the upper stories of the Empire State Building. The audience was laughing. The musicians were laughing. We pages were laughing. Everybody was laughing except the hairy guy. He never went away. He moved two feet left and stopped. He moved three feet right and stopped. And then finally the show had to end, and the music played, and the credits rolled. And somebody in the control room improvised a credit line that said "King Kong's T-shirt by Hanes."

I never again saw the hairy guy on the streets of Times Square, and soon I was off to Mexico to go to art school, and Steve Allen got his own weekly network show, competing with Ed Sullivan. That brilliant show made stars of Tom Poston, Don Knotts, Louis Nye, and a few others, doing variations on man-in-the-street interviews. I saw them much later in tributes to Allen. For a while, a variation of *The Tonight Show* featured the great jazz DJ Al "Jazzbo" Collins as a replacement for Allen, and he flopped, and then in came Jack Paar, who was a huge hit, and after him Johnny Carson, who stayed for more than thirty years, and finally Jay Leno. Every time I see Leno, I say to the screen: Open the back door and stick the camera out on the street. But there is no street where they do the Leno show in California, and now there is no Steve

Allen either. The Hudson Theater is still there, rehabbed and clean, waiting patiently for some low-key genius to come in the front door and climb onto the stage.

In 1961, working now at the *New York Post,* I was given a beat called "on the town." Each night at eight o'clock I'd go to Lindy's, at Fiftieth Street, and meet with the *Post* photographer Arty Pomerantz. We'd listen to police calls on the radio of Arty's car or sit over coffee inside the restaurant, and when something happened, off we'd go. Sometimes there was a fire in midtown. Or a gambling raid that brought dozens of sharply dressed low-level wiseguys into the Fifty-first Street station house. Or, on a good night, with some luck, we'd have a homicide at a good address. On other nights, we covered the openings or closings of Broadway shows or followed some tip from one of the press agents who used Lindy's as a base and fed items to the many gossip columns. There were seven daily newspapers in those days and each one, except the *New York Times,* had a gossip column. Those press agents were also the carriers of the old Broadway legends and most of them must have known that they were in the last days of their own time on what one columnist called Dream Street. They continued to work very hard at their craft. They worked the telephones all day, prying away at buried secrets or inventing items about their clients, and then typed out the items on small pieces of paper, each written in the style of the columnist they were servicing. Items for Ed Sullivan at the *Daily News,* for example, contained no verbs: "Judy Garland expecting . . ." Or "Tony Bennett a big hit at the Copa . . ." In the evening, the envelopes were left at Lindy's, to be picked up by secretaries of the columnists and pasted into the finished columns.

The king of the gossip columnists was, of course, Walter Winchell, who in 1962 had not been around New York in many months. The modern gossip column, with its three-dot items, was his invention, and from it flowed most of the others, along with such later variations as the supermarket tabloids, *People* magazine, and the Drudge Report. He perfected a whiz-bang style for the column, inventing language with great abandon (to get a divorce in the state of Nevada, for example, was to be "*Reno*vated"). The clipped New York urgency of the style transferred perfectly to radio, where his Sunday night audiences were gigantic, as he came on to say, "*Good evening, Mr. and Mrs. North and South America and all the ships at sea. This is Walter Winchell with the Jergens Journal. Let's go to press. . . .*" He did not restrict himself to show business. For years, six days a week, he happily served as a conduit for President Roosevelt. After the war, he signed up with J. Edgar Hoover, his frequent booth mate at the Stork Club, and that was the beginning of his long, slow decline. During the rise of Joe McCarthy he filled the column with red-baiting items, and the tone turned punishing and nasty.

By 1962, with his sour old Broadway turning rancid and his right-wing politics dominating the old mindless showbiz stuff, he was often in Florida or Arizona or out in Los Angeles. The column lost its sense of place and much of its urgency. Most of the time, the old Broadway energy of the column had become a snarl.

During my time "on the town," I saw Winchell for the first time outside Lindy's, a small, intense, Cagney-like man in a snappy gray fedora, surrounded by a praetorian guard of press agents. Suddenly, Winchell, the old vaudevillian, began a charming soft-shoe to "Once in Love with Amy," a song made famous by Ray Bolger. The intensity vanished, and for a few minutes Walter Winchell looked happy. The press agents applauded, and Winchell went back into Lindy's with most of them in tow. I couldn't help thinking of J. J. Hunsecker, played by Burt Lancaster in *Sweet Smell of Success*, the hard, corrosively intelligent movie about the world in which Winchell was once the supreme being. The streets looked black and white, and so did Winchell. One of the lingering press agents whispered to me: "It's so sad. He doesn't even know he's finished."

That night, it was hard to imagine the time of his prime, when the stretch of Broadway from roughly Fortieth Street to Central Park was a kind of tinhorn American Versailles and Winchell was the Sun King. Presidents and press agents wanted his applause. They feared his vendettas. His throne was pitched at table 50 in the exclusive Cub Room of the Stork Club on East Fifty-first Street. There he sometimes accepted the sugary compliments of old bootleggers while in the company of J. Edgar Hoover. Now the Stork was a semiabandoned ruin, locked in an endless union dispute, where the waiters sometimes outnumbered the customers. The *Daily Mirror,* the Hearst tabloid where Winchell had worked since 1929, was in desperate trouble too. In the old days, when Winchell went on vacation or took his usual Monday day off, circulation of the *Mirror* dropped by 200,000. Now it never seemed to matter if Winchell was in the paper or not, and the *Mirror* was a year away from falling into the news-paper graveyard.

Later that night, Winchell asked if he could ride around with me and Arty Pomerantz. "Hop in," Pomerantz said.

Winchell alternated that night (and on a few others) be-tween fevered monologue — *"Billy LaHiff's saloon was right over there. One night . . ."* — and moody silence. He was then sixty-five, and seemed much older. Certainly the ghosts of his lost city were everywhere. At one fire in Harlem, a young cop asked him for a press card, and he seemed stunned. Didn't this cop recognize Walter *Winchell?* Pomerantz started to explain, when a white-haired police lieutenant came over, smiled, and said, "You're Walter Winchell, right?"

"That's what they tell me," said the man who had been the most powerful journalist in America. He scribbled notes that never made their way into the newspaper. And before we drove back downtown, Walter Winchell pointed at a row of tenements. "You know," he said softly, "I used to live on that block."

Since the *Post* was then an afternoon paper, I had time to do my reporting and return to the office on South Street to write my stories before the eight-in-the-morning deadline. But even during the off-hours, when my head was filled with the Beats and Hemingway and Beckett, along with the history of New York itself, I was also drawn to Broadway. It clearly was no longer the Broadway I first saw as a boy. From about Thirty-eighth Street to Fifty-fifth Street, it was descending into a grungy mess of pa-paya stands, pizza counters, streetwalkers, and drugs.

Smelly little photo shops sold phony ID cards, mainly to underage drinkers. A few bookshops peddled magazines called *Titter* and *Laff* and others about the glories of nude sunbathing. At night, when the theaters were open on their own portion of Broadway, particularly around Shubert Alley, there was something resembling glamour. But it was swift and fleeting, the glamour of hurried arrival and even swifter departure. Some people stayed around the neighborhood for dinner after the shows, at Frankie & Johnny's, at Downey's. All over the area, nightclubs were closing. Good-bye, Copa. Farewell, Latin Quarter. The big stars were rare visitors to New York now. Frank Sinatra, Tony Bennett, and Nat Cole were playing Las Vegas, where the money was ten times what they had ever earned in New York, where many of the old big-shot New York gamblers were respectable at last, doing legally in Vegas what was once a crime in New York. Most of the old hoodlums were also New Yorkers, and they imposed on Las Vegas the architectural style they had absorbed when young: huge signs, much glitter, movement. That Times Square style lives on today on the Strip.

The old pulsing energy faded as the nightclubs died, and the stars went elsewhere. There was no huge money to be made in jazz, and big-time rock and roll had not yet arrived in the frenzy that came with the Beatles. Times Square itself was coarse, filthy, vulgar, but Forty-second Street was seedy and slightly menacing in a way that would seem, a decade later, almost innocent. At the *Post,* trying to understand what I was seeing, I read the clips and sought out some histories from the library. What was this place all about?

❁   ❁   ❁

The clips told me what was obvious: The subway was crucial to the existence of Times Square. The year of the
square's true foundation was 1904, when the long-delayed
subway first moved up the East Side from City Hall to
Grand Central, turned west at Forty-second Street, where
it stopped at what became known that year as Times
Square, and then drove north up the West Side all the way
to 145th Street. That first subway line would become the
primary symbol of New York velocity.

Until 1904, the open space where Broadway formed a
crossroads with Seventh Avenue at Forty-fourth Street
had been called Longacre Square. The area was full of stables and carriage makers, and some of the side streets were
dotted with brownstones. The new Astor Hotel was almost completed on the west side of Longacre Square, and
a German immigrant named Oscar Hammerstein had already built a few theaters, starting with the Olympia in
1895. But the subway and the *New York Times* would become joint agents of immense change.

Few could have predicted any of this drastic change in
1896, when a man named Adolph S. Ochs began his New
York career. He was then thirty-eight, the son of a German
Jewish immigrant who had served in both the Mexican
War and the Civil War and had settled in Louisville,
Kentucky. Adolph dropped out of school at fourteen and
then lived his own Horatio Alger story: office boy at the
Knoxville Chronicle, then printer's devil, then, step by rapid
step, all the way to the job of publisher—aged twenty—of
the *Chattanooga Times*. He built that fragile four-page sheet
into one of the best papers in the South. But on a trip to

New York, another opportunity presented itself, and Ochs seized the day. In 1896, using borrowed money, he bought the virtually bankrupt *New York Times* for $75,000 and began to transform it into a newspaper of solid reputation. The circulation of the *Times* when Ochs bought it was 9,000 a day. Within a year, it had climbed to 70,000.

As noted, the new publisher's reputation was established when, in the buildup to the war with Spain, Ochs refused to swim with the rushing jingoistic tide. The coverage was straight, with no rhetorical flourishes, even if the *Times* was somewhat dull compared to the shouting dailies of Hearst and Pulitzer. This decision was not entirely idealistic. Ochs's tight budget made it impossible for him to flood the *Times* with war coverage from Cuba. He ended up looking judicious, restrained, adult. As he proved that there was an audience for his sober news package, and as he turned away advertising from quacks and charlatans, he began to earn a modest profit.

By the turn of the new century, Ochs was convinced that he must move his newspaper away from Park Row. The combination of increasing traffic on the Brooklyn Bridge and congestion from the ferociously ugly post office at the foot of City Hall Park made it harder and harder to move newspapers from the presses to the customers. Ochs began looking uptown.

Ochs was not the first newspaperman to look uptown and see the future. His vision was tempered by his intelligence. He looked around first. After deciding against other sites for the *New York Times,* he settled on Longacre Square.

This was an act of faith that many (including his competitors) believed was sheer folly. Not only was the location too far from Park Row and lower Broadway, they said, it was dangerous. Ochs understood the risks. He knew that the square was a few minutes' walk from the Tenderloin, the wicked district from Fifth Avenue to Seventh Avenue, from Twenty-fourth Street to Fortieth Street. In certain ways, the Tenderloin made the old Five Points look like Mayfair. Starting in the mid-1880s (when the Five Points was losing its traditional character to reform), the Tenderloin was the most notorious district in Manhattan, packed with saloons, brothels, gambling joints, and dance halls, the whole saturnalia held together by Tammany protection and police corruption. The name itself came from a police captain named Alexander "Clubber" Williams, who is supposed to have said, when taking command of the precinct, "I've had nothing but chuck steak for a long time, and now I'm going to get a little of the tenderloin."

The legendary Clubber departed nine years later with a small fortune. The Tenderloin lived on without him. Most of the dives and "concert saloons" with their ever-available "waiter ladies" were in the shadows of the Sixth Avenue El, whose smoke-belching ugliness added to the surrounding squalor. The patrons ranged from hard-bitten Tammany pols to respectable folk engaged in slumming, foreign and domestic businessmen to true bad guys. They were catered to by professionals of the city's pleasure business, men who had learned their tough trade on the Bowery or Fourteenth Street, and the often desperate women who worked for them. The religious reformers called it Satan's Circus and, as usual in New York, they saved few souls within its rough borders.

The Tenderloin was not the only place whose existence Ochs had to consider. To the west of Longacre Square was Hell's Kitchen, stretching from Eighth Avenue to the river, Thirtieth Street to Fifty-ninth Street. The area was physically ugly, covered with slaughterhouses, railroad yards, the North River piers that handled the luxury liners, warehouses, and tenements. Many of the people were decent, most of them Irish, along with some Scots, Italians, and Africans, who worked on the piers or in the factories. But there were criminal gangs too, including the Gophers, the Parlor Mob, and the Gorillas, who methodically stole goods from the railroads and piers or operated the lowest saloons and brothels. It was a very rough part of town. A generation or two later, sentimentalists would promote the notion of the lost golden age of Times Square. They always left out the neighbors: the Tenderloin and Hell's Kitchen.

Ochs, of course, was not a sentimentalist. He must have sensed the potential dangers from the adjoining neighborhoods. Theoretically, they could be controlled by honest police or tamed with good schools and honest work. But Ochs must have understood something else: This would be the last major plaza on the island of Manhattan.

Across the centuries, a commercialized Broadway had moved remorselessly north from Bowling Green to Union Square to Madison Square and most recently to Herald Square. Each square, during its moment, was walled by commercial buildings or theaters, by hotels and restaurants, by places where time was turned into money, or time was erased by laughter or tears presented on a stage. At each square there was a pause, a widening of the Main

Stem. In its time, each square thickened with rallies, assemblies, ceremonies, with rowdy Saturday nights and exhausted Sunday mornings. Each square teemed with Knickerbockers and other luminaries, with the sons and daughters of Cork or Palermo or Minsk, and with jugglers too, and flute players and drummers and fiddlers, with dogs who could dance and snakes who could march, with barkers, policemen, anarchists, and defrocked preachers, with union men and union women, with those in search of cures for all human ailments, cures for hunger, cures for fever, cures for the pox, cures for the ache of loneliness; while peddlers passed over their counters and carts tons of oysters and clams and lobsters, roasted corn and fried potatoes, and finally hot dogs and hamburgers and shaved ice and ice cream. The squares were the great human forges of the city, drawing every kind of citizen to the common ground, to the place where the alloy was made. These squares were almost always triumphantly secular, welcoming no Torquemada, no Savonarola, reserving their adulation for home run hitters and infantrymen and heavyweight champions of the world.

Ochs understood one other large thing: After Times Square, there was nowhere else to go, no space for still another public square to the north of what was rising just above Forty-second Street. The reason was simple: The 843-acre reality of Central Park began at Fifty-ninth Street, and the terms of its creation in 1853 insisted that it be kept forever safe from commercial exploitation. When the park opened to the public in 1859, it was cherished by the citizenry and drew huge crowds, but it did not find itself within a wall of commercial businesses. Almost certainly, what was still called Longacre Square would be the last of the great squares on the island.

Ochs decided the gamble would be worth the risks. After all, he saw signs of the future already rising around Longacre Square: those early theaters, several hotels, many restaurants. The new restaurants, Rector's, Shanley's, Churchill's, were "lobster palaces" that catered to the theater crowds. Electricity was already converting Broadway in the thirties into the Great White Way. Much of the area between Forty-second Street and Central Park remained undeveloped, but Ochs was not alone in understanding what was coming. He was helped in his decision by his knowledge of the routes for the new subway and by the encouragement of his Tammany Hall friends on the board of aldermen.

The critical factor in Ochs's decision was the subway, which would stop at Forty-second Street and Seventh Avenue (in the original plan it was a mere local stop). After consolidation of Manhattan and the outer boroughs in 1898, Greater New York now had a population of four million. About 800,000 immigrants were arriving each year and they could not all live in Manhattan. The Manhattan and Williamsburg bridges were under construction, preparing to join the Brooklyn Bridge in opening Brooklyn to the New York millions, but if the immigrants lived farther from their Manhattan jobs, they would need the speed of the subway to make up for lost time. Then as now, the subway's advantage was blunt and powerful: If you went under the traffic jams, you got there faster. The projected subway would move faster than anything on the streets and three times faster than the elevated trains. For Ochs the businessman, Longacre Square would have been unworkable for a newspaper without access to the subway, and in his discussions he insisted that the new system must allow him to use the subway as a freight train too. He also wanted a change in name, as James Gordon Bennett Jr. had obtained for Herald Square. In April 1904, Ochs got what he wanted. By mayoral proclamation, Longacre Square became Times Square.

The subway plans were also revised, and the station would become an express stop, integrated with the foundations of the Times Tower, which was finished in October. The tower was modeled on Giotto's famous Campanile in Florence, rising twenty-two stories above street level (375 feet) and driving 55 feet into bedrock. The press room would be under the subway station, which allowed Ochs to move bundles of newspapers directly to subway cars. Before the end of 1904, Ochs had jammed eleven new Mergenthaler Linotype machines into that subterranean press room and moved another twenty-seven machines from the old building at 451 Park Row.

That spring of 1904, before all of that was done, Ochs left for a family vacation in Europe. Coming down the North River on the liner *Deutschland*, he moved to the rail and gazed at Manhattan island. Later, he wrote to his mother:

> The new building loomed up in all its beautiful and grand proportions, out of mid–New York, as we sailed away, and my heart swelled as I thought of association with its erection. Then it stood foremost and most conspicuous among the best buildings in the Metropolis of the World—and I

really grew sentimental. It is a beauty, and even though the $2,500,000 that went into it cost some anxieties, it is there and it will be a monument to one man's daring.

Ochs chose to officially open the new tower on New Year's Eve. Many years later, in his centennial history of the newspaper, the great *Times* reporter Meyer Berger wrote an account of that first midnight hour in the Metropolis of the World:

> On New Year's Eve in 1904, Times Square was crowded with hundreds of thousands of horn-blasting, bell-ringing celebrants, some to witness a brilliant fireworks display touched off in the Tower. Midtown skies reverberated with the thunderous bursting of flights of bombs. Skyrockets and flares streaked against the midnight sky in the first Times Square New Year's Eve show, centered around the Tower. These assemblages became traditional, with Times electricians controlling incandescent figures that spelled out the dying year, and spelled in the new. The signal for the old year's passing was a massive illuminated globe that slid down the Tower pole while the crowds far below on the sidewalk cut loose with ear-splitting din. A final burst of fireworks wrote "1905" in flame against the heavens, and the throngs screamed and shouted themselves hoarse. It was one of the greatest promotion projects of the age. The idea was Ochs'. He knew the value of such advertising.

With that first crowd of more than two hundred thousand, the New Year's Eve tradition had begun, and it would grow, continuing all the way to now. The crowds did not always wait for New Year's Eve to make Times Square their public plaza. At the end of World War II, on V-J Day, August 14, 1945, more than two million people jammed the square in an atmosphere of impending joy and relief. At 7:03, the electronic "zipper" on the Times Tower flashed the words all awaited: OFFICIAL TRUMAN ANNOUNCES JAPANESE SURRENDER. Delirium erupted. The roar of the crowd could be heard for miles.

I remember the sheer joy on my own street in Brooklyn, where so many young men had been among the nine hundred thousand New Yorkers who helped fight the war. Some had been among the sixteen thousand who had been killed. On my street, people hugged and kissed too, and some of them wept.

By 1945, the *Times* was long gone from the Times Tower, which proved to be too small and clumsy for publishing one of the country's greatest newspapers (the building was sold in 1965). The *Times* opened larger quarters down the block on West Forty-third Street, where, as I write, it remains. But the early visions of a glittering, glamorous Times Square had all vanished by the time I started going there as a boy.

In the decade after 1904, there were moments of extravagant glamour in and around Times Square. Rich young men showed up after the theater each night in the grand restaurants with members of the ensemble called the Floradora Girls and the later stars of Florenz Ziegfeld's Follies. Those lobster palaces were in the basements, so that all could make grand entrances down gleaming staircases. The rich mixed casually with the demimonde, their activities described by visiting newspapermen, and it was all part of a great loosening of the bonds of the imported Victorianism that had ruled the hypocrisies of the Gilded Age. Diamonds, wads of cash, and a sense of the forbidden were everywhere in the lobster palaces and high on the dance floors of the roof gardens atop the new theaters. They did not last.

The first of a series of shocks came with the outbreak of World War I and the arrival in 1915 of Griffith's full-length movie *The Birth of a Nation*. The world seemed to pause, as if wondering about the propriety of plunging into the mindless fun of the Floradora Girls shows while millions were being slaughtered in Europe. To be sure, new theaters kept opening, and the producers mounted many shows, but the customers seemed wary. Business was not good.

And then other things happened. Most important of all, when the Armistice ended the war, Prohibition happened, depriving the lobster palaces and the roof gardens of their liquor revenues. They soon closed. Gangsters opened speakeasies on the side streets. Bootleggers became Gatsbyesque romantic figures. Many Forty-second Street theaters converted to vaudeville or to the new motion pictures. Bigger and grander movie palaces opened, draining away the customers from the legitimate houses (the Roxy had more than six thousand seats and cost $12 million in 1927). Live theater persisted west of Broadway in the forties, as it does today, but grunge had already started eating at Times Square itself. There were few pretensions to elegance as the Jazz Age took hold and the prewar subtleties of seduction gave way to a more blatant form of youthful rebellion. Few of the elites went to Times Square anymore. It had become a more populist place of assembly.

Then the Depression happened, and Forty-second Street began what seemed a terminal decline. Vaudeville gave way to raw forms of burlesque. Drifters started showing up from other parts of the country, early versions of midnight cowboys. Mayor La Guardia closed the burlesque houses, but Forty-second Street replaced them with third-rate movies, and the place entered the stage that still lingered when I first saw the street. This was the time of the Pokerino game parlor and the Laffmovie and Hubert's Museum and Flea Circus, of dance halls and papaya stands. During World War II the street was flooded with sailors on shore leave from the ships docked on the North River. They did not often come to see a play by Eugene O'Neill.

By the mid-1960s, heroin was everywhere on Forty-second Street, and the owners of legitimate theaters lived in fear of the spreading contamination. After every earlier shock, nostalgia rose among those who remembered the good times. Now even nostalgia was no consolation. For most people, the only emotion that rose within them was disgust.

By 1990, most sane people had given up on Forty-second Street, the street now called the Deuce. It had evolved into that most dreadful sort of human invention: a metaphor. This single street (they said) stood for the future of New York, perhaps the future of all American cities. Up and down the street, ugliness prevailed. Porno shops, peep shows, and kung fu movies provided the angular light. In the shadows were the peddlers of heroin and crack, the rapists of runaways, the transvestites who looked like Diana Ross or Carol Channing on steroids and carried razors in their hair. After 1985, AIDS was part of the deal, spreading as all plagues do, secretly, silently. And lunacy was there too. In the 1970s, many crazy people were released from New York institutions, a decision that combined the need for the state to save money with the idealistic belief that the deranged would feel "normal" if they could live with other people. All they had to do was take their medicine. They didn't take their medicine. Many joined the legions of the homeless. And inevitably some wandered to the Deuce, and you would see one of them, wide-eyed and jittery, explaining that he was the lost brother of Ronald Reagan; and another hefting a tree limb, bouncing up and down, growling in a language of his own invention; and a third simply howling at the moon. Such men (there were few women) were dangerous but not truly menacing.

The menacing people hung out in the subway station at Forty-second Street and Eighth Avenue. They smoked reefer in attitudes of surly defiance. Or rose to the street in groups of ten or twelve, slamming older people on their way along the Deuce or grabbing at wallets or purses. You could see them in open daylight or at the midnight hour, moving in packs along the sidewalks, hard cases from gangs such as the Savage Skulls, their ranks swollen by a few crack-hungry freelancers. They forced middle-aged people into the gutters. Those heading for the Port

Authority Bus Terminal to grab buses for suburban New Jersey often arrived in a state of shuddering fear. The young men laughed. Most of them were young men who had never been children.

All were part of the larger story of the unraveling city. In the late 1960s, cynical landlords began burning down their aging tenement buildings in the South Bronx and in Brooklyn, paying off underage arsonists, then taking the insurance money into retirement in Florida. In Manhattan, the old seedy buildings called SROs (for single-room occupancy) were steadily converted by their owners into more lucrative apartments, and thousands of men (and some women) were forced into the streets. Another phenomenon was under way: the mass abandonment of women and children. The women were often badly educated, struggling with drugs or alcohol. The children all wore baffled faces and spoke very little, as stunned by life as any child in the Five Points in the 1850s. The fathers of those children were not there. They were in prison, or living with someone else, or, as the women would say, "in the wind."

By the 1970s, even before the Fiscal Crisis, menace was becoming more general. There were several welfare hotels near Herald Square, and children of ten and eleven formed packs, attacking the shoppers from Macy's and Gimbel's like schools of piranha fish. The newspapers called them "feral youths." Many people stopped coming to Herald Square. On the subways, where similar groups went "shopping" (as they called it), women no longer carried shopping bags that advertised the names of the stores. The kids often raided fruit and vegetable stores, and I once saw a Korean man chasing some of these kids with a machete down Eighth Avenue. In the summertime, there were very few outdoor restaurant tables anymore. There were nighttime concerts in Central Park, but many New Yorkers were afraid to attend. At a few concerts, dozens of people were mauled by the feral young gangs.

Toward the end of the 1970s, every New Yorker, male and female, white, black, and Latino, had learned to live with fear. The number of subway riders dropped. Every apartment door seemed to have three locks, including a steel bar that was jammed into a slot in the floor. Every few months, there would be news of a family burned to death in a tenement flat where the windows too were barred and nobody had a key. Movie videos were developed, and the couch potato was born: staying at home to watch a movie while eating take-out food. On Forty-second Street in the afternoons, the sidewalks were often a mash of pizza crusts, orange peels, cigarette butts, scattering newspapers, and the anonymous debris of the long night's journey into day. The marquees of the grind houses along the Deuce advertised films about emotionless sex or raw fear or both. And as time passed, a visitor heard something else in the aural compost of the street: the crunching sound of crack vials.

On Herald Square, Gimbel's closed forever. The 1930s Broadway stories of Damon Runyon now seemed like fairy tales, loaded with nostalgia. The welfare rolls would rise beyond a million, with hundreds of thousands of children now alive in the city who had never known anyone who worked. Several welfare hotels were opened on the Deuce itself. Junkie parents careened through their filthy hallways, with their children careening away from them. Some children made it on their own to the street, where sexual predators awaited them. A pedophile marketplace grew bolder, with sinister men waiting at the bus terminal for runaways, and customers vanishing into secret rooms before driving home to the suburbs. During one police crackdown in the early 1990s, some ten thousand underage human beings were rescued from this vile and terrifying underworld.

Most of the victims were black or Latino. They grew up in a world where each night they could walk to Fortieth Street and watch pimps batter their female charges. They grew up in a world of plague, where the combination of drugs, guns, illiteracy, casual violence, and the rise of AIDS was creating a nihilistic hell never imagined by Dante Alighieri. There were people who tried to help, of course, men and women of selfless compassion. They were outraged that this was happening in the richest city on the planet. Some were as utopian as those who had gone among the poor of the Five Points. Others were more practical, believing, like George Templeton Strong, that if they could save one child, they would begin the much more difficult process of saving all children. Some children were saved. Some parents were saved. But not enough.

It was no accident that many of those rootless children became adolescents with slivers of ice in their hearts. They embraced the new urban culture of cold-eyed violence. They insisted on sex without love and demanded respect without earning it. They all wanted guns and found them as easy to buy as drugs. They bought knives too, in the shops of Times Square. They donned figurative masks intended to create fear: dead eyes, blank expressions, tight lips. They adopted a style in clothes that emphasized their roots in urban poverty: unlaced heavy boots, oversize baggy jeans, baseball caps worn backward in what some academics described as a ghetto version of a postmodern statement. They were never going to work in offices. Their sound track was the music of hip-hop. Reform school or jail became their prep schools. There they learned even more about creating fear.

And the creation of fear was their only success. The Deuce became one of their theaters. They scared away African Americans and foreign tourists and New Yorkers who once sought laughter or diversion in Times Square. Even priests and cops walked with wary steps. The Deuce was the place in which the hard kids lived most fully during that brief time between a lost childhood and the penitentiary. The prophets of social doom gazed at the Deuce and its feral youngsters, and convinced themselves that nothing at all could be done. This was not the road to perdition; it was perdition itself.

There had been calls for reform for a long time, of course, starting in the 1960s, when the liberal Republican John V. Lindsay was mayor. Meetings were called, committees formed, studies made, plans drawn up. The newspapers published editorials whose tone ranged from hope to rage. But one of the last of the city's calamities struck in 1975: the Fiscal Crisis. New York was suddenly faced with certain hard realities. After decades of liberal social programs that always expanded and never contracted, the city could not pay its bills. There certainly would be no public money for a major rehabilitation of Forty-second Street, of Times Square. After all, they represented only one combined fragment of an immense city. In fact, the Fiscal Crisis led to cutbacks in some services that were absolutely necessary. As just one example, thousands of policemen were laid off, which pleased the hard-core criminals and encouraged some of the amateurs. Crime in the city quickly soared, to nobody's surprise. Everybody agreed that Forty-second Street was worse than it had ever been. Even reformers seemed to lose heart. I remember asking one policeman on the Deuce what he would do about the terrible street.

"Brick it up," he said.

Very few New Yorkers expected a happy ending to the squalid saga of Forty-second Street, and yet a reasonably happy ending was what we got. Sometimes miracles do happen. In the 1990s, through a combination of planning, will, intelligent politics, and sheer luck, the Deuce was reclaimed. The first moves came on the frontiers of the street. The city first cleaned up Bryant Park, on the eastern side of Sixth Avenue, turning it into a sylvan gem to be used by ordinary citizens instead of pushers and junkies, the scene of concerts and fashion shows and simple afternoons on benches. Between Ninth and Tenth avenues, a giant housing development called Manhattan Plaza was opened in 1977, and after failing as luxury housing, became a subsidized home for writers, artists, musicians, and actors, along with older citizens. That helped stabilize the western end of the terrible Deuce. Across the street from Manhattan Plaza, seven theaters were soon combined into what was called Theater Row, bringing the concept of Off-Off-Broadway to a haven only a few blocks from the more conventional theaters. The Broadway theaters had for too many years been the venues for shows packed with tourists and exhausted salesmen and their clients while theater itself happened elsewhere (there were, of course, exceptions to this generalization). Now, suddenly, the Broadway of Shubert Alley was within walking distance of Off-Off-Broadway. Tentatively at first, and then with growing confidence, another kind of life began to rise around the new theaters and Manhattan Plaza: restaurants, grocery stores, dry cleaners.

At the same time, a new cast was appearing in Times Square, made up of inspired citizens, real estate people, members of foundations, hardworking bureaucrats, drafters of zoning laws, and architects. Most were not well-known to the public but were encouraged by the politicians in their primary goal: to save Times Square, starting with Forty-second Street. Their efforts over two decades began to work, with increasing New York–style velocity. They thought the area could be saved without being bricked up or converted into a faceless new version of Rockefeller Center. They insisted that the loose, populist character of Times Square could actually survive progress.

At first, the changes were small, incremental. The Port Authority Bus Terminal was expanded and then cleaned up by its own police officers, who forced the regiments of vagrants off the premises. Special plainclothes cops watched for runaways, saving them from the predators, gently persuading them to go home. Times Square was becoming the visual symbol of changes that were taking place across the entire city.

In his last year, Mayor David Dinkins added five thousand new police officers to the force. His successor, Rudolph Giuliani, and his police commissioner, William Bratton, showed how to use them. They employed computers in a system called COMSTAT and insisted on accountability from their commanders. That tale has been well told in a thousand newspaper and magazine articles, and though Giuliani gave himself a variety of unnecessary problems through his brusque personal style, the new system began to work. Crime rates plunged.

Giuliani had some good luck too. Wall Street and the NASDAQ began to boom, making money available for projects that were impossible during the austere times. The crack fad slowly ended, as ghetto kids backed away from the drug. They had seen what it did to their older brothers and sisters and their parents. Within the poorer communities, many people started calling for a renewed sense of personal responsibility, most clearly voiced at the Million Man March in Washington in October 1995. Speaker after speaker said that black men must take care of their children and guide them to a fully human future, and when the march was over and everybody went home on the buses and trains and in crowded automobiles, that process, steady and slow, actually began to take place. Meanwhile, national welfare reform was enforced locally, and the welfare rolls would fall during Giuliani's term by more than a half million. At the same time, the largest immigration wave in a century was under way, with more than a million people from China, the Dominican Republic, Russia, Korea, and Mexico arriving in the city, bringing a new version of the work ethic in their baggage. The traditional New York alloy was being revived.

Then strange things began to happen, most obviously on the Deuce. The grind houses slowly closed, one or two at a time. The welfare hotels closed too, along with the porno shops. The crowds of young hard guys began to thin. The Disney people announced grand plans for the decayed old New Amsterdam Theater, built in 1903, once the home of the Ziegfeld Follies. They began to restore it in 1994 with money from the city (and did the work with extraordinary care). The Disney name attracted other investors. Soon, the newspapers were running many stories of things to come. On another level, change could be witnessed in glimpses. For the first time in many years, I saw women in the subways carrying Macy's bags. Others even risked what they had not risked for two decades: a subway nap.

One summer night in Giuliani's second year, I walked to a building on Twenty-second Street and Broadway where my wife had a small office. We were going to dinner together, and I told her I'd wait for her downstairs, outside the building. The front garden was surrounded by a low polished brick wall. I sat on the wall and watched people go by the way I had when I was a young man on the stoop on East Ninth Street. A white-haired man and his heavy-set wife passed, murmuring intimately in the warm downtown air. The restaurant across the street had four small sidewalk tables, lit by hurricane lamps, each chair full. A young woman ran past me and leaped for her young man and they hugged each other. Three young black men ambled by in the other direction, dressed in the summer version of the gang-banger uniform. They were talking about the following month, when they would enter the City University. A man in his sixties came out and sat ten feet away on the brick wall beside a garden light, nodded at me, and began to read a newspaper. A Latino man passed with a transistor radio in his hand. He was tuned to the Mets game. And I thought: It's over.

Then my wife came out of the building and I hugged her in that little piece of my city and hers, and all she wanted to know was why I had tears in my eyes.

Chapter Eleven

ENVOI

THE CLICHÉ IS true. Nothing lasts forever. As noted, there is almost nothing physical left of the Dutch town. Not much has survived from 117 years of the British colony except the language and the names of places and the paths of certain streets. And yet the Dutch and the British would recognize the place, as would the Knickerbockers, who were descended from their inevitable merger. It might take a few astonished weeks as they adjusted to the height of buildings and the advances of technology. But those original Dutchmen, and the English who accepted and then refined their hardheaded wisdom, would recognize the enduring presence of certain templates. The original settlers knew that the only way human beings could live together here was by practicing tolerance. Sometimes it was a reluctant tolerance. Sometimes it was tolerance combined with the wink and shrug of hypocrisy. But in the end, it was a tolerance that insisted on one fundamental truth: There are people here who are not like us, and we must accept them in order to live.

Those original New Yorkers must have known, too, that a living city is made through a process of retreat and advance, decay and revival, corruption and reform. That was one of the lessons of European history, going all the way back to the Greeks and Romans. The details have always differed, but similar cycles, no matter what the details, have been part of the history of New York. As I write, we are living in a wonderful period in the city's life, in spite of, and possibly because of, the worst calamity in our long history. One result of that cyclical history, of course, is that the city and its people are full of contradictions. We moan about the decay of Times Square and Forty-second Street, and then when they are brought back to life, too many of us bemoan something called "Disneyfication." We pretend to be tough and can weep at the news of a child killed in an accident. We sometimes have a rude way with strangers but go out of our way to help those strangers find their way. We like to brag that we are generous people, but we vigorously protest any new tax that might help the weak. No surprise: Eventually, begrudgingly, we pay, which is why New York is the most heavily taxed city in the United States. This is the city, after all, that made Walt Whitman celebrate each noisy, crowded day, and sing his chants democratic. But it is also the city from which Whitman fled, to live the last eighteen years of his life in New Jersey. In his poetry, Whitman made a virtue of his contradictions. In our lives, so do many of us. New Yorkers often bitch and moan about the impossibility of a decent life in such a place. Some even leave. Almost all of them return. I like to believe that they can't live without contradiction.

Like so many New Yorkers, I've tried to live the time of my life as fully as possible. But there has simply never been enough time to know all that I wanted to know. One example in my Manhattan is Harlem. I'm a resident of Downtown, and Harlem, in its way, defined Uptown, but I still felt possessive about it, although I knew it only in glimpses. When I was young, I would go there to listen to musicians, sitting some evenings in Small's Paradise on 135th Street and Seventh Avenue or in the boisterous rows of the Apollo Theater. In the summer of my return from the navy, I saw Duke Ellington standing with a friend outside Frank's Restaurant. He was the only true American aristocrat I've ever seen, but I was still too timid to say hello and give him my gratitude.

In the fall of 1960, I was sent by the city desk to the Hotel Theresa on 125th Street to cover the action that was swirling around the presence of Fidel Castro. He had come to New York for a meeting of the United Nations General Assembly, checked in with his people at a hotel in Murray Hill, hated it, and left for Harlem. There he would hold separate meetings with Nikita Khrushchev of the Soviet Union and Egypt's president Nasser. But affairs of state were only part of the story. Outside the Theresa, crowds gathered for a glimpse of young Castro. Some of them cheered his arrivals and departures. But there were anti-Castro Cuban exiles on the street too, and some black

Americans who agreed with their congressman Adam
Clayton Powell that Castro was simply using Harlem as a
stage set for his own purposes.

Among the anti-Castro Cubans was a man who was an
eerie double for Fidel. He was tall, had the Fidel-style
beard, wore the horn-rimmed glasses that Fidel then favored, held a huge (unlit) cigar, and was dressed in fa-
tigues. The photographers loved him, and a UPI
cameraman named Andy Lopez, who had covered Fidel's
triumph in Cuba, was among them. Somehow, in spite of
security, the photographers rented a room on a middle
floor of the Theresa. They gave it to Fidel's double. Then,
as Fidel groupies appeared among the crowds in front of
the Theresa, the photographers whispered to them about
the chance to meet their hero in private. Up they would
go. To this day there must be women who are certain they
once slept with the bold hero of the Sierra Maestra, when
he and they were young.

Across the years, I came to know Harlem in other ways.
I visited such places as the Schomburg Center for
Research in Black Culture on 125th Street, the Abyssinian
Baptist Church, and the Frederick Douglass Center,
where young writers held workshops. I saw Malcolm X
make a speech to a crowd of almost two thousand people,
his language vivid, his volcanic anger simmering beneath
almost every word. Alas, I covered too many murders that
didn't get into the newspaper, because they took place at
the wrong addresses. I covered a few fires, and one riot
that did not approach in horror the eruptions in Watts,
Detroit, and Newark. I listened to black nationalists on
street corners and got accustomed to being called a "blue-

eyed devil." I sat and talked to the families of black American soldiers who had gone off to Vietnam and came back in body bags, forever young.

Many Harlemites were welcoming to me, speaking about the things they feared. They were the same things all New Yorkers feared: drugs, guns, the feral young. They were often angry with the police, for what they did (with clubs or guns) or what they didn't do (cracking down on drug dealers). Like all New Yorkers, the Harlemites often contradicted themselves. But I admired their intelligence, their courage, and their clear-eyed skepticism. Yes, there was still too much injustice if you were a person of color. But they were New Yorkers. The skepticism seldom collapsed into empty cynicism. They believed that life in Harlem would get better because life in New York would get better. "This is my town, man," one Harlemite said to me during some of the worst of the crackhead years. "I ain't going anywhere. We gonna beat these bastards."

By the time of Giuliani, the change was already under way. Many blacks were annoyed with Giuliani, and a few infuriated, but he and his police commissioners were saving black lives. Black-on-black crime declined, and most violent crime in New York had been committed, sadly, by blacks against blacks. More and more young African Americans were graduating from college and, unlike the educated generation immediately before them, they were staying put in New York. In Harlem, they began reclaiming many of the broken-down brownstones, returning them to life. Other New Yorkers noticed. For the first time in eighty years, whites were competing with blacks for the same Harlem houses, and certain blocks were being inte-

grated. Some unreconstructed sixties-era black nationalists objected to the arrival of the whites, but their rhetoric
sounded racist or anachronistic or both. In the years of the
boom, most Harlemites were too busy working to join any
campaign against the gradual change. Many African
Americans had died over the years in the name of integra-
tion. How could it now be resisted?

Around the same time that Disney and others were
transforming Forty-second Street, similar changes were
under way on 125th Street. The former basketball star
Magic Johnson opened a thirteen-screen multiplex for
first-run movies. Video stores opened, and record stores,
and a Ben & Jerry's ice cream place, along with clothing
stores and restaurants. Yes, this was about being middle
class, but Harlemites had little sympathy for the romance
of poverty. They knew too well what it was. For Harlem
near the end of the twentieth century, as for so many other
parts of New York, the plague years seemed to have
ended.

But I never got to know Harlem the way I know other
parts of the island's geography. Again, the main reason
was simple: I never paid rent there. I came as a visitor and
then went home to some other place. I've read the histo-
ries° of Harlem and the many fine novels, but they don't
create the knowledge that comes from being part of the
dailiness of a place. You have to live in a place to absorb

°For a way into this rich history see the classic *Black Manhattan* by James
Weldon Johnson and *Harlem: The Making of a Ghetto; Negro New York, 1890–1930*
by Gilbert Osofsky. Or start with the Harlem chapter in *New York City* by Eric
Homberger. And the novels of Ralph Ellison and Albert Murray are indispensable.

its truest rhythms, to read its whispered scripts, and to know the names of dozens of people and not a mere three or four. I've known Harlem the way I know, say, Paris, or even the Upper East Side. The surface is there for me, and the spirit of the place. But now there isn't enough time left in my life for me to find that other, deeper Harlem. On some nights, in the loft I share with my wife downtown, I apologize to myself.

As a New Yorker, I ache for certain places and times and people. But the recurrence of that ache is obvious proof that they were alive and so was I. They existed in the world, and I was there to see them. I'm among the most fortunate of men. Much of my life was spent in a ringside seat at the spectacle of history. But being a newspaperman wasn't the only factor in my education. I saw my city exuberant with life after 1945 and was a boy in a place where everything seemed possible and where I was never alone. I was part of this larger thing too, this city, this living alloy that was Irish and Jewish and Italian and African, this New York.

How full of marvels was the world! One of the marvels is that I got to see Roy Campanella coming to the plate, a bat in hand and men on base. I saw Jack Roosevelt Robinson rounding third, heading for home. I saw Willie Mays. And I saw them in the company of thousands of roaring human beings, glad people in a glad place in a glad time, all of them members of my tribe, the New York tribe. Nobody can ever tell me that such moments were trivial, mere examples of mindless entertainment and diversion, part of the bread and circuses devised by those who rule us. Such moments were possible only among people who ruled themselves.

And what gifts were granted to us in our rude democracy. Some were indeed trivial, although made more important by loss. There are New Yorkers in their thirties who never once read W. C. Heinz in the *Sun*, or Red Smith and Jimmy Breslin in the *Herald-Tribune*, or Dan Parker in the *Daily Mirror*, or Frank Graham in the *Journal-American*. They never ate the ice-cream cone called a Mello Roll either, or candies called Houtons, Kits, Sky Bars, or B-B Bats. They never played stickball. They never held a spaldeen in their hand on a Saturday morning in a street empty of cars and full of hours. They don't know what game was played in the Polo Grounds. They never saw El Morocco or the Copa, the Latin Quarter or the Chateau Madrid, with the gangsters at the rear tables, all wearing pinkie rings, and the Wall Street big shots down front, and the tall women in feathers and frills on stage, with the highest cheekbones and creamiest skin in the universe. They never saw the Palladium.

The young still have their cherished moments too, of course, glamorous nights and stars they will remember when they are old. But I don't make much of an effort to understand Britney Spears. Forgive me, but I saw Billie Holiday. Up on the stage at Carnegie Hall one final time in the 1950s, her voice a ruin, singing those songs written by Jews and Irishmen and transformed by Lady Day into autobiography. Her autobiography, and mine too. I listened to her records for hours on end, and the blues entered me to stay for life, that music of the midnight city that we shared. She was at once one of the gifts my city gave me and part of my tribe.

The gifts were endless. Where else could you find so many free schools and libraries, those places where you could invent your own life? They were free because the children of the poor Irish and the poor Jews never forgot the time when all such doors were closed. The poor of New York made the rich better. They voted for politicians who, in spite of their own weaknesses, made the city stronger, more prosperous, more just. The politicians were too often corrupt, but in the end the poor got water, the poor got hospitals, the poor got sanitation, the poor got schools and libraries. The poor of the nineteenth century physically built the city in which all of us now live. They dug the subways and laid the tracks. They paved the streets and erected the bridges and the skyscrapers. Too many of them died while doing those jobs. That's why so many of them had a certain amount of contempt for those whose antics filled too many inches in the newspapers. After all, poor silly Mrs. Astor, with all her fancy dress balls, had never put one brick upon another. When she died, nothing was left behind except her name and the story of her many follies.

There was a sense among those working people, almost from the beginning, that you would do all right in New York if only you followed the rules. Where I came from, the rules were relatively simple. Work. Put food on the table. Always pay your debts. Never cross a picket line. Don't look for trouble, because in New York you can always find it. But don't back off either. Make certain that the old and the weak are never in danger. Vote the straight ticket.

For a long time, these were the rules all over the city. We got into our deepest trouble in the 1960s, when some of these rules were discarded. I'm part of the New York generation that saw the city glitter and then slowly begin to dim and then to fall into a sustained version of purgatory. If we had died in 1990, we'd have ended our days in a city plagued by drugs, guns, and despair. Somehow our luck held. We have lived long enough to see the city gather its will and energy and rise again, its people playing by the old rules. And every day, we see the thrilling results, sometimes in subtle changes. In my time in New York, I saw shopping-bag ladies arrive, their rusting supermarket carts lumpy with debris wrapped in plastic bags. They slept in doorways, they babbled on corners, they multiplied and were everywhere, and then, abruptly, they were gone. The reason was simple: Those women were weak and abandoned and forlorn, and members of the New York tribe came to their rescue.

I never see streetwalkers anymore either, not even down by the meat market below Fourteenth Street, where they once gathered in cartoony profusion. Each evening at dusk, they jangled their immense earrings and their chains and offered themselves for a price to cruising suburbanites. The hookers were almost all junkies, but they could laugh at the New Jersey men in their cars with the blue license plates, calling them "blue bozos." There were few laughs on their street corners as they plied their joyless trade. Most cops and judges shrugged at their presence in years when the city was rife with more savage crimes. It seemed streetwalkers would be among us forever, a part of New York since the early nineteenth century. And then, as the twentieth century turned into the twenty-first, the streetwalkers vanished.

I'm not sure where they went. Some surely went to the graveyard. But I hope the living found the secret place where they'd be free of smack and pimps and disease. As I write, the true Manhattan streetwalkers now are cigarette smokers, banished by law from restaurants and bars and dancing places, gathered in shivering knots on nights when the temperature is in the teens. Their voices carom against the surrounding buildings, waking families from exhausted sleep. They make up a new floating population of noisy narcissists in a time when the city fathers insist that even drunks must be healthy. One thing is certain: Nobody in power seems to remember the lessons of Prohibition.

Meanwhile, the island is vivid with energy. In that sense, Times Square has once again become our most perfect symbol: noisy, plural, brash, vulgar, shifting, slightly dangerous. We have other symbols. The Statue of Liberty. The Empire State Building. The Chrysler. But all are static. All are remote from the people themselves, too often these days closed to visitors by security guards. Even in the age of terror, Times Square, like the city itself, is open to all.

That openness is essential to living here. It is based on choice. You can choose to look at the Vermeers in the Frick or walk around Chinatown. If you live downtown, uptown is also yours, a subway ride away. So are all the places in this book and more. The wanderer in Manhattan must go forth with a certain innocence, because New York is best seen with innocent eyes. It doesn't matter if you are young or old. Reading our rich history makes the experience more layered, but it is not a substitute for walking the streets themselves. For old-timer or newcomer, it is essential to absorb the city as it is now in order to shape your own nostalgias.

That's why I always urge the newcomer to surrender to the city's magic. Forget the irritations and the occasional rudeness; they bother many New Yorkers too. Instead, go down to the North River and the benches that run along the west side of Battery Park City. Watch the tides or the blocks of ice in winter; they have existed since the time when the island was empty of man. Gaze at the boats. Look across the water at the Statue of Liberty or Ellis Island, the places to which so many of the New York tribe came in order to truly live. Learn the tale of our tribe, because it's your tribe too, no matter where you were born. Listen to its music and its legends. Gaze at its ruins and monuments. Walk its sidewalks and run fingers upon the stone and bricks and steel of our right-angled streets. Breathe the air of the river breeze.

And look up: There are falcons in our sky again, safe at last from the perils of DDT, returned to full life after a long hard time. They can be seen moving through the upper stories of the tall downtown towers, those spires of the magic city, where they also build their nests and teach their children. They fly over the places where the Dutch once lived and the British watched plays in powdered wigs and Africans insisted upon their humanity on streets where they were owned by others. On explorations uptown, the falcons can see the spires and the bridges and the endless roll of rooftops moving north and west and east. Their movements might at first seem aimless. But be patient. Near the end of day, with the sun heading for New Jersey and the sky suddenly mauve, you can see the falcons wheeling and turning, heading downtown, heading for home.

SUGGESTED READING

THIS ESSAY IS based on memory, reporting, and reading. Much reading, over decades. My own library contains more than five hundred books of New York City history, along with memoirs, novels, and works of journalism set in New York. I own many books of New York photographs, along with extensive files of newspaper and magazine clippings. There were other books too, over the years, many of them now lost. They have contributed in some way to this essay, but it would be impossible to list them all.

Certainly, every student of New York must consult several key books: *The Epic of New York City* by Edward Robb Ellis, *Gotham* by Edwin G. Burrows and Mike Wallace, *The Encyclopedia of New York City* edited by Kenneth T. Jackson, *The New York Chronology* by James Trager, *The Iconography of Manhattan Island* by I. N. Phelps Stokes. These, along with the diaries of George Templeton Strong and Philip Hone, are indispensable. All can be found in bookshops or libraries.

But there is a growing list of other books on New York City; many of them were of great help in writing this volume. Each has something new or original to add to our understanding of the city and its people. All provoke the two responses every writer longs for: "I didn't know *that,*" and "I never *thought* of it that way." I am grateful to all of the authors, living or dead. They helped me see my native place.

Here is a partial list:

Adler, Jacob. *A Life on the Stage.* Translated by Lulla Rosenfeld. New York: Applause, 2001.

Alpert, Hollis, and Museum of the City of New York. *Broadway! 125 Years of Musical Theater.* New York: Arcade Books, 1991.

Amory, Cleveland. *Who Killed Society?* New York: Harper, 1960.

Anbinder, Tyler. *Five Points: The 19th-Century New York City Neighborhood That Invented Tap Dance, Stole Elections, and Became the World's Most Notorious Slum.* New York: Free Press, 2001.

Asbury, Herbert. *The Gangs of New York.* New York and London: A. A. Knopf, 1928.

Auchincloss, Louis. *Edith Wharton: A Woman in Her Time.* New York: Viking, 1971. In addition to his many superb novels, short stories, and essays set in New York City.

Augustyn, Robert T., and Paul E. Cohen. *Manhattan in Maps, 1527–1995.* New York: Rizzoli International Publications, 1997.

Bascomb, Neal. *Higher: A Historic Race to the Sky and the Making of a City.* New York: Doubleday, 2003.

Bender, Thomas. *The Unfinished City: New York and the Metropolitan Idea.* New York: New Press, 2002.

Berger, Meyer. *The Story of the New York Times: 1851–1951.* New York: Simon & Schuster, 1951.

Bianco, Anthony. *Ghosts of 42nd Street: A History of America's Most Infamous Block.* New York: William Morrow, 2004.

Birmingham, Stephen. *Our Crowd.* New York: Harper & Row, 1967.

———. *The Grandees: America's Sephardic Elite.* Harper & Row, 1971.

Bliven, Bruce. *Under the Guns: New York, 1775–1776.* New York: Harper & Row, 1972.

Breines, Paul. *Tough Jews: Political Fantasies and the Moral Dilemma of America Jewry.* New York: Basic Books, 1990.

Cahan, Abraham. *The Rise of David Levinsky.* New York: Harper & Brothers, 1917; Penguin, 1993.

Carlson, Oliver. *The Man Who Made News: James Gordon Bennett.* New York: Duell, Sloan and Pearce, 1942.

Chapman, John. *Tell It to Sweeney: The Informal History of the New York Daily News.* Westport, CT: Greenwood Press, 1977, 1961.

Churchill, Allen. *Park Row.* New York: Rinehart, 1958.

Cohen, Patricia Cline. *The Murder of Helen Jewett: The Life and Death of a Prostitute in Nineteenth-Century New York.* New York: Knopf, 1998.

Diner, Hasia R. *Lower East Side Memories: A Jewish Place in America.* Princeton, NJ: Princeton University Press, 2000.

Diner, Hasia R., Jeffrey Shandler, Beth S. Wenger, eds. *Remembering the Lower East Side.* Bloomington: Indiana University Press, 2000.

Dunlap, David W. *On Broadway: A Journey Uptown Over Time.* New York: Rizzoli, 1990.

Finson, Jon W. *The Voices That Are Gone: Themes in Nineteenth-Century American Popular Song.* New York: Oxford University Press, 1994.

Fitzgerald, F. Scott. *The Crack-up.* Edited by Edmund Wilson. New York: New Directions, 1993.

Folpe, Emily Kies. *It Happened on Washington Square.* Baltimore: Johns Hopkins University Press, 2002.

Fox, Dixon Ryan. *The Decline of Aristocracy in the Politics of New York: 1801–1840.* New York: Columbia, 1919; Harper and Row, 1965.

Fried, Albert. *The Rise and Fall of the Jewish Gangster in America.* Revised edition. New York: Columbia University Press, 1993.

Gilbert, Rodman. *The Battery.* Boston: Houghton Mifflin, 1936.

Gilfoyle, Timothy J. *City of Eros: New York City, Prostitution and the Commercialization of Sex, 1790–1920.* New York: W. W. Norton, 1992.

Goldberger, Paul. *The Skyscraper.* New York: A. A. Knopf, 1982.

Gordon, Michael A. *The Orange Riots: Irish Political Violence in New York City, 1870–1871.* Ithaca, NY: Cornell University Press, 1993.

Grace, Nancy. *New York: Songs of the City.* New York: Billboard Books, 2002.

Gray, Christopher. *New York Streetscapes: Tales of Manhattan's Significant Buildings and Landmarks.* New York: Harry N. Abrams, 2003.

Hale, William Harlan. *Horace Greeley: Voice of the People.* New York: Harper, 1950.

Harlow, Alvin F. *Old Bowery Days: The Chronicles of a Famous Street.* New York: Appleton, 1931.

Harris, Luther S. *Around Washington Square: An Illustrated History of Greenwich Village.* Baltimore: Johns Hopkins University Press, 2003.

Head, Joel Tyler. *The Great Riots of New York: 1712–1873.* Indianapolis: Bobbs-Merrill, 1970.

Henderson, Mary C. *The City & the Theatre: New York Playhouses from Bowling Green to Times Square.* Clifton, NJ: James T. White, 1973.

Homberger, Eric. *Mrs. Astor's New York: Money and Social Power in the Gilded Age.* New Haven: Yale University Press, 2002.

———. *New York City: A Cultural and Literary Companion.* Northampton, MA: Interlink Books, 2002.

Howe, Irving. *World of Our Fathers: The Journey of the East European Jews to America and the Life They Found and Made.* New York: Harcourt, Brace, Jovanovich, 1976.

James, Henry. *New York Revisited.* New York: Franklin Square, 1994. Also the novel *Washington Square* (New York: Vintage Books, the Library of America, 1990) and other essays and fictions available from Library of America.

Koeppel, Gerard T. *Water for Gotham: A History.* Princeton, NJ: Princeton University Press, 2000.

Landau, Sarah Bradford, and Carl W. Condit. *Rise of the New York Skyscraper: 1865–1913.* New Haven: Yale University Press, 1996.

Lockwood, Charles. *Manhattan Moves Uptown: An Illustrated History.* Boston: Houghton Mifflin, 1976.

Lopate, Phillip. *Waterfront: A Journey Around Manhattan.* New York: Crown, 2004.

Moody, Richard. *The Astor Place Riot.* Bloomington: Indiana University Press, 1958.

Morris, James McGrath. *The Rose Man of Sing Sing: A True Tale of Life, Murder, and Redemption in the Age of Yellow Journalism.* New York: Fordham University Press, 2003.

Morris, Jan. *Manhattan '45*. Baltimore: Johns Hopkins University Press, 1998.

Motley, Willard. *Knock on Any Door*. New York: Prentice Hall, 1947.

O'Connor, Richard. *Hell's Kitchen: The Roaring Days of New York's Wild West Side*. Philadelphia: Old Town, 1958, 1993.

Patterson, Jerry E. *Fifth Avenue: The Best Address*. New York: Rizzoli International Publications, 1998.

Pritchett, V. S. *New York Proclaimed*. New York: Harcourt, Brace and World, 1965.

Reed, Henry Hope. Photographs by Edmund V. Gillon Jr. *Beaux-Arts Architecture in New York: A Photographic Guide*. New York: Dover, 1988.

Revell, Keith D. *Building Gotham: Civic Culture and Public Policy in New York City, 1898–1938*. Baltimore: Johns Hopkins University Press, 2002.

Rosenberg, Charles E. *The Cholera Years: The United States in 1832, 1849, 1866*. Chicago: University of Chicago Press, 1962.

Sanders, Ronald. *The Downtown Jews: Portraits of an Immigrant Generation*. New York: Harper & Row, 1969.

Sante, Luc. *Low Life: Lures and Snares of Old New York*. New York: Farrar, Straus & Giroux, 1991.

Schoener, Allon. *Portal to America: The Lower East Side 1870–1925*. New York: Holt, Rinehart & Winston, 1967.

Shaw, Irwin. *Short Stories: Five Decades*. Chicago: University of Chicago Press, 2000.

Silver, Nathan. *Lost New York*. Expanded and updated edition. Boston: Houghton Mifflin, 1967, 2000.

Spann, Edward K. *The New Metropolis: New York City, 1840–1857*. New York: Columbia University Press, 1981.

Taylor, William R., ed. *Inventing Times Square: Commerce and Culture at the Crossroads of the World.* New York: Russell Sage Foundation, 1991; Baltimore: Johns Hopkins University Press, 1991.

Traub, James. *The Devil's Playground: A Century of Pleasure and Profit in Times Square.* New York: Random House, 2004

Turner, Hy B. *When Giants Ruled: The Story of Park Row, New York's Great Newspaper Street.* New York: Fordham University Press, 1999.

Wald, Lillian D. *The House on Henry Street.* New York: Holt, Rinehart & Winston, 1915; New York: Dover Publications, 1971.

Wertenbaker, Thomas Jefferson. *Father Knickerbocker Rebels: New York City During the Revolution.* New York: Cooper Square Publishers, 1969.

Wharton, Edith. *A Backward Glance: An Autobiography.* New York: Simon & Schuster, Touchstone, 1998. In addition to her many works of fiction, including *Old New York,* all available in Library of America editions.

White, E. B. *This Is New York.* New York: Harper & Bros., 1949; New York Bound edition, 1999, with an introduction by Roger Angell.

White, Samuel G., and Elizabeth White. *McKim, Mead & White: The Masterworks.* New York: Rizzoli International Publications, 2003.

Wilentz, Sean. *Chants Democratic: New York City & the Rise of the American Working Class, 1788–1850.* New York: Oxford University Press, 1984.

Wolfe, Gerard R. *New York, a Guide to the Metropolis: Walking Tours of Architecture and History.* New York: McGraw Hill, 1988.

READING GROUP GUIDE

Downtown

My Manhattan

by Pete Hamill

It All Started with
Bomba the Jungle Boy

**Pete Hamill talks with the *Birmingham News*
about some of the pleasures of reading**

What are you reading?

I'm currently reading *Between Two Rivers*, a superb novel by
Nicholas Rinaldi. Before that, it was Thomas Kelly's
Empire Rising, another first-rate novel. And before *that*, I
spent a month reveling in the new Edith Grossman translation of *Don Quixote*, the best novel ever written — and the
first.

Who are your favorite authors?

In no particular order: Gabriel García Márquez, Edith
Wharton, Cervantes, Edwidge Danticat, Stendhal, James
Joyce, William Kennedy, Chekhov, Elmore Leonard, the
great nineteenth-century Brazilian Machado de Assis,
Carl Hiaasen, William Trevor, Dickens (over and over

again), Carlos Fuentes, Faulkner, William Butler Yeats, Thomas Mann, Oscar Wilde, James T. Farrell, Philip Roth, Marcus Aurelius, Norman Mailer, Seamus Heaney, Robert Louis Stevenson, Graham Greene, my brother Denis, along with . . . I go on. Forgive me. For me, life will always be a case of so many writers, so little time.

Any types of books that are your favorites?

I like those books — fiction or nonfiction — that make me more human. Those that show me the hidden lives of strangers. Those that stir me to compassion and pity and joy. As I get older, I'm reading again those Books I Thought I'd Read When Young. The *Quixote*. Dante's *Inferno*. Dickens. Stendhal. Balzac. I read a new book and alternate with one of those classics, and even the classics feel like new books. That's why they are classics, I suppose. And they are almost all even better than I remembered them. There's nothing quite like reading a book for the second time, after having lived a life.

Any particular time of the day that you do your reading?

I like late afternoon, after the day's work is done. And I can't ever fall asleep without reading something. I try to read at least one poem a night, like a prayer.

Do you have a favorite book?

Not really, but I do try to read *Huckleberry Finn* once a year. Mr. Clemens created the highest American art, and Huck and Jim are his finest creations. Along with his wonderfully fluid use of the American language.

What's your first book memory?

The first book I ever read was *Bomba the Jungle Boy at the Giant Cataract*. The author was "Roy Rockwood," surely a house name for some third-rate publisher. I was ten. The book carried me off to the jungles of South America, crossing rivers, fighting wild animals, evading villains. I still have a copy. Years later, I heard from Louis Auchincloss that the Bomba books (it was a series) were his own favorites. He and I have lived very different lives, but we are joined forever by *Bomba the Jungle Boy*.

The complete text of this interview first appeared in the Book Chat column of the Birmingham News on December 26, 2004. Reprinted by permission.

QUESTIONS AND TOPICS
FOR DISCUSSION

1. Having read Pete Hamill's *Downtown,* what would you say are your favorite impressions of New York? What did the city represent to you before you read this book? Has your perspective changed?

2. Hamill highlights a number of key figures in New York's history — some of them well known, others unsung heroes behind the scenes. What qualities does the author most admire about these heroes and heroines? Among them, who stands out for you? How do they reflect the changing tides of New York?

3. What do you think the initial settlers had in mind for New York City? How might they view present-day New York?

4. Hamill occasionally uses the term *alloy* to describe certain features of New York City. What do you think the author is trying to convey with this term?

5. Describe your own "downtown." What do you like best about it? What kind of history can be gleaned from the buildings, the people, and the streets?

6. Early on Hamill writes, "This book is littered with casualties of time and greed and that vague reality called progress" (page 17). Discuss examples of greed and progress presented in the book. In the growth of a city, is one possible without the other?

7. The author draws a distinction between nostalgia and sentimentality, calling New York "the capital of nostalgia." What does he mean by this comparison? Do you agree with his treatment of the two terms?

8. Oz is one of the first images Hamill associates with New York City. Is the author's analogy apt? Explain your answer.

9. Hamill notes that "In New York, the present becomes the past more rapidly than in any other world city" (page 50). He also says, "There was no point in permanently bemoaning change. This was New York. Loss was part of the deal" (page 17). How does Hamill's own experience of New York bear out these two statements?

10. According to Pete Hamill, even native New Yorkers overlook some of the best elements of the city. What details does he feel many people miss? Which parts of Hamill's New York would you most like to visit and experience for yourself?